JOAN OF ARC AND RICHARD III

JOAN OF ARC

A N D

RICHARD III

SEX, SAINTS, AND GOVERNMENT

IN THE MIDDLE AGES

CHARLES T. WOOD

New York   Oxford
OXFORD UNIVERSITY PRESS

Oxford University Press

Oxford   New York   Toronto
Delhi   Bombay   Calcutta   Madras   Karachi
Petaling Jaya   Singapore   Hong Kong   Tokyo
Nairobi   Dar es Salaam   Cape Town
Melbourne   Auckland

and associated companies in
Berlin   Ibadan

Copyright © 1988 by Oxford University Press, Inc.

First published in 1988 by Oxford University Press, Inc.,
200 Madison Avenue, New York, New York 10016

First issued as an Oxford University Press paperback, 1991

Oxford is a registered trademark of Oxford University Press

Library of Congress Cataloging-in-Publication Data
Wood, Charles T.
Joan of Arc and Richard III: sex, saints,
and government in the Middle ages / Charles T. Wood.
p.   cm.   Bibliography: p.   Includes index.
1. Great Britain—Politics and government—1066-1485. 2. France—Politics
and government—1328-1589. 3. France—Politics aqnd government—987-1328.
4. Monarchy—Great Britain—History. 5. Monarchy—France—History.
6. Joan, of Arc, Saint, 1412-1431. 7. Richard III, King of England.
1452-1485. 8. Sex—Political aspects—History. 9. Christian saints—
Political activity—History. I. Title.
DA176.W66 1988 87-35023
942.04—dc19 CIP
ISBN 0-19-504060-0
ISBN 0-19-506951-X (pbk)

Preface

This book began as a study of representative institutions in England and France, but at some now-unremembered point it took on unexpected dimensions, those suggested by the sex and saints of its subtitle. For in the process of research it became increasingly clear that the questions traditionally posed in this field had failed to do justice either to the available evidence or to the outlook of the people who had created it. The participants in medieval government appeared to have interests and concerns quite at variance with those of the modern historian, and unless the resulting work managed to convey something of their thought processes, something of the problems they saw and the manner in which they dealt with them, it seemed unlikely that its conclusions would prove any more satisfying than those provided in endless earlier works of political and institutional history.

Back in the 1950s, a stern Stuart Hoyt used to warn undergraduates that if they did not understand St. Bernard, they could not possibly understand the Middle Ages. Since I, then the grader in one of his classes, knew full well that I myself had not the slightest insight into the motives of saints, this warning gave no little impetus to my own quest for enlightenment, and if I still do not pretend adequately to understand Bernard, it is also true that my attempts to do so had much to do, over time, with the evolving nature of my historical investigations. In particular, at some metaphorical level the concerns thus engendered undoubtedly influenced the approach I began to use in a series of articles, all of them aimed at trying to fathom the views and actions of people in conflict, people who claimed with differing degrees of success and failure to represent the communities in which they lived. Then, as patterns gradually emerged, Hoyt's warning took on new form as I started to sense that, if I did not understand Joan of Arc and Richard III, I could never hope to grasp the nature of the governments that they sought, respectively, to save or to seize. For it seemed to me then, as it does now, that their careers might well provide the key needed to solve the enduring mystery of why two countries, the histories of which were so closely related, should have developed in such contrasting ways. In crisis upon crisis, after all, England had chosen to return to a limited and increasingly representational form of government, whereas France, though no stranger to representative institutions, seemed rather to prefer a path in which, ultimately, the authority of its kings came to be accepted—in theory, at least, if not always in practice—as absolute, divinely ordained, and therefore beyond the possibility of human review or amendment.

Nevertheless, as I came better to know my protagonists, I saw too that any meaningful understanding of their lives would depend not just on knowledge of their careers, but even more on insights gained from the study of earlier lives and earlier crises. This book, then, could be no mere double biography. Rather, it had to be a series of studies, loosely linked, all of which would culminate in, and gain purpose from, the lives of Richard and Joan. Their careers would be the centerpiece that would justify the whole, and in what follows, I can only hope that this vision has been at least partly realized.

Research for this book has stretched over many years, but none of it could have been done without generous assistance. To Dartmouth College I owe thanks for sabbatical leaves and other research funds, the ingenious sources of which often seem well-nigh medieval. Moreover, Dartmouth's support has often been augmented by a variety of grants and fellowships. Early on, for example, the American Philosophical Society provided a travel grant that made it possible for me to study the manuscript sources for Richard III long before his quincentenary encouraged their publication. Similarly, in 1980–81 I was fortunate enough to receive a fellowship from the American Council of Learned Societies, itself made possible by funds received from the National Endowment for the Humanities. That grant was then immediately followed by a fellowship in legal history from the American Bar Foundation, a group venturesome enough to risk some of its resources on an applicant who claimed that the origins of statute law were to be found in the perceived wishes of the Holy Spirit, a view that attracts little support from practicing lawyers today. Lastly, this preface is itself being written thanks to a fellowship from the John Simon Guggenheim Memorial Foundation, a charitable institution that thought it was making an award to investigate the political uses of Arthurian mythology. That mythology is present, too, as review of the discussions of Henry II and Joan of Arc will demonstrate, though there is much more to come. To all these bodies, then, my deepest gratitude.

Authors often complain, scholars among them, that theirs is a lonely calling, but the truth of the matter is rather more complex. To put thoughts into words can prove a painful process, for it involves nothing less than what the Rhyme-Prose of Li Po once called an attempt "to catch heaven and earth in a cage of form." On the other hand, if authors continue to make the attempt, it is not infrequently because, over time, others have made clear to them that the effort is worthwhile—and have then pitched in themselves with generous offers of assistance. Such help goes far toward relieving the loneliness. In my case, needed aid has come in many and frequent forms, most of which I have tried to acknowledge in the notes at the back of the book. There are, however, instances in which my indebtedness exceeds anything that can be properly expressed within the confines of a note. To Francis Oakley, for example, I owe my introduction to many of the ideas that shaped my thinking on collegial bodies, such as parliament, and to the late William Huse Dunham I am grateful for endless encouragement early on that usually took the form that he was "mighty sure" that he himself had thought of it all years ago. At the other extreme, to Elizabeth A. R. Brown I owe constant reminders that one needs evidence, precise and specific, before one can make persuasive judgments, and she has been an invaluable source of leads in those instances where my own knowledge of documentation was limited. Peter Hammond, long an officer of the Richard III Society, has provided similar assistance in the areas of his own expertise, and since they include an unmatched mastery of English coronation procedures, that assistance extended into the reign of Richard II as well. James Gillespie and George Stow regard me as a Ricardian of the third kind, an allegation that Peter Hammond would firmly deny, but in no way have their own convictions as partisans of

viii   *Preface*

the second Richard lessened their cheerful willingness to instruct me on how best to infringe on their turf. And I have done so from the borrowed London flat of Susan Reynolds, a scholar whose typewriter I use and whose ideas on medieval communities I follow at such moments as I am not breaking her crystal and china. She will be happy to know, then, that even though it was my turn to do dishes tonight, Susan my wife has done them instead, one of the many ways in which she, too, has helped to transform the merely possible into a reality.

Since roughly half of this book is based on work earlier published in other forms, I am further indebted to a variety of journals, publishers, and people for permission to reuse these pieces, almost invariably in heavily revised form. In the order in which these materials appear, they are: Princeton University Press for permission to reprint a new version of chapter 24 of William C. Jordan et al., *Order and Innovation in the Middle Ages: Essays in Honor of Joseph R. Strayer*, copyright © 1976 by Princeton University Press; to the *Iowa State Journal of Research* for the use of two short passages from "Shakespeare and the Drama of History," *Iowa State Journal of Research*, 60 (1986); and to the Society for French Historical Studies for use of "The Mise of Amiens and Saint Louis' Theory of Kingship," *French Historical Studies*, 6 (1970). Also to The University of Chicago Press, acting on behalf of the North American Conference on British Studies, to reprint "The English Crisis of 1297 in the Light of French Experience," *Journal of British Studies*, 18 (1979); to Charles Scribner's Sons, acting on behalf of the American Council of Learned Societies, for permission to borrow two reworked passages from "England: 1216–1485," *Dictionary of the Middle Ages*, ed. Joseph R. Strayer et al., 4 (1981–); and to the North-Holland Publishing Company, Amsterdam, for use of "Celestine V, Boniface VIII and the authority of parliament," *Journal of Medieval History*, 8 (1982). Lastly, to the editors of *Traditio* and the Fordham University Press for permission to reprint revised versions of Part I and small snippets of Part II of "The Deposition of Edward V," *Traditio*, 31 (1975); and to Ralph A. Griffiths for his assurances that I need no one's permission to reuse one brief passage from "Richard III, William, Lord Hastings and Friday the Thirteenth," *Kings and Nobles in the Later Middle Ages*, ed. Ralph A. Griffiths and James Sherborne (Gloucester, 1987).

In conclusion, a word about the sources used in the text. Whenever translations were already available, I have employed them, so citing that fact in the notes. With one or two possible exceptions, though, I have also returned to the originals, checking them for the accuracy with which they have been translated. As a result, I have on occasion silently amended doubtful words or passages just as I have felt free to make spellings, names, and punctuation conform to my own usage. When such changes are significant, I have attempted to explain the reasons for the change in the notes. One doubts, sadly, whether either Joan or Richard would have appreciated the niceties involved.

London   C. T. W.
Octave of the Epiphany, 1987

Contents

PART I

THE DYNASTIC
CONTRAST

In 1958, France's Fourth Republic fell victim to forces unleashed by Algerian revolution. By September, most Parisians no longer feared a military *coup*, but violence remained the nightly norm and there seemed little reason to believe that the imminent reign of Charles de Gaulle would prove much better than that of the paratroopers he claimed to supplant. During the early October week preceding a vote on his new constitution, no fewer than seventeen movie theaters provided commentary by reviving Charlie Chaplin's *The Great Dictator,* and after the vote, a store founded in 1797 could wryly advertise: "Among our best former customers—one consul, two emperors, three kings, and four republics."

Across the Channel, such evidence merely confirmed the obvious, that the fragile political institutions of France were in no way a match for those of England. To the popular mind, French history seemed little more than an endless tale of chaos and discontinuity, whereas that of England—or of the United Kingdom of Great Britain and Northern Ireland that had technically replaced it—was the story of inexorable progress toward unity and forms of government that could properly express it. Nor was this just a popular notion. In 1954, for example, from the calm retreat of Sevenoaks, Kent, the distinguished medievalist Helen Maud Cam had watched the problems of French Prime Minister Pierre Mendès-France with historical detachment. As he struggled to address the multiple crises posed by decolonization, regional particularism, and the need for modernization in all aspects of life, she could only observe: "I have great admiration for the present Premier of France, but of course he faces difficulties that go back to the Middle Ages. Poor France, not to have had a Norman Conquest!"[1]

That view reflects the judgment of generations of English historians. If the France of the 1950s seemed a nation divided against itself, unable to create lasting forms of government or even lasting ministries, such problems were taken to be a permanent feature of French political life. After all, even the apparent cohesion of Roman Gaul had only masked the fragmentation of its underlying Celtic structures, and with the disintegration of Rome, that fragmentation had intensified as each new Germanic tribe had succeeded in establishing its own successor kingdom.

JOAN OF ARC   This statue once stood in Algiers, but was moved to Vaucouleurs, Meuse, shortly after the Algerian Revolution. (*Photograph by the author*)

3

In the eighth and ninth centuries, Pepin and Charlemagne may have momentarily reimposed order with the military success and imperial dreams of their new dynasty, but Carolingian unity had quickly crumbled under the weight of renewed invasion and civil war. By the eleventh century, about all that remained were heroic legends telling of a common past and a present reality consisting largely of semiautonomous territorial principalities. Although bonds of homage were supposed to link each territorial lord to the king, in practice most such men found that, thanks to growing differences in language, law, and culture, their lands had little in common with the rest of France. Small wonder, then, that the France of one system of laws, one system of weights and measures, had had to await the modernizing efforts of the French Revolution, for under the Old Regime, no king had ever possessed the kinds of power needed to transform his divided realm into a single community. Yet even the Revolution had proved distinctly a mixed blessing because varied reactions to its terrors had then led to still more ways to cut up the body politic.

Conversely, if England had long since achieved a strong sense of political unity, it was argued that this, too, had been the product of lengthy historical development. Like Gaul, Roman Britain had fallen to Germanic invaders, and also like Gaul, its land had quickly become a vast patchwork of successor kingdoms. After that, however, English experience began to differ markedly from the French. Whereas Charlemagne's empire had failed to survive, in the late ninth century Alfred the Great had rallied the forces of Wessex not just to stem the tide of Danish settlement, but also to lay the foundations for a truly national monarchy. The final century of Anglo-Saxon rule had then sketched in the principal elements of its superstructure, but it remained for the Norman Conquest to complete what Alfred had so nobly begun.

In simplest terms, the victory of William the Conqueror meant that, from 1066 on, each generation had seen one individual guiding the political destiny of England. Moreover, thanks to lands confiscated from the vanquished, the Norman kings found themselves endowed with a demesne, the resources of which greatly exceeded either those of their Anglo-Saxon predecessors or of their cross-Channel rivals, the Capetians. Lastly, because even the mightiest of William's followers had received their reward for service in the form of lands scattered widely over England, none—not even the marcher lords—enjoyed the kind of territorial power so typical of France and so necessary for successful resistance to, or even independence of, the unifying royal will. English kings could therefore rule from the center. As a result, harsh and resented though their government frequently was, its continued existence had forcibly brought people together and, in so doing, had gradually smoothed out or eliminated their provincial differences. In turn, though, this very success had had paradoxical consequences, ones to which Joseph Strayer gave their classic expression fifty years ago:

> England developed parliamentary government because her early kings were strong. France developed absolutism because her early kings were weak. The strong English kings prevented the formation of provinces and forced the whole country to accept the authority of the central assembly which was part of their government. The French kings were too weak to wipe out provincial boundaries or to create an assembly which was universally respected. They had to govern personally if they were to govern at all, because they could not govern through a Parliament.[2]

On the surface, this case appears to stress only the long-term effect of strong kings, but its arguments rest on further implicit assumptions about the ways in which the Norman Conquest had increased the contrast between the two countries. If, for example, English kings had greater success in preventing the formation of provinces, it should be noted that theirs was the lesser challenge, not always the greater strength. After all, English shires had seldom experienced the autonomy of French counties, and they were fewer in number, smaller in size. Thus, even though both monarchies drew upon roughly similar resources for much of the twelfth century, resources adequate to Norman and Angevin needs proved inadequate in the case of the Capetians, men faced with the much larger problem of controlling vassals as powerful as the count of Flanders or the duke of Normandy. The fiefs they ruled were vast; their wealth, extensive. And when pressed by the king, each such vassal could justify a defiant course of action through appeals to centuries of tradition. They were not, then, an easy nut to crack.

On the other hand, English earls were far from numerous, and because the Conqueror's land settlements had denied them a territorial base, no English king faced comparable difficulties. If the government of French provinces remained in the hands of provincial leaders, in England only the king ruled the shires. In them royal sheriffs looked after governmental affairs while earls had to content themselves with the administration of estates, the dispersed nature of which prevented the easy acquisition of public authority on the local level that had made the counts and dukes of France into such formidable opponents of every attempt to unify through centralization or, more cautiously, a limited insistence on standardization.

Still, these differences are far from the full story. Modern France is over four times the size of England—212,658 square miles versus England's 50,331—and while the disparity was less marked during the Middle Ages, a time when France had not yet attained its present frontiers, it was nonetheless significant. England's relative smallness made its totality easier to grasp. For example, when William I decided to survey the state of his realm, a sour Anglo-Saxon Chronicle could only report: "So very narrowly did he have it investigated, that there was no single hide nor a yard of land, nor indeed (it is a shame to relate but it seemed no shame to him to do) one ox nor one cow nor one pig was there left out, and not put down in his record."[3] By way of contrast, Domesday inquests would have been a patent impossibility in eleventh-century France, and that the problem long continued, an ignorance encouraged by size, is nowhere more evident than in the fact that as late as 1318 Philip V found it necessary to ask local officials for the names of all prelates and nobles, of all "notable towns and places," to be found in their jurisdictions. Somewhat lamely the king explained that he "often had occasion to write them," but under the circumstances one wonders just how.[4]

In addition, although both countries were ruled by former invaders, the modesty of England's dimensions appears to have interacted with the realities of foreign invasion and its timing in ways that created a different dynamic, a different relationship between the king and his barons—and among the barons themselves. By 1066, centuries had passed since the Franks had swept into Gaul, and even in the case of Normandy more than a hundred and fifty years separated Rollo and his Viking followers from their exclusively French-speaking descendants. As a result, and at a time when improved economic circumstances had made state-building into a general phenomenon, in no part of France did distinctions remain between victor and vanquished. Instead, settlement brought change, for what had once been linguistic and ethnic differences were then inexorably transformed into provincial ones based on place.

After Hastings, however, and especially after William had completed his conquest of the North, the structure of English society, of English government, bore little relationship to what had evolved in France. Because a few thousand Normans displaced a much larger landed class, because, therefore, the average Anglo-Saxon land-holding had been smaller than its Norman replacement, and because William could bestow these holdings only as they came into his hand, those who had accompanied him found that the rewards for their labor were both slow in coming and usually granted in bits and pieces along the routes of their completed campaigns. Nothing here suggests a considered policy, a deliberate attempt to achieve harmony through that process of conscious checkerboarding so stressed by nineteenth-century historians. Instead, the Norman settlement emerges as a very hand-to-mouth operation, one run by a king whose chief concern lay in meeting the demands of avaricious supporters. And if, on occasion, his generosity included titles of meaningless territorial worth, they, too, were but sops to the greedy while they waited for land.

Nevertheless, since one of the hard facts of medieval life was that poor communications always made it easier to bring people to the source of their food than vice versa, this dispersed pattern of land-holding meant that the Normans were constantly on the move, exhausting the resources of one manor and then proceeding on to the next. Doubtless this constant movement increased mutual contact, but the likelihood that such contact would have fruitful consequences was enhanced by fear of the Anglo-Saxon world through which they journeyed. Foreign in tongue, alien in outlook, and few in number, the Normans were inevitably perceived, and perceived themselves, as outsiders. As a result, and to paraphrase Ben Franklin, they had to hang together lest they be hanged separately. In France, if most nobles had little in common because, in part, they so seldom met, in England this kind of early interactive experience lay at the heart of what would later become and be called the community of the realm.

By the thirteenth century, the effects of these dissimilarities were often discernible, but nowhere more clearly than in the contrasting assumptions that underlay decisions to resist the kings of either realm. In 1241, for example, when Hugh the Brown, count of La Marche, rose in revolt against Louis IX and Blanche of Castile, he framed his complaints in awesomely provincial terms, ones totally blind to any conception of France as that higher good to which all men owed their ultimate earthly allegiance:

> The French have always hated the Poitevins and continue their hate. They wish to grind everyone underfoot and to possess everything in their ancient domains and in the conquered countries. They treat us with more contempt than they do the Normans and the Albigensians. A valet of the king does his will in Burgundy, Champagne, and in other lands; the barons dare to do nothing without his permission. They are as serfs before him.[5]

A generation later, though, when Edward I sought to emphasize the royal origins of all baronial justice, the grounds for English resistance took notably different form. To implement his policy, the king created assizes and ordered each baron to appear and explain by what warrant he held his court. Walter of Hemingburgh reports that the earl of Warenne responded to his summons by drawing a rusty sword which he then threw down in front of the startled judges before angrily exclaiming:

> See, my lords, here is my warrant. My ancestors came with William the Bastard and conquered their lands with the sword; with the sword will I defend them against anyone who wishes to usurp them. For the king did not conquer and subdue the land by himself, but our fore-fathers were with him as partners and helpers.[6]

Although nothing in Hemingburgh's account would encourage the belief that this scene ever occurred, the attitudes conveyed are fully consistent with those expressed in more reliable contemporary sources. By the time of Magna Carta the barons were already calling themselves "the community of the entire country," while at Oxford in 1258 they would claim to represent "the whole community of the land" or even to be, in their own persons, "the community of England." The speech of Hemingburgh's earl surely echoes those sentiments. Still, because such terminology tended to surface only in times of crisis, it has frequently been misunderstood. Thanks largely to the myths fostered by seventeenth-century opponents of Stuart rule, historians long alleged that the English tradition of limited monarchy had arisen in response to conflict; more specifically, that a community of the realm had come into being mainly to check the king; and hence that, since neither side could crush the other, standoff and compromise had been the ineluctable outcome.

Yet the facts testify to a more complex reality. The Conquest had required cooperation, after all, and the way in which the Normans received possession of their fiefs ensured that under normal conditions it would long continue. In the putative words of John of Warenne, "William the Bastard . . . did not conquer and subdue the land by himself, but our forefathers were with him as partners and helpers." Moreover, if this speech expresses a grievance, it finds its source not in the need for conflict, but in the conviction that Edward I and his justices have failed in their historical obligation to preserve that harmonious partnership which the earl saw as the essence of proper relations between monarch and baron. In clause after clause, too, both Magna Carta and the Provisions of Oxford had already sounded similar themes.

Kings may have dismissed such claims as overblown and presumptuous, but they had a future, one that underscores still another distinction between England and France. In England, two parties—king and community—came to think of themselves as guardian spokesmen for the realm, and because they did, they found themselves usually in agreement, able to work together. In turn, this shared sense of guardianship also meant that their episodic conflicts would never threaten the unity of the land. On the other hand, the divisions of France encouraged the view that only the king could speak for the kingdom—indeed, that he alone *was* its community. If so (and so briefly put, the case is doubtless overstated), absolutism becomes a logical response to specifically French conditions, for its justification of a transcendent royal authority provided the means needed to counter faction and to lay the foundations for an enduring state. In its absence, chaos would have ensued, fragmentation not unlike that experienced by Germany after papal challenge in the eleventh and following centuries had deprived its rulers of their status as the undoubted vicars of God. That being the case, though, it follows that England's failure to embrace absolutism may have resulted from nothing more profound than the simple fact that its kings were to find in practice that they could reign quite well without it.

Still, widely accepted as these views undoubtedly are, they reflect neither the concerns that most animated medieval people nor the context within which they viewed their world. Everything suggests that the outlook of the Middle Ages was markedly different from the ones that followed it, but that reality has seldom prevented historians from attempting to interpret medieval experience almost entirely on the basis of their own decidedly nonmedival assumptions. Instead of using the particularities of the surviving evidence to explain developments in terms compatible with the views of participants, accounts such as the above have all too often relied on the application of modern concepts to a society that was profoundly innocent of them. As a result, the paired histories of England and France have typically ignored what the medieval record itself has had to say, and always to their detriment. By replacing the past's own testimony with the belief, usually unconscious, that the present was the goal toward which that past was relentlessly heading, this approach has so reshaped history that it becomes little more than the story of inevitable state-building and the emergence of that all-embracing and destructively self-serving sovereignty that came in the end to justify it. Like life, no past was ever that simple.

Even more to the point, the evidence makes clear that the Middle Ages themselves knew a different story. As in the modern account, the medieval version of the histories of France and England may well still culminate with Joan of Arc, the peasant maid who saved her land, and Richard III, the wicked uncle whose evil deeds long set the standards for villainy. Yet if Joan's career remains quintessentially French, Richard's inescapably English, the reasons for their prominence take on sharply different forms. No longer is Joan the representative of a nation incarnate, a woman whose fervent expression of French nationalism foreshadowed the world to come. And no longer, either, is Richard III merely "hell's black intelligencer," that "bunch-backed toad" or "abortive rooting hog" whose death ushered in the blessings of Tudor rule and the Renaissance. On the contrary, both are transformed by a medieval understanding of their roles, an understanding that sheds fuller light on that process whereby Joan's France and Richard's England should have come to prefer such different forms of government.

Nevertheless, if this new version is no longer the story of institutions gradually growing in response to impersonal forces and contrasting conditions, neither is it one that begins just with Joan and Richard. For too much of importance had preceded them. Before the meaning of their careers can be adequately assessed, we must first know something of the realities with which each had to contend, realities rather different from those usually stressed. Moreover, because their lives gained importance from their impact on monarchy, perhaps the logical place to begin is with the ways in which the royal families of both lands attempted to justify and transmit the powers of kingship from one generation to the next. The road thus chosen may be littered with the accidents of history, among them the accidents of sex and of sainthood, but more surely than most, it is the one that will return us to Joan, Richard, and what they can tell us about the varied nature of governments.

1

Queens, Queans, and
Kingship

In the spring of 1314, scandal rocked the court of France. It was alleged that two of King Philip the Fair's daughters-in-law, Marguerite of Navarre and Blanche of Burgundy, had for three years been involved in an adulterous relationship with two knights, Philip and Gautier d'Aunay. The royal response was immediate: Marguerite and Blanche were imprisoned in Chateau Gaillard while their unfortunate lovers were subjected to a public execution that (depending on which chronicler one cares to believe) may or may not have included such popular delights as emasculation, flaying, drawing, hanging, beheading, and quartering, all followed by long and open display of the remains.[1]

Scarcely a decade later, England endured similar scandal, this time involving the queen herself, but with quite different results. When Isabella became the mistress of Roger Mortimer, the future earl of March, the final outcome was scarcely Mortimer's execution or the queen's imprisonment. On the contrary, in 1326 the two lovers raised troops, invaded England, and overthrew the cuckolded Edward II. In the following year, these events led to that monarch's forced abdication and the accession of Isabella's son, Edward III.[2] And even when, in 1330, Edward III turned against his mother and her paramour, the charges for which Mortimer was executed related almost exclusively to his bad rule and complicity in the murder of Edward II. The closest the government came to raising the question of adultery was in a vague and ambiguous claim that "the said Roger falsely and maliciously caused discord between the father of our lord the king and the queen his wife."[3] A true statement, surely, but not very revealing. As for Isabella, though her role in government came to an end, no charges were brought. She was permitted freedom of movement and £3000 per annum as a widow's portion. Some found her an unlikely widow even though she did end her life as a Poor Clare.[4]

Chroniclers contemporaneous with these events serve only to reinforce the sense of difference between them. In France, every chronicle alludes to the adulteries of 1314 in straightforward detail;[5] in England, however, sources were more circumspect. Most explicit are Thomas Walsingham and the Chronicon of Lanercost, and they appear hesitant to say much more than: "Intimacy was suspected . . . as public rumor testified." More typically, Avesbury argues that "as things more secretly done must not be spoken about, I shall be silent."[6]

Since the problems of medieval government have usually been thought of within a framework of modern assumptions, historians have never concerned themselves with the implications of these striking differences. Traditionally, the English have viewed the overthrow of poor, benighted Edward II as scarcely worthy of explanation, and if Edward III chose not to blacken his mother's name, that, too, was perfectly understandable. Similarly, if the French mention the scandals of 1314 at all, they pass off their consequences either as striking proof of the Capetian court's puritanical morality, or as a foreshadowing of difficulties and dissensions to come.

Nevertheless, when these events are studied comparatively and within the framework of a royal office to which men could lay claim only by virtue of legitimate hereditary succession, new questions and possible interpretations arise. In this regard, for example, it seems not unreasonable to explore the possible problems these adulteries posed in terms of succession to the throne. After all, both cases involved women whose progeny would in the normal course of events have been expected to rule, so one would assume that uncertainties about legitimacy of birth would inevitably have been reflected in disputes about the person to whom the crown should pass after the death of either cuckolded king.

In fact, that appears to have happened in France, where the accession of Philip V and the concomitant exclusion of women from rights of succession cannot be fully understood without reference to the adulteries discovered in 1314.[7] For Louis X's wife, Marguerite of Navarre,

stood convicted of a liaison that was alleged to have started a year
before the birth of her one child, Jeanne. And contemporaries *did* draw
the appropriate conclusions. As the Chronicle Attributed to Jean Des-
nouelles puts it: "King Louis had two wives: the first was the daughter
of Mahaut, countess of Artois, and this queen committed misdeeds of
the body for which she was separated from the king and imprisoned in
Chateau Gaillard. This queen had one daughter of the king, as she
claimed, but for the misdeeds of her mother she lost her lands."[8]

The issues here are tricky. At Louis' death in 1316 Jeanne was only
four, and everything suggests that a significant prejudice already existed
against the rights of women.[9] Yet the chronicle cited above never takes
that position, and the various agreements negotiated between the regent,
Louis X's brother Philip of Poitiers, and the duke of Burgundy further
demonstrate that her rights were far from nugatory.[10] And when the
royal council reviewed the matter during the pregnancy of Louis' second wife, the duke continued to maintain his position, arguing (as John
of Saint Victor reports it) that "King Louis, while alive, recognized her
as a legitimate daughter."[11] Such views, which have to do not with sex
but paternity, are not lightly to be disregarded, even if advanced out of
self-interest. It seems likely, therefore, that succession devolved on
Philip V largely because, given Jeanne's possible illegitimacy, he was
Louis X's closest blood heir.

In France, then, doubts about legitimacy played a significant role in
changing the anticipated royal succession. But what of England? How
should the transfer of power to Edward III be seen? Here we are on
shakier grounds thanks to the reticence of available sources, but the
general dimensions of the problem are nonetheless clear. First, Queen
Isabella was an acknowledged adulteress. Admittedly her relationship
with Mortimer appears to have ripened only in 1325,[12] while Edward III
had been born in 1312, but the possibility always exists that she had had
earlier lovers. This is especially the case when the question of her
husband's own sexual preference is raised. For historians have long
speculated (albeit in discreet and muted tones) about the extent of Edward II's apparent homosexuality.[13] And men in the fourteenth century
were equally suspicious. Froissart claims that Hugh Despenser's private
parts were cut off "because he was . . . guilty of unnatural practices,
even with the king, whose affections he had alienated from the queen by
his wicked suggestions."[14] Geoffrey le Baker presents Edward's
murder as a symbolic reenactment of sexual perversion,[15] and the

Chronica de Melsa sums it all up with the statement: "Edward especially delighted in the vice of sodomy."[16] Clearly, then, we have a much more explicit case than chroniclers present with regard to Isabella's adultery, something that may in itself have interesting implications.

Still, all these charges may not be true.[17] Edward may, in fact, have been the father of his supposed offspring. He certainly recognized them as his, and he was always with Isabella at the appropriate and necessary times before the birth of each of her children.[18] Moreover, many of those who are homosexual in orientation remain bisexual in practice, and in this regard it is possibly significant that even though the queen began complaining to her father, Philip the Fair, about her husband's friendship with Piers Gaveston almost immediately following the wedding,[19] Edward III was born only after the barons had hurried this despised royal favorite to his final reward. On the other hand, it is equally plausible that Isabella, who was twelve at her marriage in 1308, had become fertile only later.

Be that as it may, in the context of the present argument the actual truth of the matter is largely irrelevant. What matters is the much simpler question whether people of consequence in 1326–27 would have had plausible grounds for challenging Edward III's legitimacy. On that issue there is no logical basis for doubt: an adulterous queen married to a presumptively homosexual king leads necessarily to the thought that the progeny of one may not have been the progeny of the other. *Honi soit qui mal y pense.*

That contemporaries had such doubts is nowhere better illustrated than in the differences already noted between French and English chronicles. French authors could write openly because their adulterous queen had been punished and her daughter excluded from the succession. But in England, where nothing of the kind had happened, to write too explicitly about Isabella's extramarital activities was inevitably to bring into question the paternity of her son, the king. For those with doubts, the one sensible solution was silence, and if chroniclers inadvertently reopened the subject with their treatment of Edward II's sexuality, that seems entirely understandable: the deposed king's eccentricities provided both a tempting theme and ample explanation of (not to mention justification for) the events that had brought young Edward III so precipitately early to the throne. In terms of his succession, the late king's sodomy was a relatively safe subject; the queen's adultery was not.

If so, the *coup d'état* of 1326–27 acquires new interest. The proposed king was a minor, just fourteen, and his sponsors, Isabella and Mortimer, were hardly popular.[20] Nevertheless, given Edward III's age, the lovers were clearly going to rule in his name unless the opposition could devise means for getting rid of them. And the opposition did try, as demonstrated by the events surrounding the final days of Edward II at Berkeley Castle. For everything shows that the new regime had no initial thought of murdering him, but moved in that direction only after revolts aimed at rescue and restoration began to break out.[21] That people so opposed Isabella and Mortimer that they were prepared to chance the return even of a hopeless incompetent suggests the degree of hostility with which the regnant adulterers were viewed. But the announcement of Edward's death cut off this avenue of resistance, and that seems momentarily to have ended the matter. The opposition quieted down, not to reemerge until three years later when Edward III solved the problem by having Mortimer executed.

This chain of events is troubling. If, as is always assumed, succession to England's throne had become predominantly hereditary, and if there were reasonable grounds for challenging Edward III's legitimacy—at least on the part of those who wanted to be rid of Mortimer and Isabella—a more logical solution would have been to deny that legitimacy and to proclaim the next clearly legitimate heir as king, in this case Thomas Brotherton, earl of Norfolk, marshal of England, and the elder of Edward II's two half-brothers born of Edward I's second marriage, to Margaret of France. In many respects Norfolk would have been an ideal candidate. Though an early supporter of Isabella and Mortimer's invasion and their subsequent *coup,* he was scarcely an ardent follower of the upstart earl of March. Rather, it was simply a question of his disliking Hugh Despenser, the fallen king's favorite, even more.[22] If, ten years before, Philip V had seized the crown of France by taking advantage of the consequences of his sister-in-law's adultery, what better way for Thomas to solve the governmental crisis than by imitating Philip's example and claiming the throne himself? Yet he never tried, and nothing in the surviving evidence even remotely suggests that the idea ever occurred to him or to anyone else. Given the French precedent, this silence is surprising. We must ask, therefore, why such similar events in neighboring realms should have had, at roughly the same time, such contrary results.

Part of the answer may lie in the field of private law, particularly in the customs governing illegitimacy and rights of inheritance. At first glance this hypothesis may appear unlikely because in theory both countries sought rigorously to deny that bastards had any rights transmitted from parents.[23] In practice, however, there were significant differences. The French appear always to have applied this principle, whereas the English showed a marked willingness to adjust theory to circumstances so that children of adulterous unions could be given some chance of succession. In 2 Edward II, for example, the king's justices heard a case in which the plaintiff alleged that one Thomas of Boudon was not, as he claimed, the son of Hervey, but rather that of William of Rusting. Bereford, J., replied:

> What you have said as yet will not suffice . . . , for he says that he was holden and acknowledged as Hervey's son all his life and he is "in" as heir. And as to your averment that he is son of William of Rusting, how could one try such a matter? . . . It cannot be known who begot him; the only proof of filiation is the presumptive proof.[24]

Not content with this denial, Spigurnel, J., then added:

> May be he was begotten and born upon and of one Margery as you have said, and that he was acknowledged and holden as son of Hervey in his, Hervey's, lifetime. That lies within the knowledge of the country. But as to what you say about his being William's son, that cannot be known for the reason already given. So it is better in this case to be acknowledged and holden as son, albeit you really are not heir, than to be the very heir in blood but not acknowledged and holden as such.[25]

Even more germane to the question of female adultery are the reminiscences of Hengham, J., from the Year Books of 32–33 Edward I:

> I remember a case in which a damsel brought an assize of *mort d'ancestor* on the death of her father. The tenant said that she was not next heir. The assize came and said that the [alleged] father after that he had married the mother went beyond the seas and abode there three years; and then, when he came home, he found the plaintiff who had not been born more than a month before his return. And so the men of the assize said openly that she was not his heir, for she was not his daughter. All the same, the justices awarded that she should recover the land, for the privities of husband and wife are not to be known, and he might have come by night and engendered the plaintiff.[26]

Or, as Metingham, J., put the case under similar circumstances:

> Who so bulleth mine kine,
> Ewere [always] is the calf mine.[27]

In the thirteenth and early fourteenth centuries, then, English common law with regard to disputed paternity based itself on two principles: first, that "the privities of husband and wife are not to be known"; and second, that "it is better to be acknowledged and holden as son, albeit you really are not heir, than to be the very heir in blood but not acknowledged and holden as such." If so, the relevance to Edward III is immediately apparent. Edward II had consistently recognized him; indeed, he appears to have agreed to abdication only after becoming convinced that this was the one way to ensure that the boy would succeed.[28] The privities of husband and wife being beyond review, the possibility thus arises that even those hotly opposed to Isabella and Mortimer had no choice but to accept Edward III if they, like their sovereign, were to "keep . . . the laws and customs given to them by the previous just and God-fearing kings."[29]

Here, however, further questions arise. Simply to quote from Edward II's coronation oath is to underscore the fact that royal succession involves matters of public, not private, law. And by the opening decades of the fourteenth century it was becoming clear that there could be sharp differences between them. As a result, to search out the rules governing private inheritance may not be terribly instructive about the law of legitimacy as it applied to the crown. To understand it, one must first explore the prerequisites of kingship, looking for the conditions that had to be met before a man could legally exercise the right to rule.

During the early Middle Ages, both kingdoms appear to have developed remarkably similar theories of legitimacy, theories in which lawful kingship depended on three essential elements: kin-right or, in words of the time, a "throne-worthiness" based on some form of blood membership, even illegitimate, in the ruling dynasty; election or recognition/acceptance by the community (however defined) of one's successful candidacy; and, finally, religious coronation, the most important element of which was unction.[30] But over time, and particularly in the course of the eleventh and early twelfth centuries, these requirements underwent subtle modification. Again, though, these changes would appear at first glance to have continued roughly in parallel on both sides of the Channel.

First, even though the redefinition of the family in more nuclear terms was a phenomenon discernible throughout Europe at the time, in royal families it had a special effect: that of underscoring and increasing the inheritance rights of a ruler's own children. Furthermore, in France this tendency was reinforced by the appearance of the *rex-designatus* or king-designate system, whereas in England it found support in a related inclination, not quite so marked, to provide for the succession during an incumbent's lifetime.[31] Second, the reforms of Gregory VII led to a downgrading of the importance of coronation and unction. Hitherto, they had not infrequently been viewed as one of the sacraments; as such, they had become one of the principal supports of sacral kingship and of a monarch who was himself directly the vicar of God. After Gregory, however, these claims were diminished, one result of which was that both England and France seem to have begun the thirteenth century with an outlook and ambiance much less receptive to religious and sacramental justification for kingship than had been the case fifty or a hundred years earlier.[32]

Moreover, the evidence suggests that these changes led to further consequences. For example, if election or recognition tended to disappear as a necessary precondition to a candidate's installation as king, by implication it would appear that heredity alone was coming to be the prime criterion and that primogeniture was increasingly seen as its principal component, one that was beginning to overshadow all other elements in the king-making process. As a symbol of this kind of transformation, the accessions of Philip III in 1270 and of Edward I in 1272 come readily to mind, for in both instances the new kings dated the start of their reigns from the time of their fathers' deaths and not, as had previously been the case, from that of their own coronations.[33] Since, however, coronation rites are inherently antidynastic, at least in principle,[34] these twin events have often been seen as the final victory of heredity over those other factors, election and crowning, which had earlier been of equal importance in the king-making process.

The striking feature of this interpretation, one common to most of the literature, is its insistence on the continuing similarity of England and France. By 1300, both monarchies are judged to have become overwhelmingly hereditary, and if the ruler of one is found to have had unusual attributes (thaumaturgic powers, say, or inviolability of person),[35] so, too, is the other. Yet this view is highly suspect. Accurate though it may be within limits, it fails adequately to note significant differences in emphasis that were already beginning to develop. And these differences are crucial to an understanding of why, in public law, female adultery in France should have deprived women of whatever slim claims they had on the throne, whereas in England it led to the deposition of a reigning king and the substitution of his putative son. Or, to put the matter a bit more cautiously and the other way 'round, the very fact that the two adultery crises had different consequences suggests that dissimilarity in public law, though seldom noted, may have had a greater importance than is generally assumed.

Although measurement of such differences is fraught with difficulty, it seems safe to say that from 987 onward, the actions of the French monarchy tended to favor the creation of a legitimate, sanctified, and hereditary succession, much more so than was the case in England. Indeed, insofar as repeated use of kings designate worked toward that end, one could argue that a hereditary throne had been the goal from the moment that, only months after his own accession, Hugh Capet decided to associate his eldest son in the kingship. But such thoughts enjoyed little initial acceptance, and it is not until 1165, when Arnoul of Lisieux wrote Louis VII to congratulate him on the birth of Philip Augustus—a boy, the bishop said, who would rule by right of birth alone—that one can say with any confidence that blood had begun to supersede election as the prime criterion for elevation to the throne.[36]

To some extent, the early Capetians faced difficulties simply because they had come to power a century before new modes of family structure and family rights began to appear. Such changes were largely a by-product of Hildebrandine reform. But even as older views of the family disappeared, that phenomenon itself posed still more problems since the fact of the matter was that the Capetians were usurpers, men who had wrested the throne from the Carolingians, a dynasty whose right to rule the pope had guaranteed under pain of excommunication in 754. Hugh had claimed, of course, that his elevation to the kingship had been the dying wish of the last Carolingian, Louis V, and the first century of Capetian rule had seen a number of royal marriages with women of at least vaguely Carolingian descent. In addition, Louis VI's adoption of the Oriflamme, the supposed banner of Charlemagne, tended further to associate the new dynasty with the old.[37] Nevertheless, these ties proved insufficient in the changed circumstances of the late twelfth and thirteenth centuries, or so it would appear, for how else is one to explain the profound significance attached to Philip Augustus' Carolingian (albeit maternal) blood, the double Carolingian descent of his son Louis VIII, and the decision to abandon the *rex-designatus* system after seven generations of use?[38]

From the time of Philip Augustus, then, hereditary right came to prevail, a right dependent not on Capetian but Carolingian legitimacy—itself a dynasty that was carefully linked to Merovingian beginnings.[39] Under Louis VIII "Charles" reemerged as a family name, and during St. Louis' reign the royal tombs at Saint Denis were rearranged—Carolingians on one side, Capetians on the other—with Philip Augustus and Louis VIII providing the bridge and union between them.[40] In the reign of Philip III the process then appears to have reached full flower with the synthesis, in the *Grandes Chroniques,* of older myths and legends into the so-called *Reditus Regni ad Stirpem Karoli Magni,* a piece of royalist propaganda that both legitimized the reigning dynasty and justified its territorial ambitions by showing its Carolingian roots.[41]

So strong did the claims of heredity become that it began to be claimed that a king assumed his full powers previous to, and without legal need for, coronation.[42] Here, however, a caveat should be entered, for if blood right became the predominant element in determining royal legitimacy, that blood carried with it associations strongly linking the kingship to religious mission and rites. The Capetians traced their origins to Clovis, first baptized among the Franks, and to Charlemagne, the recently canonized emperor. Thus it seems scarcely surprising to find them emphasizing the capital importance of their unction, brought by a dove from heaven for that first baptism; nor is it remarkable that their crusading ardor should have been justified by constant reference to the zeal of the great Charles so vividly portrayed in *The Song of Roland.*[43] All the same, everything—even these religious elements—depended on blood, for only in its purity, seminally transmitted,[44] was there any guarantee that past greatness would be realized again in times to come.[45]

In short, thirteenth-century France enjoyed a kingship that was increasingly sanctified on the basis of legitimate dynastic descent. "Royal" and "most holy" became nearly synonymous;[46] unsuccessful attempts to underscore the point with the canonization of Philip Augustus turned into successful ones with the elevation of his grandson;[47] and Rigord could unblushingly (and inaccurately) refer to Louis VIII as "the only begotten son of King Philip," a formula the credal and christological implications of which seem unmistakable.[48] Small wonder, then, that Beaumanoir, who enjoined justice as a duty on all sovereigns, did so "more especially" in the case of his own lord Robert of Clermont, "who is a son of the king of France";[49] or that Matthew Paris, who called Louis IX "the king of mortal kings," should have agreed with that monarch in finding it preferable "to be the brother of such a king, whose lineage of royal blood has exalted him to rulership of the Franks" than to be merely the emperor, "whom voluntary election alone exalts."[50] As William of Plaisians put it when attacking Boniface VIII: "Seeking to destroy the faith, he has long harbored an aversion against the king of France, in hatred of the faith, because in France there is and ever was the splendor of the faith, the grand support and example of Christendom."[51]

Although more could be said, the evidence seems already sufficient to show that by 1314 France had become a holy land populated by God's chosen people and ruled over by a king who was suitably styled "most Christian."[52] And because these concepts had become embedded in the fabric of public law, reinforcing blood-right legitimacy with a sense of awful mystery, it becomes clear why the adultery scandals of that year should have provoked a crisis. Regardless of sex, no child of a possibly adulterous union could ever have been allowed to succeed in such a realm, and if Philip V manipulated the situation to his own advantage, he was justified by much more than personal, private ambition.

Strikingly, though as Ernst Kantorowicz noted almost a generation ago, "similarly exalted elaborations of mystic endowments of the royal house by grace and nature were hardly found in England at that period."[53] Given the difficulties inherent in trying to understand the causes of non-events, one can never fully explain why these developments never occurred. Nevertheless, it seems likely that accident, stimulated by the reality of trans-Channel possessions, provides as good an explanation as any.

After Hastings, William the Conqueror found himself in a position markedly similar to that of Hugh Capet a century earlier, and he responded in much the same way, dredging up all manner of semiplausible reasons to justify his newly minted royal title. Edward the Confessor had promised him the crown, he said, and he further claimed kin-right, somewhat dubiously citing the fact that the Confessor's mother Emma had been the daughter of his own great-grandfather, Richard I of Normandy. Next, God had demonstrated the justice of his cause in battle and, finally, he had been properly crowned after an equally proper election by the Witan of England.[54] And in these arguments, all the elements of traditional kingship were clearly present.

From this point on, though, English experience began to diverge from the French. As befitted a duke of Normandy, William selected his first son to succeed in the duchy and only the second to rule in the kingdom. Moreover, the suspicious displacement of Rufus by Henry I served further to emphasize the lack of clear rules, and even though Henry himself tried to speak to the issue by having his one legitimate son recognized as king designate,[55] the drowning of that son in the wreck of the White Ship ended this hope: Henry's death was to bring in its train a disputed succession, the elevation of Stephen, and twenty years of anarchy.

In twelfth-century England, calculation and chance made it impossible for the principle of election to be harnessed and focused by the use of designation, a practice that had slowly transformed France into a monarchy that followed strict rules of hereditary primogeniture. On the contrary, sons were lacking or died young;[56] cross-Channel possessions tended to encourage blurred and fragmented ambitions;[57] and in at least four cases—Henry I, Stephen, Henry II, and John—the crown was either seized by force or devolved on a man whose own accession denied the rights of those whom a more hereditary approach would have seen as heir or heiress presumptive. And these difficulties were compounded by the failure to develop any widely accepted dynastic myths comparable to the *Reditus Regni ad Stirpem Karoli Magni*. The Conqueror had claimed kinship with Edward the Confessor, and Henry I had reinforced the point by marrying back into the Anglo-Saxon royal line, but these tendencies came early and, like the Carolingian alliances of Hugh Capet and his immediate successors, they carried little dynastic weight.[58] Besides, Henry's failure to produce a legitimate son who outlived him necessarily put a damper on whatever positive effects these efforts may have had.

Unhappily, too, by the turn of the century, when French propagandists were for the first time beginning to explore the benefits of a more grandiose approach, earlier English efforts along similar lines had already failed. Soon after Henry II's accession, for example, the new king started to press for the canonization of Edward the Confessor, hoping thereby to highlight not just his own impeccably Anglo-Saxon ancestry, but also the sanctity with which his line had been blessed. And by 1161 this stratagem appeared to be working, for in that year the pope agreed to proclaim the Confessor's sainthood.[59] Nine years later, though, the martyrdom of Becket wrecked the whole enterprise since, inevitably, that tragedy caused most people to draw rather different conclusions about Henry's relationship to—and with—saints. Indeed, if chroniclers mentioned his ancestry at all, it was often to show that the origins of the Plantagenets lay in the marriage of an early count of Anjou to Melusine, the daughter of Satan. As St. Bernard had put it earlier in the century: "From the Devil they came, and to the Devil they will return."[60] This was not, surely, very promising mythic material on which to build a dynasty.

Toward the end of the reign, Henry returned to the task with a new ploy. By then, the legends of Arthur had gained unprecedented popularity and if, in Geoffrey of Monmouth, Merlin foretold that the red dragon of Brutus' line would ultimately triumph over the white dragon of the Anglo-Saxons who had momentarily defeated it,[61] in that prophecy Henry saw opportunity. In point of fact, it is not unlikely that his fresh solution to dynastic uncertainty became the model for those later Capetians who were to counter the ominous prophecy of St. Valéry about the end of their line by arguing that with Philip Augustus the kingship had at last returned to its Carolingian roots.[62] Whatever the case, Henry's approach proved very simple, no more than an acceptance of Constance of Brittany's suggestion that his first-born grandson and potential heir be named Arthur. Again, though, disaster ensued. Only two at Henry's death in 1189, the boy was to find that his rights, though first confirmed by his uncle Richard the Lionheart, would then be denied by the accession of John, a true son of Melusine who was later to ensure that this Arthur would enjoy a sleep from which he would never awake.[63]

Arthur's murder soon had further consequences, not the least of which was its negative impact on the Plantagenets' final attempt to establish a dynastic cult; this one based on the creation of a magnificent mausoleum at the Angevin abbey of Fontevraud. In 1189, Henry II's burial there had been largely the product of chance, he himself having preferred the austerities of Grandmont, but when Richard joined him ten years later, and especially after Eleanor of Aquitaine had been laid to rest between husband and son in 1204, it became clear that, like Louis IX whose subsequent arrangements at St. Denis would pursue a similar strategy, the Plantagenets had grasped the extent to which the shrewd placement of family tombs could be used to enhance claims of hereditary legitimacy. Unfortunately, however, by that point rumors of Arthur's passing had already begun to increase the difficulties caused by John's unwise marriage to Isabella of Angoulême, a marriage that had led to his condemnation by Philip Augustus as a contumacious vassal. The result was not just the intensification of widespread revolt, but the appearance of conquering French armies that were forever to remove Fontevraud from Plantagenet control. Thus, even though John's widow was ultimately allowed burial there, he himself was not. Only his heart and that of his son Henry III ever made it to the abbey, after which there was nothing.

Bereft of dynastic myth and endowed with no more than weak principles of heredity, the English monarchy, unlike the French, was therefore forced to rely on coronations for much of its legitimacy. For example, when Richard came to the throne, the Chronicle of Benedict of Peterborough continued to refer to him as no more than count of Poitiers before his investiture in Normandy; then as duke following that ceremony; and as king only after his crowning in England.[64] Similarly, Henry III lacked the essential powers of kingship before his majority as declared in his final coronation,[65] and even though Gregory VII and his successors had consistently denied the sacramental efficacy of unction, the mid-thirteenth-century bishop and thinker Robert Grosseteste found it still not improbable that the full legal prerogatives of office came only with anointing.[66] One understands, then, why coronation oaths and charters had much greater significance in England than in France:[67] they stood as testimony to the relative weakness of the hereditary principle and hence to the monarch's need, given the resultantly great comparative strength of election and crowning, to bind himself with a set of near-contractual obligations to those whose willingness had made him king.

The confusions of the situation became evident during the reign of Edward II. On the one hand, he could write that he was "ruling in the hereditary kingdom of England."[68] On the other, he was to prove equally insistent about the centrality of unction. As the poet Richier had pointed out, only in France had the coronation oil come from heaven; "[i]n all other places kings must buy their unction from merchants."[69] In 1318, however, Edward came into possession of a miraculous oil that the Virgin had vouchsafed to St. Thomas Becket in a vision, prophesying to him that the fifth king after Henry II—that is, Edward II—would be "a man of integrity and champion of the Church."[70] That Edward, weak and beset by enemies, immediately sought papal permission for a second coronation goes without saying; similarly, that he should have sought salvation through blatant imitation of the French is wholly unremarkable. What needs to be stressed, though, is that his decision to emphasize the efficacy of renewed unction had the effect of undercutting all his otherwise hereditary arguments. This was to have long-term consequences.

Yet for the moment, Edward's contrary theories served only to emphasize the confusions in English public law about justifications for kingship. Given a common law that chose not to delve too deeply into questions of paternity; and given a kingship, the authority of which depended more on election, anointing, and the coronation oath than it did on legitimate heredity, one begins to see both why Isabella and Mortimer were able to depose Edward II and why Edward III, once crowned and of age, could rule without opposition. There was nothing in the traditions of English monarchy to prevent it.

Nevertheless, this is but half the story, for if the events of the twelfth and thirteenth centuries had helped to shape quite different theories of royal legitimacy in England and France, theories that help to explain the differing results of queenly adultery, it is equally true that those results themselves—the exclusion of women from rights of succession and the deposition of a reigning monarch—were further to intensify the legal and constitutional differences that distinguished the two realms. In France, whereas assemblies had merely found, on the accessions of Philip V and Charles IV, that "a woman cannot succeed to the kingdom of France,"[71] by 1328 experts in canon and civil law were being called upon to present more elaborate justifications, all aimed at demonstrating, contrary to the pretensions of Edward III, that it was impossible for a female to transmit rights of succession that she did not herself possess.[72] In this way a purely hereditary succession was preserved even as France changed dynasties. Although these theories were not to reach full flower until Charles V—or even Charles VII—France was well on its way to inventing the Salic law.[73] And if coronations retained their importance, that was largely because they came to be viewed as a kind of wedding sacrament, a religious ceremony that served to unite legitimate kings with their bride, the kingdom, until the parting of death.[74]

In England, however, the deposition of Edward II could only further confound unsettled principles. A draft coronation manual, apparently from the 1330s, cautiously provided that a lay assembly was to elect the king prior to coronation and that the presiding archbiship could not begin the solemnities until "the people" had confirmed this election.[75] Richard II found parliamentary recognition useful to insure, as he hoped, the succession of his designated heir, Roger Mortimer,[76] and if this same unfortunate monarch agreed to abdicate, in surrendering the royal title he was equally certain that he could not renounce its spiritual honor, something that had been "in-oiled" in him by his unction.[77] One understands why Henry IV, his hereditary claims rejected by the very commission he had appointed to review them, should have thought it desirable to buttress his dubious rights by anointing with that oil, serendipitously rediscovered, that the Virgin had given to Becket.[78] Lastly, although in theory the Yorkists based their claims on principles of strict heredity, in practice each of them found, like the Lancastrians before them, that if (in words of Bagot's case) he "was not merely a usurper," that was because "the crown was entailed on him by parliament."[79] When England reached this point, it was well on its way to the wonders of the Tudor constitution, one that allowed Bloody Mary and Elizabeth—both bastards in the new Protestant world—to succeed to the throne purely by virtue of parliamentary enactment.[80]

These events may sound suspiciously like a story of Isabella the She-Wolf's revenge, but they serve to emphasize just how far apart French and English theories of royal legitimacy had drifted by the end of the Middle Ages. And the implications are enormous. One sees, for example, why it was so much easier to depose a king in England than in France. Because their experiences had differed, one found that it could accommodate both theory and practice to the possibility of an unexpected ruler; the other could not. Thus the madness of a French Charles VI could lead to civil war, as could the madness of his grandson, the English Henry VI. But where Charles remained secure on his throne for forty years, Henry had the misfortune to be deposed not once, but twice. The difference is instructive.[81]

Little wonder, then, that Charles VII, his rights of inheritance denied in the Treaty of Troyes and his royal paternity challenged by later rumors about the adulterous behavior of his mother ("a great whore," Louis XI called her),[82] should have been subject to so many fits of doubt and crises in leadership. And it is here, finally, that we again encounter Joan of Arc, this time with fuller understanding, for it was to take her mission, bringing assurances from heaven that he was truly king and proving it with coronation at Reims, to convince him that he alone had the right to rule. For surely God would have struck him dead at that triumphant moment had his title been in any way tainted or suspect.[83]

How different the realm of England! There, kings had to depend on power and ability, not sacredness of blood, and in their coronation oaths they gave witness not to an indissoluable marital bond but more to a contract with those people, their subjects, whose laws they swore to uphold. Thus, if the logical outcome in one kingdom was the divine-right preaching of Bossuet, in the other it was the social-contract theories of John Locke. This is, perhaps, still Isabella's revenge— the contrary consequences of the queanly conduct of queens—but that is the chance one takes when venturing forth on a road littered with the accidents of history.

2

The Child Who Would
Be King

In 1377, those recording the death of Edward III had little difficulty in dating it, for all agreed that it had come on June 21, "the Sunday immediately preceding the feast of St. John the Baptist."[1] Nevertheless, finding a date for the coronation of Richard II, his ten-year-old grandson, seems to have posed greater problems. There was a general consensus that the ceremony had taken place on July 16, but after that, agreement broke down. Responsibility for planning the event had rested with John of Gaunt, steward of England and the young king's uncle, so if the solemnities occurred at midweek, and not on a Sunday as was more typical in English practice, the change doubtless reflected his conscious choice. It was one the uncle never explained, but a clue to his reasoning may lie in the dating used in his formal report to the Chancery, one in which the coronation is said to have taken place on "Thursday, the morrow of the translation of St. Swithun."[2] Still, however much this date may reflect his motives, it failed to find favor. Only one chronicle followed him in using it, while most joined Thomas Walsingham in preferring "Thursday, the eve of St. Kenelm the king," or, as at least two had it, "Thursday, the eve of St. Kenelm the king and martyr."[3]

Since, these days, St. Swithun calls to mind little more than the threat of rain, whereas Kenelm's name conjures up nothing at all, a brief exploration of their medieval significance may prove instructive. Unlike people in the modern world, Gaunt's contemporaries would have known, and known instantly, that Swithun had died as bishop of Winchester, later to be buried under his cathedral's drainspout, thereby leading to his subsequent legend. Even more to the point, they would have known that his career owed its impetus to Egbert, from 802 to 839 the king of Wessex, who had first made him royal chaplain and then tutor to Ethelwulf, his son and heir. Lastly, they would certainly have recognized that after Ethelwulf's own accession, it had been he who had installed Swithun at Winchester.[4]

The model presented by Gaunt's choice of date was thus a bit ecclesiastical in tone, but not without its secular suggestiveness. The nephew was young, so in need of guidance, but lest the message be missed, the uncle repeated it in ways that were equally direct, equally subtle. At the coronation, he saw to it that the king and his entourage were all clothed in a sparkling—and untraditional—white, the symbolic meaning of which served to emphasize the purity and childlike innocence of the boy he was crowning.[5] In point of fact, this strategy appears to have first emerged during the mourning period that the royal family observed for Edward III at Sheen. When, for example, a delegation from London arrived there, seeking reconciliation with the Gaunt it despised—and whose wrath it feared in return—Gaunt begged Richard to assent to an accord and then sought similar reconciliation with the bishop of Wincester, Swithun's distant successor. Walsingham's reaction to the scene may have been naive, but in its underlying concern it demonstrates the extent to which Gaunt knew full well just what he was doing: ''O happy auspice that a boy so young should of his own accord show himself so solicitous for peace; that with no one to teach him he should know how to be a peacemaker!''[6] Like Swithun before him, Gaunt would fill the void by becoming a teacher, and also like Swithun, he expected reward.

If so, the Kenelm response was devastating. According to legend[7]— and in this case, most of the details are legendary—Kenelm was the son of Kenulph, king of Mercia. When Kenulph died in 821 (a genuine fact), Kenelm succeeded, though aged only seven. But these events served only to enrage Cynefrith, the boy's older sister, depriving her as they did of the riches and power that possession of the crown alone could provide. Therefore she approached Askebert, Kenelm's tutor, and with the promise, in Caxton's translation, of ''a great sum of money and also her body at his will,''[8] she soon persuaded him to slay their new king. This he accomplished by cutting off the lad's head in the

forest of Clent, after which he buried the remains under a hawthorn
bush. In Milton's none-too-heroic rendition:

Low in a Mead of Kine under a Thorn,
Of Head bereft li'th poor Kenelm King-born.[9]

Yet all was not lost, for from Kenelm's unburied head, made radiant by
the purity of his innocence, "a milk-white dove with golden wings
soared up to heaven."[10] Without hesitation, the dove then flew to Rome
where, spotting Leo III saying mass, it dropped a message (on parch-
ment, one hastens to add) that landed right on the high altar of old St.
Peter's. Unfortunately, the message turned out to be written in English,
but as luck would have it, an English pilgrim was attending mass that
day and he quickly translated the unknown words for an eager pope.
They revealed the whole sad story, both of the murder and of where the
body now lay, though the latter problem should have posed few problems in any event since, when the cardinal-legate dispatched by Leo
actually reached the site, he found the thornbush topped by a pillar of
heavenly light.

After disinterring the body, monks from Winchcombe bore it rever-
ently back to their abbey for permanent rest. Yet one further obstacle
remained, for as they neared home, whom should they meet but the
wicked Cynefrith, seated in a window reading? Interrupted by the
chanting of the monks and quickly guessing the identity of the body
they bore, she leapt to her feet and began reciting the ninetieth psalm
backwards, apparently her way of cursing the whole triumphant proces-
sion. At this point, God finally intervened: Even as Cynefrith stood
reading, her eyes dropped from their sockets and she herself fell dead,
consigned in eternity to the flames of hell. And for those with doubts
about the validity of this tale, before Henry VIII's dissolution of
Winchcombe, evidence of its total veracity was graphically available.
For one of that monastery's most prized possessions—most prized, that
is, after the body of St. Kenelm himself—was the book from which
Cynefrith was reading that day, a psalter on the ninetieth psalm of
which devoted pilgrims and monks alike could still see the two tracks of
blood left by her falling eyes.

Such, then, is the story that lay behind the date chosen by those who
distrusted John of Gaunt and feared his intentions. In its richness, the
legend of St. Kenelm drives yet another nail into the coffin of those who
claim that medieval society had little affection for children, and that this

loving concern extended even to princes of a historicity greater than Kenelm's is nowhere better demonstrated than in the care exercised by Edward IV in the rearing of his elder son, also named Edward and nephew of the future Richard III. In 1473, for example, and just before the boy was about to turn three, the king sent him to Ludlow, the Welsh castle in which he himself had been raised. Then, on September 28, he issued precise instructions for the education of his heir.

As envisaged, princely life was to be far from idle. Young Edward was expected to rise "at a convenient hour, according to his age"; then immediately to hear matins in his chamber; and, finally, as soon as he had dressed, to attend mass in his closet or chapel. After mass, he could at last eat breakfast, but until his midday dinner he was to give over his time to "such virtuous learning as his age shall suffer to receive." Indeed, even dinner provided little respite since, in the best monastic tradition, it was to be accompanied by the reading of "such noble stories as behooveth a prince to understand and know." After dinner, it was back to virtuous learning again, though in the late afternoon the boy was also to be instructed in "such convenient disports and exercises as behooveth his estate to have experience in"—presumably the martial arts, but possibly also a few games and hunting. Then came evensong, followed by supper, and it was only after that meal that this three-year-old was allowed to enjoy "all such honest disport as may be conveniently devised for his recreation." Still, recreation must have been brief, for bedtime came at eight, at which point servants were told to "enforce themselves to make him merry and joyous towards his bed." Further, attendants including a physician and surgeon were to keep watch throughout the night lest disease or human harm intrude; and, to diminish the risk of more subtle contamination, no member of the household was permitted to be "a customable swearer, brawler, back-biter, common hazarder, [or] adulterer." In short, because Edward IV considered his son "God's precious sending and gift, our most desired treasure," he did everything within his power to ensure that this child would receive "virtuous guiding," protected from even the most contingent dangers.[11]

If, at three, the future Edward V had to endure such a regimen, its stern thoroughness testifies to the loving care with which his tutors were to prepare him for the rigors of life. To rule in a violent age required talents not easily acquired, and if Edward IV attempted to provide them, one further suspects that the very violence of the times served greatly to enhance the affection with which all children were viewed. In a period when the life of man could prove nastily brutal and viciously short, even the callous saw childhood as an interval not governed by the rules of maturity, and the extraordinary devotion Christians displayed on Holy Innocents' Day can only underscore the extent to which children were never, never to be made pawns in the deadly games played by their fathers.[12] That was, after all, a world they would be entering quite soon enough. Edward V was to do so at twelve, still too young to be a player, and it was the revulsion caused by his fate, that of a new Innocent whom a new Herod had slaughtered to preserve his crown, that was instantly to transform Richard III into the very archetype of perfect villainy. Moreover, precisely because children were incapable of playing these dangerous games, the legend of the little princes in the Tower, like that of St. Kenelm it so starkly resembles, goes far toward explaining just why the Middle Ages so feared regencies and minority rule, just why they so often invoked the verse from Ecclesiastes (10:16): "Woe to thee, O land, when thy king is a child, and thy princes eat in the morning!"

The ongoing debate over the so-called invention of childhood has tended to obscure other issues. In particular, the tendency to ask only about those qualities that make a child a child has left in abeyance an even greater question: that of what turns children into adults and therefore defines a society's criteria for maturity. For those criteria can vary enormously. In the United States, for example, one can vote at eighteen but drink only at twenty-one. The laws of some states provide that one can get married without parental consent at fourteen if female, sixteen if male, and in criminal proceedings Vermont statute specifies that one can be charged as an adult at ten, provided the crime be serious enough.[13] In northern New England, it seems, only minor crimes make minor defendants.

Similar anomalies pervade medieval law. The Establishments of St. Louis declare that a peasant becomes an adult at fifteen and that, as such, he can hold land and render the services owing. On the other hand, a gentleman can possess land and have his lordship or inheritance only at twenty-one, the age also specified for the bearing of arms, so presumptively that of full knighthood as well.[14] And comparable variety marks the laws of England, a realm where knighthood again came at twenty-one, but one where, right down to 1837, a person could serve as a testamentary executor at seventeen and make a chattel will at fourteen.

Majority came for the English socman at fifteen, and in Bracton's words, it came for the bourgeois whenever he was "of age to count pence, measure cloth, and conduct his father's business."[15]

Unintentionally humorous though Bracton may be, the very practicality of his definition demonstrates a point too frequently missed, that ages of majority often depend on implicit assumptions about newly attained functional capacities. For example, the minimum age for marriage used to be determined by the onset of puberty, the point at which boys and girls could be reasonably thought to have developed the ability to reproduce themselves. In much the same way, if it could be shown that medieval kings came of age at twenty-one (and a few did),[16] then it would follow that the definition of maturity in a ruler was heavily dependent on the qualities needed for successful lordship and knighthood, the capacity for which was acquired only at that age.

As it happens, though, twenty-one was rarely considered the age of royal majority in either England or France. In both countries, kings came of age at times—and for reasons—that were as varied as those defining the maturity of their subjects. Thus, when Philip Augustus drew up a will in 1190, he provided that during his absence on crusade, France was to be governed by a council of regency. Further, in the event of his own demise, the regency was to continue until Louis, his two-year-old son, "comes to the age when he can rule the realm through the grace of the Holy Spirit" or, as Philip put it in another passage, until "he comes to the age when he can rule the realm through the counsel of God and his own understanding."[17]

Now, unless one becomes a knight primarily by putting on the new armor of Christ, these requirements are not those of knighthood. Rather, they seem most closely linked to ideas more usually associated with the changes wrought by the sacrament of confirmation, a principal consequence of which is precisely a strengthening of the recipient's capacity to cooperate with the Holy Spirit. In the twelfth century, however, confirmation was supposed to follow baptism almost immediately and was in any event almost never administered after the age of seven, in canon law the age of reason. As a result, even though Philip's language has clear sacramental associations, it is difficult to believe that he wanted the royal majority of his son somehow tied to the specific age of confirmation. To have intended that would have been to run the risk of little St. Kenelm all over again since, of course, seven is impossibly young in political terms for effective kingship. Fourteen, canon law's age of discretion, seems a more plausible possibility, though whatever Philip's intent, in no way did it involve mere fighting capacities. On the contrary, his phrasing shows that he knew that above all else, Louis would need mental abilities, ones that would come long before twenty-one and would require active cooperation with the divine.[18]

Nevertheless, if Philip Augustus tried to establish an age of majority that was relatively young, future queen mothers were soon trying to push it in the opposite direction. In the case of Blanche of Castile, St. Louis' mother, regency powers came during 1226 with the accession of her son, at twelve too young to rule, and she continued to govern long after he had become twenty-one. Indeed, Louis appears to have gained full autonomy only in 1244 when, aged thirty, he swore the crusader's vow.[19] Even more strikingly, nineteen years later Marguerite of Provence, St. Louis' wife, made her son, the future Philip III, swear that he would remain a ward and under her tutelage until he, too, had reached thirty, an oath which it took both royal and papal intervention to break.[20] And if one ponders the significance of thirty, the implications, while twofold, are unmistakably clear: First, in canon law it is—and was—the minimum required for the investiture of bishops; and second, though related, it is the age at which Christ is traditionally thought to have begun His ministry.[21] It was, then, a marvelously appropriate point at which to begin one's reign over the holy kingdom of France, though not entirely a practical one, as even St. Louis recognized.

Five generations and nine kings later, Charles V showed that he agreed with his ancestor's judgment. Faced in 1373 by a wife who "had become so ill . . . that she lost her good sense and memory,"[22] and worried by potential consequences if his own death were unexpectedly to bring their still minor son to the throne, he tried the following year to make the queen's contingent regency as short as possible by reducing the royal age of majority, an action the son, Charles VI, renewed and confirmed in 1392. In a supposedly perpetual edict, the elder Charles specified that kings, "having attained the fourteenth year of their age," were to be consecrated; that they were to have "rule and administration"; and, lastly, "that everything that they did was to take place as though they were adults of twenty-five years."[23] The king attempted to justify the change by pointing out that fourteen was legally the age of discretion, and he then further cited a number of biblical instances in which God had called children like David and Solomon to the rule of His people.[24] Charles VI added no new justifications in 1392, but in

1409, when declaring the twelve-year-old dauphin Louis of Guyenne old enough to preside over the council, he explained that this action had flowed from the fact that his son was now "coming to the years of puberty and to the age of being able to endure pain and of having the care and diligence needed to listen and attend to what we would want him to do."[25] Thus reasons of practicality and law joined those of religious effectiveness to define the capacities expected in rulers of France.

If, however, small mention has been made of England so far, that silence reflects a simple reality, that there is little to say. For a striking difference between the two realms is the extent to which English kings or others in power failed to develop clear principles for determining the age of royal majority. St. Dunstan may have deferred the coronation of Edgar the Peaceable for fourteen years, until 973 when the king was thirty, but in no way did this imitation of Christ deny or delay Edgar's earlier right to rule.[26] Besides, it proved a precedent without issue since, after the Conquest, no other coronation was similarly postponed. After all, Richard II was crowned at ten, and if, in that same year, a commons petition asked that all councillors and officers of the crown be approved in parliament until such time as the king was "of full age to know both good and evil,"[27] the petition came to naught while the biblical approach of its language, though revealing about the innocence imputed to children, was never repeated.

It would appear that people expected Henry VI's adult responsibilities to begin at fourteen or, as the chancellor phrased it in 1427, "at such time as God wills he should come to years of discretion,"[28] but the reality proved vastly more complicated. Even Ralph Griffiths, the king's most thorough biographer, seems frequently baffled, offering events dated from 1436 to 1442 as significant steps on the road to royal maturity and then summing up his own resulting uncertainties with a brilliantly evasive: "Henry only gradually, and without formal announcement, began to explore the extent of his prerogatives."[29] It must be added immediately, though, that the problem here lies less with Griffiths than with England's lack of rules. Their absence makes it almost impossible to decide with certainty just when any minor king came of age, the one exception being Edward III insofar as his anti-maternal *coup* at seventeen defines the start of his adult years with brutal precision. In this action he resembles no other ruler so much as Louis XIII of France who, while still fifteen, ended the regency of his mother Marie de Medici in 1617 through the simple expedient of having her lover Concini assassinated. As he then announced: "I am king now."[30] And, like Edward, since there was no one to gainsay him, he clearly was.

Nevertheless, in most instances minorities came to an end only gradually, and over a period of years. If the transition took six years for Henry VI, it proved equally long for Henry III and even longer for Richard II, a monarch who turned fourteen in 1381, but who proved incapable of breaking free of the Lords Appellant and of declaring his own majority until 1389, when he was twenty-two.[31] In France, too, the ending of a minority could be equally difficult, and this in spite of greater precision in law. Charles V died in 1380, for example, and after some debate, Charles VI was duly crowned even though he was then just short of his twelfth birthday or, in other words, over a year younger than the age of coronation laid down in his father's perpetual edict of 1374. After that, however, things went rather less expeditiously for the young king. At the start of his fourteenth year, he asked for recognition of his adulthood as envisaged in the edict, but the council of regency refused to grant it—and continued to refuse right down to 1388. At that point, Charles finally took matters into his own hands. Keeping his strategy secret from the council, he approached the archbishop of Reims and persuaded him to proclaim the royal majority in an unexpected announcement from the steps of his cathedral.[32] Since, at that point, Charles had already entered his twenty-first year, little wonder that he should have decided to underscore his father's intent by confirming his edict some four years later.

In a sense, these problems arose at least partly because neither England nor France was ever to develop formal rites of passage through which kings could gain politically effective recognition that, at some age certain, they were leaving childhood behind and becoming adults. This lack vastly complicated the politics not just of minority rule, but also of determining who had the power to end it and why. In the sixteenth century, the emergence of the *lit de justice* as France's most solemn judicial occasion led to attempts to solve the problem with majority *lits,* imposing ceremonies at which a king's newly attained status as legal adult was formally recognized,[33] but as Concini's fate proves so graphically, political behavior often failed to conform to the dictates of law. Moreover, if French history suggested no easy answers, neither did that of England. Its one advantage, an accident only, lay in the fact that insofar as England experienced no minorities after 1552, its needs were less pressing.

It bears repeating, though, that coronations alone never gave proof of majority, for minors who remained minors were frequently crowned: In France before 1500 they included Philip I, Philip Augustus, Louis IX, Charles VI, and Charles VIII; in England, Henry III (more than once, in fact),[34] Richard II, and that one monarch who received youthful coronation in both lands, Henry VI. During the fourteenth and fifteenth centuries, English practice implied that even in the case of a child, coronation ended protectorates, but if the king was not yet of age, minority government continued under different guise until full adulthood was reached, whenever that might be.[35] In fact, the one coronation in the later Middle Ages that may be said to have conferred or enhanced a right to rule was not that of a child at all, but that of Charles VII, a man for whom this ceremony took on unprecedented importance as a kind of protojudicial ordeal and quasi-sacramental confirmation of a title earlier beclouded by legal doubt.[36]

Still, despite occasional similarities, sharp contrasts were much more common and hence help to distinguish the French and English approaches to coming of age. For example, the English were much less insistently religious in their rhetoric. If the commons assumed in 1377 that a knowledge of good and evil would prove Richard II's maturity, such phrasing was highly unusual in England, whereas it would have been commonplace in France. Further, in wills and edicts or merely by letters patent and simple declaration, it was usually the kings of France themselves who defined the composition of minority governments and tried, with varying degrees of success, to dictate how long they should last. Only in the absence of specific instructions from the departed king were others allowed to act, others who might include (depending on the time period involved) "the estates-general, or the high nobles of the realm, or the council of state, or the parlement."[37]

On the other hand, when the dying Henry V attempted to provide for the minority of Henry VI in a last-minute codicil to his will, the lords of parliament rejected the document and went on to declare that "the king that dead is, in his life neither might by his last will nor otherwise alter, change nor abridge without the assent of the three estates, nor commit or grant to any person, governance or rule of this land longer than he lived."[38] In other words, no English king could bind the future beyond his own lifetime, and if minority rule required adult decisions, only the living could make them. As the council put the case to Bedford in 1427, given the king's "tenderness of age," responsibility for "the politic rule and governance of his land . . . belongeth unto the lords spiritual and temporal of his land at such time as they be assembled in parliament or in great council, and else them not being so assembled unto the lords chosen and named to be of his continual council."[39]

Here further differences emerge. If woe came to a land when its king was a child, that was the inevitable consequence of the infighting that was sure to arise between and among those who ruled in his name. Both countries recognized the problem, of course, and both tried to prevent it, but their ways of doing so were remarkably disparate. In France, regencies were family affairs, dominated by the royal princes, but the person named as regent was almost invariably the queen mother. Such an arrangement may seem a trifle anomalous in a land that so rigorously excluded women from rights of succession but, in a sense, that was precisely the point. Because queen mothers could have no claims of their own, in theory they would lack ambition. Their very lack of prospects made them into promising figureheads who could preside over the bickering of others and make decisions that were less likely to founder amidst charges of selfish greed.[40]

By way of contrast, in the aftermath of Magna Carta, England entered its first minority after the Conquest under difficult circumstances. Because John had died amidst renewed rebellion, his own wishes were hardly crucial, though the first response to his passing was not inconsistent with arrangements he had solemnly made at the time when Innocent III had finally agreed to lift the interdict he had imposed on England. Nine days after the king's death, there assembled at Gloucester the magnates who had served him faithfully, and on the same day, October 28, 1216, the papal legate Guala and other bishops "publicly anointed and crowned" the nine-year-old Henry III in St. Peter's Abbey there. In return, the new king did homage to Guala for England and the lordship of Ireland, also promising to pay the sums owing the pope under the terms of his father's settlement with Innocent.[41]

It looked for the moment, then, as though Guala alone might emerge as regent of England, but events proved otherwise. When, immediately thereafter, Magna Carta was reissued in drastically shortened form, although its legal force derived from its issuance in Henry's name, in fact the seals under which it was dispatched were those not just of Guala, but of William Marshal, earl of Pembroke. Moreover, if Guala soon became *rector regis,* "governor of the king," concurrently William received the title of *rector regis et regni,* "governor of the king and the kingdom." Although the significance of this difference has been endlessly debated, the point to note here is simply the fact that these arrangements—without queen, without members of the royal family—bore little resemblance to those being almost simultaneously fashioned in France for the minority of Louis IX.[42] Even more strikingly, at least one of those who would be prominently involved in the minority government, Hubert de Burgh, later recalled that its authority had derived only in part from the pope and not at all from the late king, for as he testified in 1239:

> On the death of King John in the time of war, the Marshal was made governor of the king and of the realm, by the counsel of Guala then legate, and of the magnates then gathered round the lord king. When peace was re-established, the Marshal remained governor of the king and of the kingdom. . . . Afterwards the dignity of majority was asked for, from Pope Honorius, at the suggestion of the archbishops, bishops, earls and barons.[43]

In short, and contrary to French assumption when minorities occurred, Hubert claimed that during Henry's youth the government had derived at least part of its authority from the community, not from the royal family or the wishes of predecessor kings. Henry VI's lords of parliament were to maintain little else.

In spite of such seeming continuity, though, it could doubtless be argued that because Henry III came to the throne under unusual circumstances, the accidents of his minority cannot be taken as precedent. Nevertheless, accident seems always to recur in England, and even chance events, if repeated, can form the basis for law. As it happened, too, the next minority was equally unusual, that of Edward III, a boy whose path to the kingship was greatly accelerated by the armed might of his mother. And here, also, there was a similar outcome. Isabella failed to become regent (as would have been her due in the land of her birth); instead, a great council of prelates and magnates again met at the time of the coronation and itself devised a standing council of twelve to handle the affairs of government. It consisted of four bishops, four earls, and six barons, and if Isabella failed to head it, this time a member of the royal family did receive the honor: Henry, earl of Lancaster and the new king's cousin.[44]

Royalty fared less well in 1377. Contrary to John of Gaunt's ambitions, the settlement excluded all three of the royal uncles, including Gaunt, from participation in the council. Rather, on the day after Richard II's coronation, a great council appointed a smaller continuing body to assist the chancellor and treasurer, a select group of twelve consisting of two bishops, two earls, two barons, two bannerets, and four knights bachelor. Edmund Mortimer, earl of March and father of Richard's possible heir presumptive, received membership, but it was not, in fact, a full council of regency. Its powers were restricted; tenure was limited to a one-year term not renewable until two more years had elapsed; and the king's person remained under the care of his mother who, without title, acted as his guardian and as head of court. As for the royal uncles, their sole duty was to prevent bribes.[45]

As events were soon to illustrate, neither the French nor the English approach proved entirely satisfactory. The France of Charles VI's minority was filled with avuncular controversy, while the England of the Peasants' Revolt and the Lords Appellant was scarcely better. As a result, a new idea began to gain favor, the legal fiction that there need be no regencies at all since the king could be viewed as always adult, and only the crown as perpetually minor.[46] Thus, for example, the lords of Henry VI's council had it announced in 1427 that "howbeit that the king as now be of tender age nevertheless the same authority resteth and is at this day in his person that shall be in him at any time hereafter."[47] Similarly, the parlement of Paris addressed the minor Charles IX in 1563 in parallel terms, explaining: "When, Sire, you were only one day old, you were as adult with regard to justice as though you were thirty."[48]

In effect, to adopt this fiction was to make the still mentally incompetent king into the symbolic head of government, the hope being, apparently, that the very innocence of his being would temper discord and strife among those who had to do the actual governing in his name. It seldom worked out that way. In France, the usefulness of the approach was first tested not in a minority, but during one of Charles VI's periodic bouts with insanity. The first time madness had struck him, his wife Isabeau of Bavaria had served as regent, but by 1403, when illness recurred, fear of her own political involvements, of her partisan partiality, had transformed her into an unacceptable candidate. On the other hand, acrimony had become so pervasive among the princes of the blood that agreement on one of their number was equally impossible.

The solution finally adopted was a variant of the adult-king theory. Charles would remain theoretically in charge; there would be no regency; and the actual business of government would be handled "by the advice, deliberation, and counsel" of the queens, the warring princes, other members of the lineage, the constable, the chancellor, and the wise men of the council. This decision was first announced in April 1403 and then reformulated as a perpetual edict on December 26, 1407—or, in other words, scarcely a month after the duke of Burgundy had seen fit to have the king's brother Louis of Orleans assassinated.[49] The beneficial effects of such a system seem far from apparent.

English experience proved little different during the minority of Henry VI. Gloucester warred continually with Beaufort, and if outward tranquillity ever descended on the council, it was a consequence not of legal theory, but of the conciliatory skills of Bedford, called home from France to restore order. The obvious difficulty was that in the practical world of affairs any theory of perpetual adulthood was apt to seem highly implausible when confronted by the reality of a king who was either a babe or a madman. Besides, there could be times when having an acknowledged child on the throne had clear advantages. Insofar as law had long held that none had the right to cede the property of a child, minorities became periods when the king's possessions were effectively inalienable. Even as early as Henry III it was held that no valid grants could be made in perpetuity before his majority,[50] and in the 1240s Louis IX was to find it exceedingly useful to claim, when instituting his *enquêteurs,* that his own youth relieved him of all personal responsibility for any acts of misgovernment committed by his mother's officials during her regency.[51] Richard II took the same position, albeit with less beneficent intent, when proclaiming his majority in 1389;[52] and when the theory of a minor crown had the effect of making only its property inalienable, not that of the perpetual adult who wore it, men were still to find occasional profit in stressing the true age of their kings. At the Congress of Arras, for instance, the English found it advantageous to argue in 1435 that they were unable to enter into serious negotiations with the French—in particular, that they were unable to cede the land needed to achieve peace—until Henry VI had come of age and could give his personal assent.[53]

In practical terms, then, the theory of an adult king could lead to endless difficulties, but nowhere more clearly than in the case of Henry VI and his cousin Richard Beauchamp, earl of Warwick. On June 1,

1428, the legally adult king, aged six, sealed a letter in which, acting entirely on his own authority, he appointed Warwick his tutor and guardian. In the letter's words, the earl's principal task would be "to teach us and make us learn." Here, though, an obvious problem arose, one that Henry solved by again using his adult authority: "[A]nd if," he wrote, "we estrange ourself from learning or trespass or do misdeeds contrary to the teachings and will of our said cousin," then the new tutor has royal permission "to punish us reasonably from time to time . . . as other princes of our age have been accustomed to be punished both in this our kingdom and elsewhere." The letter then goes on to say that if, at any time, Henry or someone acting on his behalf should try to change these provisions, Warwick is to pay no attention.[54]

Nor is this the end of the story. Four years later, on November 29, 1432, Warwick approached the council with a nagging problem. He pointed out that the king, now ten, was increasing in years, stature, "and also in conceit and knowledge of his high and royal authority and estate, the which naturally causes him, and from day to day as he groweth should cause him, more and more to grouch with chastising and to loath it." As a result, the harried earl asked the council to promise "that they shall firmly and truly assist him in the exercise of the charge and occupation that he hath about the king's person, namely in chastising of him for his defaults." Lastly, Warwick closed by asking the council to back him up in the event that Henry should "conceive indignation" against him, a request to which all present gave willing assent.[55] So much for the realities of legal adulthood in the Lancastrian nursery.

In a sense, though, Warwick's was a universal dilemma, for in England and France alike, the child as king posed problems that neither kingdom could solve. Yet in their several attempts they reveal much about their differing political structures, the one a land in which the king's wishes prevailed, even beyond the grave; the other a realm in which chance and belief had made possible the participation of men not drawn from the royal family—sometimes, indeed, to the exclusion of that family. Still, the two countries retained some similarities, for on both sides of the Channel minorities were a period in which politics prevailed over law, and at no time more clearly than when the majority of a king had not only to be proclaimed in theory, but accepted in practice. In that instance, there were no rules in either land, and kings often became adults not because they had reached some magical age, but because, like Edward III and Louis XIII, they simply announced the fact of their majority—and then made it stick. Perhaps the point was best though nonroyally put in Christopher St. German's treatise from 1523, *Doctor and Student*. After the student points out that majority under the common law comes only at twenty-one, he asks whether the man who makes a highly profitable land transaction at twenty can later cancel it on grounds of minority. To which the doctor responds:

> Me seemeth that, forasmuch as the law of *England* . . . is grounded upon a presumption, . . . that infants commonly afore they be of the age of twenty-one years be not able to govern themselves, that yet, forasmuch as that presumption faileth in this infant, that he may not in this case ask the land again that he hath sold to his great advantage.[56]

The doctor's is, possibly, a proper rule for kings as well. If so, the real truth is that the child-kings of England and France came of age only when, unlike the martyred St. Kenelm or Edward V who followed him, they were able to show through success in governance that the presumption of infancy had failed.

PART II

KINGS AND THEIR KINGSHIP

IN SPITE of the insights gained from minorities and dynastic policy, the nature of kingship itself remains elusive. And little wonder, since that nature was constantly changing. In the beginning, at the time of the Germanic migrations, kings had functioned primarily as tribal chiefs, warriors who led their people in battle. Then, as settlement occurred, they began extending their authority to times of peace, often in the face of stiff resistance. The result was chaos. Gibbon was doubtless extreme when he described the situation as despotism tempered by assassination, but in his aphoristic disdain there resides a germ of truth: in the early Middle Ages limits on kingship were often imposed by nothing more subtle than brute opposition to it.

With conversion to Christianity, new concepts appeared. The ideal king was now to serve as the shepherd of his people. His duty, seldom realized in practice, was to care for his flock by protecting it, preserving its laws, and providing for its salvation. Above all else, kings remained warriors, but because their actions took place within an increasingly Christian context, their conduct became subject to religious judgment. Indeed, the extent to which rulers instituted religious reform only after experiencing political disaster suggests a growing tendency to assume that success in this life would come uniquely to those whose own purity of purpose had merited the favor of God. As Alcuin expressed at least part of these views when writing for Charlemagne, "in accordance with the aid of divine piety," the king's duty was "to defend on all sides the Holy Church of Christ from pagan incursion and infidel devastation abroad, and within to add strength to the Catholic faith by our recognition of it."[1]

By the thirteenth century, if kings ruled by the grace of God, their actual capacities were best conveyed by the title they bore: *dominus rex,* "lord king."[2] As lord, rulers enjoyed the profits of holdings that were just beginning to be called the domain in France but that had long been known as the demesne in England. Here, though, qualification is in order. In English usage, "demesne" was overwhelmingly a landed concept and comprised those manors held directly by the king. On the

---

THE WILTON DIPTYCH *Overleaf*   Backed by saints, a kneeling Richard II prepares to receive the banner of St. George as heaven's gift. (*The National Gallery, London*)

other hand, "domain" in the French sense took in not just lands under the immediate seigneurial control of the king, but also the fiefs of minor lords who lacked high jurisdiction or, in other words, the right to judge serious offenses. Nevertheless, for present purposes the difference is immaterial; to be *dominus* in either land also meant having lordship over other men, vassals both great and small, who had sworn their allegiance in ceremonies of homage and fealty.

Here notions of kingship begin to obtrude, the *rex* side of the title. As king, rulers enjoyed a more transcendent authority, one that burdened them with obligations even as it provided possibilities for the expansion of their powers. Above all else, it was the king's duty to protect the Church and, as Henry II found to his regret, the penalties for failing to meet it could be heavy. Still, this obligation brought advantages as well, those regalian rights that permitted kings to receive the revenues of vacant bishoprics and to participate in the selection of prelates. Second, the king was the guardian of law, what was coming to be called the font of justice. To him belonged the responsibility for preserving the right relationships in society, and if, at the start of the century, this duty was fulfilled primarily through the judgments of his courts, by its end it would further involve legislative activity, the creation of law. Because, however, people continued to believe that law made the king, not the king the law, implicit limits were thereby placed on royal action. To exceed the law was to risk being viewed as a tyrant, and tyrants, men knew, were rulers that no Christian need obey.

Lastly, though inseparable from the above, to be king meant being the defender of one's realm and guardian of its people. In a sense, this was primarily a military obligation, but it related to the preservation of justice as well since to repel foreign invasion was also to prevent possible subjugation to alien laws, unsanctioned by God. Moreover, in times of emergency, the king could call on others for support, aid that was initially military in form and then became increasingly financial as the century wore on. At a more general level, though, the duties of defender and guardian created much broader responsibilities. If, for example, it was the sovereign's duty to maintain peace and to insure that justice prevailed, it followed—and would be more and more claimed—that any king had the right to intervene anywhere in his kingdom to make certain that, in the default of others, this duty was met. The germ of these ideas had long been present in both England and France, but

nowhere did they find more succinct expression than in Edgar the
Peaceable's coronation oath of 973:

> In the name of the Holy Trinity I promise three things to the Christian
> people my subjects: first, that God's Church and all Christian people
> of my realm shall enjoy true peace; second, that I forbid to all ranks of
> men robbery and all wrongful deeds; third, that I urge and command
> justice and mercy in all judgments, so that the gracious and compas-
> sionate God who lives and reigns may grant us all His everlasting
> mercy.[3]

Broadly speaking, then, monarchy on either side of the Channel
shared many assumptions, and yet the specific evidence has already
shown that differences were not only great, but growing. French kingship was more strictly dynastic and imbued with a sense of sacred
mission, whereas almost of necessity its English counterpart had had to
devise more flexible rules and at the same time displayed little ability to
fashion compelling myths through which to express its eternal destiny.
Yet these were no more than tendencies over time, and from them it
would be difficult to understand either why individual kings behaved as
they did or how, in turn, their actions and outlook helped to shape
conceptions of kingship as well as the course of their countries' history.

In this regard, three kings merit attention—Louis IX, Edward I, and
Richard II—all of them monarchs who inherited much from the past,
but also men whose own accomplishments, and reactions to them,
placed an indelible stamp on the political culture of their lands. Louis
was the crusader and saint, a king whose reputation for justice was to
make his reign the model of kingship to which all subsequent reformers
would demand a return. Edward, his nephew, was no saint, but his
reputation as a law-giver was equally as great, and the way in which he
responded to opposition not only clarifies the nature of English kingship
in operation, but also the nature of the forces with which it had to
contend. Lastly, if Richard, too, seems a man of great talent, his reign
was to end in disaster amid charges that his high conception of office
had violated every fundamental precept of English rule. In short, to
understand these kings is to learn more of the world that could produce
both Joan of Arc and Richard III.

3

St. Louis and
the Mise of Amiens

Because the Mise of Amiens was the arbitral judgment in which Louis IX attempted to quash the Provisions of Oxford, French historians have never studied it with care. For them, it has seemed no more than an incident from English history, and therefore unworthy of note. At the same time, English historians have proved equally negligent. After all, the Mise reflects only the views of an outsider, a mere foreigner, and it surely did nothing to end the disputes between Henry III and his barons. One might have expected that constitutional historians of the traditional school would have seized on this judgment as a wonderful opportunity for attacking the absolutist proclivities of the French, but in fact their interpretations were few, brief, and remarkably restrained. Even Bishop Stubbs, so often criticized for bias these days, found it possible to be judicious. "The king of France," he wrote, "had his own idea of the dignity of royalty, and was too humble and charitable not to credit other men with the same desire of doing their duty which was predominant in himself."[1]

The only hostile note—and a muted one at that—comes from R. F. Treharne, possibly the warmest recent supporter of the barons and Simon de Montfort, their leader:

> [F]or many in England, the Provisions of Oxford, despite all that Henry alleged against them, had stood for something very big—for an

ideal of justice and good government, of reform in law and in administration, not to be forsaken at the bidding of a foreign king, however
saintly. . . . There is no question of Louis' eager zeal for justice . . .
or of his sincere desire for good government, and [earlier] negotiations . . . suggest that . . . he had [once] entertained some sympathy
with Simon's position. But Louis was a King who held a high ideal of
the dignity and authority of his office, and to him the constitutional
checks which Simon desired to impose upon the royal authority must
have seemed such an invasion of royal rights and duties as to be
almost sinful, impious and sacrilegious.[2]

   Unsupported and general though these interpretations may be, they
begin to raise troubling questions about the true nature of St. Louis'
political ideas as they underlie his reasoning in the Mise. French schol-
arship is of little help in solving this problem since few of the recent
works on the thirteenth century are directly relevant, and the range of
their views is enormous. It is a curious fact of French historiography
that no full-dress study of the reign has appeared since Lenain de Tille-
mont's antiquarian classic of the eighteenth century, and the resulting
vacuum has encouraged endless interpretive controversy. Among
French historians of the present century, for example, Langlois gave
thanks that France in the thirteenth century had been strong enough to
afford the luxury of a weak and peace-loving king,[3] whereas Fawtier
was equally insistent that if absolutism had its origins in the Middle
Ages, St. Louis was its founder.[4] Finally the American William Jordan
adds that "even when we pay due regard to the impressive accomplishments of the saint-king's predecessors, it may still be said, and quite
truthfully, that it was Louis IX who was chiefly responsible for giving
substance to the hitherto vague sense of the identity, purpose, and
destiny of the kingdom of France."[5] Which authority, if any, is one to
believe?

   In this context of uncertainty the Mise of Amiens takes on obvious
interest since it is one of the few documents in which Louis IX was ever
forced by circumstances to express his views on the rights and duties of
kings. It is, then, a piece of evidence rather more concrete than the
familiar royal sayings reported by Jean de Joinville, statements that may
accurately reflect Louis's general outlook, and yet ones that suffer from
the shortcoming that they were informal remarks of the moment, and of
uncertain authenticity at that. Even if accurate, none is a well-consid-
ered and official pronouncement like the Mise.

Although the train of events leading to Amiens is generally familiar, a few of its features need emphasis. By 1258 Henry III's hopeless mismanagement had so angered the English barons that they imposed on him the so-called Provisions of Oxford. In brief compass, the Provisions attempted to limit his powers by insisting that his chief ministers should receive their appointments from a small council of barons, not from Henry himself; that these ministers should swear their oaths of office only to this council; and, lastly, that all those who held governmental positions were to be Englishmen and not foreigners such as the king had been accustomed to appoint in times past. Three times a year, the councillors, possibly joined by others, were to meet in parliaments, at which times they were "to examine the state of the kingdom and to consider the common needs of the kingdom and likewise of the king." Other clauses then dealt with a variety of other matters, notably the reform of local justice.[6]

Unsurprisingly, Henry III did not take kindly to these arrangements. His complaints assumed various and often petty forms, but all of them repeatedly stressed the obvious, that the Provisions of Oxford denied him the essence of his kingship.[7] On several occasions Henry carried his grievances to the pope, thanks to John his feudal overlord as well as pontiff, and in due course two popes, Alexander IV and Urban IV, freed him from his oath to observe the Provisions. Acting solely in their papal capacity, they argued that the oath had been given under duress and was therefore invalid. Further, they ordered the Provisions quashed in their entirety, though they hastened to add that all articles beneficial to the Church were to continue to have force.[8]

In no way did these bulls end the dispute. The barons were occasionally troubled by them,[9] but their qualms did not prevent continuing opposition to the king. Given the balance of forces on either side, arbitration, though hotly rejected when initially proposed, began to appear increasingly desirable. Finally, in December 1263, Henry, Simon de Montfort, and their followers arrived at a mutual agreement to take their differences to St. Louis for judgment, solemnly binding themselves to observe his decision.[10]

The following month, January 1264, Louis rendered his opinion, ruling for Henry III in all respects. First, he found against the Provisions "especially since it appears that the supreme pontiff by his letters has proclaimed them quashed and annulled." Second, after rejecting in detail every specific restriction that the Provisions had placed on kingly authority, he added a more positive and general statement: "Likewise we declare and ordain that the said king shall have full power and unrestricted rule within his kingdom and such status and such full power as he enjoyed before the time aforesaid," that is, before the issuance of the Provisions of Oxford. Finally, in closing he made the following reservation, his one concession to the baronial opposition: "By the present ordinance, however, we do not wish or intend in any way to derogate from royal privileges, charters, liberties, establishments, and praiseworthy customs of the kingdom of England, existing before the time of the same provisions."[11]

This statement, then, is the essence of the Mise of Amiens, and if one can unravel St. Louis' intentions there, it may be possible to grasp what those intentions reveal about his views on the nature of kingship and government. This is, however, no easy task since, as the quotations demonstrate, Louis was far from explicit about the reasoning that informed his judgment. Indeed, Treharne has argued that no one can ever know his true thoughts on the matter because, as he points out, the Mise is little more than a restatement of the arguments that Henry's lawyers had presented in the pleadings that preceded Louis' decision. Thus, says Treharne, if anyone's position is reflected in the Mise, it is that of the king of England, not of France.[12] Nevertheless, even though the technicalities of this case are undeniably correct, as a comparison of documents would show, they overlook an obvious point, that Louis IX based his judgment on the reasoning of his royal brother-in-law because, presumably, that reasoning accorded well with his own—or at least with his own as he found it desirable to express views publicly.

This last qualification is made necessary by the problems arising out of Louis' statement that he was voiding the Provisions "especially since it appears that the supreme pontiff by his letters has proclaimed them quashed and annulled." From Henry's long efforts to gain that end, and from his lawyers' insistence on its importance in their presentation at Amiens, it would appear that the king of England actually believed in the efficacy of papal judgments. Yet everything suggests that the attitudes of the saintly king of France were rather more complicated. Though no absolute proof is possible, the whole tendency of French monarchical policy at least since the reign of Philip Augustus had been so contrary to any acceptance of papal sovereignty over matters of state that it becomes difficult to take at face value Louis' seeming acceptance of it here. Under Philip Augustus, for example, the king had stoutly opposed papal intervention in such widely divergent matters as the Albigensian Crusade, Philip's border wars in Normandy, and in the hotly disputed question of succession to the Empire.[13] Moreover, that his grandson was of similar mind is fully demonstrated by his flat refusal in 1245 to accept, or even aid, Innocent IV's deposition of Frederick II; by his unwillingness to back sentences of excommunication with temporal sanctions in the absence of a concurring royal inquest; and by the sharp memoir commonly known as "The Protest of St. Louis" that was presented to the pope in 1247.[14]

Since such arguments can easily be overstated, possibly the safest approach would be to suggest that St. Louis' attitude toward papal claims to sovereignty in political matters was not unlike that expressed in 1261 by the English barons toward the sovereignty of Henry III. When Henry complained that the council as envisaged at Oxford was failing to follow his "necessary and honest commands," the barons replied that they would willingly "obey the king as their lord," but only when, and insofar as, his orders were "reasonable."[15] In much the same way, when Louis IX found his views in accord with the pope's, as he did in the case of the Provisions, he showed no hesitancy in acknowledging papal superiority. In order to understand his conception of monarchy, though, it is important to recognize that he was no more hesitant in denying that superiority in those instances where he found the pope's views not to be "reasonable." Papal sovereignty might therefore be recognized from time to time, but for all practical purposes the king of France claimed freedom from its jurisdiction.

Nevertheless, because independence alone cannot prove the extent of one's power, some attention should also be paid to the amount of royal authority actually permitted by the Mise. In this regard, Louis was exceedingly vague, saying only that "the said king shall have full power and unrestricted rule within his kingdom and such status and such full power as he enjoyed before the time aforesaid." This passage would be difficult to interpret in any event, but the problems involved are intensified by the use of such words as full power, status, and kingdom—*plena potestas, status,* and *regnum*—words over the meaning of which scholars have wrestled for years.

It is clear, though, that these words, especially "full power" and "kingdom"—are so crucial to St. Louis' reasoning that their meaning must be reexamined, even at the risk of provoking controversy. Given the context provided, his intent in using "full power" is possibly easiest to grasp since, even though the term can be highly ambiguous in matters of procuration and representation, it seems less so here. In particular, the phrasing of the document demonstrates that "full" power in no way means "complete" or "absolute," an interpretation that would be possible only if the term's first appearance were not later qualified in the same sentence by the provision allowing Henry only "such status and such full power as he enjoyed before the time afore-said." The restrictions thus introduced certainly suggest that the enjoy-ment of "full power" can give the king little claim to absolute authority.

In fact, the limitations on that authority are then amply explained by Louis' final statement, that he did not intend his decision "to derogate from royal privileges, charters, liberties, establishments, and praise-worthy customs of the kingdom of England existing before the time of the same provisions." If such limitations, notably Magna Carta in its royally approved form, were to continue to have force even after Henry had recovered full power, it follows that this power, far from being absolute, continued in Louis' mind to be constrained and defined by custom and law, an old medieval notion, perhaps, yet one that, when reaffirmed in the Mise, gives significant testimony to the extent of St. Louis' traditionalism.

On the other hand, this traditionalism acquires an unexpected poten-tial as soon as one begins to explore the implications of "full power and unrestricted rule" in relation to the possible meaning of "kingdom." In the first half of the thirteenth century there had been a sharp increase, both practical and conceptual, in French royal authority. Moreover, as the king increased his strength, men's understanding of what was meant by his kingdom underwent similar change. At the start of the century, both Philip Augustus and Louis VIII appear to have thought of their realm as a judicially defined entity, one frequently consisting of nothing more than the domain or, more precisely, those areas over which they exercised an immediate and direct jurisdiction. In the sense here intended, principalities like the duchy of Burgundy or the county of Flanders were not parts of the kingdom of France insofar as their people and lands fell outside the normal competence of royal courts. Over time, though, the situation began to change. Royal powers of justice broke free of this narrowly domainal reasoning, and through use of a variety of techniques succeeding kings proved so successful in broaden-ing the concept of their kingdom and of the jurisdiction of their courts that by the end of the century the lawyers of Philip the Fair would confidently assert that "everything within the limits of his kingdom belongs to the lord king, especially protection, high justice and dominion."[16]

No one would dispute the fact that St. Louis was himself intimately involved in these developments. Through his care, the parlement of Paris was established; bailiffs and seneschals received more precise but growing jurisdictions; and *enquêteurs* were created to insure that the legal rights of all men, not least the king, would continue to be respected.[17] Moreover, in his foreign policy St. Louis displayed a similar interest in strengthening the territorial and jurisdictional integrity of the realm, notably in the Treaty of Corbeil (1258) with Aragon and the Treaty of Paris (1259) with England. In these treaties Louis surrendered much—the old Carolingian Spanish March to Aragon and legal title, though in fief, to much of the old duchy of Aquitaine to England—but at the same time he enhanced his own position throughout southern France by attempting to settle all the endless disputes over jurisdictional rights that had long clouded the king's claims to authority. As he put it himself when defending the Treaty of Paris against the objections of his councillors: "it seems to me that what I give [Henry] is given to good purpose, since he has not hitherto been my liegeman, but will now have to do me homage."[18] Nor should this justification be taken lightly, for the treaty involved not only the simple renewal of an homage long broken, but also the infeudation of lands that even longer had been purely allodial.[19]

These policies help to explain what is undoubtedly the most perplexing aspect of the Mise: its formal judicial character. Treharne has quite properly remarked that Henry, Simon, and their partisans had agreed only to arbitration, but that they actually received a solemn legal decision in which Louis IX functioned as a judge, deciding which party had the better right, and not as an arbiter trying to find some acceptable middle ground on which both parties could agree, regardless of right.[20] Without an understanding of the changing nature of royal judicial concepts, the legal foundations of the Mise would become inexplicable, for how could the king of France claim formal jurisdiction over a dispute involving only the realm of England?

It seems certain that St. Louis wanted such a jurisdiction, if only to help Henry. Although their relations had not always been cordial, and even though the negotiations leading up to the Treaty of Paris had been far from easy, once the English baronage had raised the standard of revolt, Louis was quick to come to the aid of his beleaguered fellow king and brother-in-law. For example, one clause of the treaty specified that Louis was to pay Henry funds to defray the cost of maintaining five hundred knights for two years, funds that were to be used "only in the service of God, or of Holy Church, or to the profit of the realm of England, to be determined by the consent of loyal Englishmen and the magnates."[21] Nevertheless, when Henry broke with the barons and rejected the Provisions of Oxford, Louis proved willing again and again to advance money against this sum purely for Henry's use in the resulting civil war. Fittingly, though, the original language was changed so that the funds could be rather more ambiguously employed "in the service of God or to the profit of the king of England."[22] Nor was financial assistance the only form of aid provided, for Louis and his circle were also active in attempts to restore peace by bringing the barons to heel. Little wonder, then, that on April 18, 1260, Henry should have exclaimed to Louis: "After God you are my salvation."[23]

Still, the hard fact remains that in no way did a desire to help provide the necessary legal justification for changing the expected arbitration proceedings into a formal judicial hearing followed by solemn and presumptively binding judgment. Treharne argues in explanation that the form used at Amiens, the so-called *petitio libelli,* was adopted not only because it was familiar to English and French alike, but more especially because both Henry and his recalcitrant barons had frequently resorted to it in their previous quarrels.[24] Yet this formalist argument evades the central issue, Louis' seeming lack of jurisdictional competence, and Treharne, seeing the point, then capitalizes on it to insist that Louis' highly royalist decision became inevitable, and can be understood, only in that context:

> Since neither customary nor positive law could be applied, Louis could judge only by natural law. To Louis, with his religious conception and idealization of kingship, natural law could give only one answer in a dispute between a lawfully anointed king, demanding undiminished restoration of the royal power and rights which he held immediately of God, to whom alone he was responsible, and his barons seeking to control that divine right through a committee of subjects according to a constitution devised by men.[25]

The obvious difficulty with this interpretation is that the Mise of Amiens is singularly devoid of appeals to natural law or to some medieval precursor of divine-right kingship. On the surface, then, the case seems weak, so it becomes preferable to explore other alternatives, among them the possibility that Louis, anxious to help Henry, had finally succeeded in persuading himself that he did in fact have a quite proper jurisdiction over the dispute. Given the limited and inconclusive nature of the evidence, such a hypothesis must be viewed as highly tentative, but for all that, it remains suggestive.

The idea of arbitration was far from new in 1264, Simon de Montfort having proposed it three years earlier. Nevertheless, each time one side had offered it as a potential solution, the other had raised objections, with the result that no progress had previously been made. In 1263, however, St. Louis intervened directly. As various English chronicles report the incident, notably the Flores Historiarum, the Annals of Dunstable, and the Continuation of the Gesta Regum of Gervase of Canterbury, Henry and his wife persuaded Louis to summon Henry and the English barons to the French court, the legal basis for this summons being the assertion that they were all, thanks to their French holdings (real or claimed), vassals of the king of France. Once assembled, the barons were to be arraigned on charges of rebellion against Louis' vassal Henry. Simon and his followers naturally protested, arguing that they "were not bound to answer for their actions in the court of the king of France, but that they should be judged In the court of the king of England, by their peers and by faithful men of oath." When the nobles of Louis' own court supported this position, one that echoed Chapter 39 of the original Magna Carta, the plan was abandoned and further negotiations then led to the proceedings at Amiens.[26]

One never knows, of course, how much weight to put on chroniclers' tales, but this one has the ring of truth. It finds support not only in Louis' obvious desire to help Henry, but also in fragmentary evidence in the *Calendar of Patent Rolls,*[27] the high value Louis placed on Henry's vassalage when defending the Treaty of Paris, and especially in the ever-expanding nature of French royal justice and jurisdiction during the reign and the century. Thus it seems not unlikely that at Amiens in 1264, Louis reverted to his reasoning of the previous year. If so, the highly judicial character of the Mise resulted not from dependence on natural law, but rather from Louis IX's conviction that Henry's liege homage had created a French jurisdication even in those cases when Henry was acting solely in his capacity as king of England.

Although such a failure to distinguish between a man and his various offices should doubtless be seen as yet another instance of St. Louis' old-fashioned traditionalism, it has enormous implications. If a king could so easily manipulate the obligations of vassalage, he could radically increase his jurisdictional powers. As a result, even though the Mise of Amiens failed in its attempt to quash the English barons, men who operated on quite different beliefs, the judgment itself and the principles upon which it was based give striking proof of the ways in which traditionalism could be harnessed, possibly without conscious thought about it, to revolutionary ends. Louis IX may have had no more in mind than the creation of an acceptably legal framework within which he could most effectively give aid to Henry, but the result was a precedent that would demonstrate to successors more ambitious than he how vassalage could provide a vehicle for rapid growth in the scope of royal judicial competence. Thus, while it remains true that St. Louis' insistence on full power for Henry should be qualified by a sense of the limitations that medieval men placed on the use of such power, it seems equally clear that the Mise formed a part of that process through which the conceptual limits of both the kingdom of France and its jurisdiction were being profoundly transformed, thereby altering the very basis for French political life.

In final illustration, it may be instructive to ponder the assumptions underlying St. Louis' statement that he did not "wish or intend in any way to derogate from royal privileges, charters, liberties, establishments, and praiseworthy customs of the kingdom of England existing before the time of the same provisions." This reservation would appear to have new implications, for, even though French royal charters had long contained a seemingly similar clause, earlier practice had been simply to grant or ordain something. "saving the rights of others," but without in any way specifying the origins of those rights. Here, however, Louis makes the flat assertion that, except for the "praiseworthy customs of the kingdom of England," the only rights that are safe from his possible derogation are those that can be shown to have derived from specific royal grants.

Although the royalism of this phrasing may derive in part from the peculiar circumstances under which the Mise was issued, it also testifies to a growing conviction, implicit in St. Louis' creation of the *enquêteurs* and explicit in Edward I's later establishment of those *quo warranto* proceedings that so exasperated John of Warenne,[28] that all rights, especially of justice, were exercisable only upon proof that they had once been directly and formally received from the king. Indeed, even the limitation of St. Louis' acceptance of the customs of England to those that were "praiseworthy" suggests a parallel point, for it recalls his famous advice to his son to uphold the good law while putting down the bad, an admonition which, if followed and accepted, would give the king control not just over specifically "royal privileges, charters, liberties, [and] establishments," but over pure custom as well.[29]

In the 1280s, Beaumanoir could assure St. Louis' brother Robert of Clermont that "every baron is sovereign in his barony," but he found it necessary to add that "the king is sovereign above all others."[30] In practice, that had not always been true, and if the process of change had begun with Louis VII and Philip Augustus, it took on new dimensions with Louis IX, ones that were destined to last. For Louis was a saint, a reality long recognized even before his death. To the Englishman Matthew Paris, he was "the king of mortal kings"; to one of his own subjects, he was simply "Louis the Just." And though Joinville once told him that he had "no desire as yet to kiss [his] bones," the implications of that "as yet" were to be fully realized when this bluff comrade-in-arms dedicated an altar to his name and then asked Louis X to bestow "some relics of the true body of the saint . . . so that those who visited his altar might increase their devotion."[31] Little wonder that Henry and his barons should have so willingly agreed to Louis' arbitration.

Yet that is far from the whole of the story. Saints are different from ordinary people, and Louis IX participated fully in that difference. It was, for example, a king's duty to seek advice, and Louis did so consistently. On the other hand, he seldom followed that advice, when offered. Rather, he appears always to have assumed that his own convictions gave more accurate expression to divine intent that did those of his sinful subjects. As a result, he knew far better than they which were the good laws and which the bad, and so felt perfectly free to make an unfettered choice between them. In much the same way, he could accept the Treaty of Paris and act as judge in the Mise even though his policies in both cases were not those of his barons. In short, Louis believed, and believed deeply, that kingship conferred a status notably superior to that enjoyed by even the noblest of his nobles. Moreover, when his views differed from theirs, they went along with his judgment because the very sanctity of his life had convinced them that his decisions were apt to have merit. The result over time was the creation of a monarchy that so revered the memory of "the good king St. Louis" that future rulers would often assert that they, too, were under no obligation to seek the consent of their subjects. Such a conclusion goes well beyond the specifics of the Mise, of course, but in no way is it contradictory of them. On the contrary, the Mise of Amiens provides a lens through which the nature of French kingship comes much more sharply into focus, and precisely because that focus emphasizes the ways in which the Capetian monarchy established its claims and created a political culture, this document becomes vastly more important than its English commentators have made it appear. If so, then the peace-loving St. Louis seems to have been a luxury that France could well afford.

4

Edward I and the
Confirmation of the Charters

Among the familiar sights crowding the landscape of English history
from the dooms of Ine to that crown plucked from a hawthorn bush at
Bosworth, few are more deeply cherished than the crisis of 1297 and the
so-called "Confirmation of the Charters" to which it gave rise. Despite
differences in detail, historians have shown remarkable agreement in
seeing it as the one defeat suffered by St. Louis' nephew Edward I in
what was otherwise a long and notably successful reign.[1] Stubbs set the
pattern, calling the "result singularly in harmony with what seems from
history and experience to be the natural direction of English progress,"[2]
and Wilkinson is only one among the many who have more recently
elaborated on that theme:

> The crisis of 1297 . . . placed a definite check on the tendencies
> which Edward I had shown, to ignore the deep principles of the
> constitution under stress of the necessities which confronted the na-
> tion. . . . It was a landmark in the advance of the knights . . . toward
> political maturity. It helped to establish the tradition of co-operation
> and political alliance between the knights and the magnates, on which
> a good deal of the political future of England was to depend. . . .
> What the opposition achieved, in 1297, was a great vindication of the
> ancient political principle of government by consent . . . [T]he crisis
> of 1297 . . . decisively prevented any arbitrary use of the king's
> power, to obtain military service from his subjects beyond that pro-
> vided by ancient service or freely rendered on a basis of consent.[3]

Such an interpretation makes very good sense within the confines of a wholly English historiography; there is little in the evidence itself that would lead one to challenge it. Nevertheless, if English sources appear to support this view, at least when seen in a purely English context, nearly contemporaneous events in France, and the interpretation long placed on them, serve to raise troubling doubts about it. For the France of Philip the Fair faced many of the same problems, military and financial, as did the England of Edward I, and the ways in which Philip's government attempted to cope with its difficulties suggest that Edward I may not have experienced anything like the reverse in 1297 that is commonly assumed. Moreover, if he did not, then a new sense of English kingship begins to emerge, one markedly different from the French, doubtless, and yet one much more politically adroit, much less ensnared in constitutional conflict, than the traditional story has made it seem.

During the 1290s, the French monarchy, like its English counterpart, had relied primarily on feudal levies in creating an army, and it had financed its wars with a combination of sales and hearth taxes, clerical tenths, and, from 1295 on, with property taxes first of a hundredth, then of a fiftieth. The last fiftieth was levied in 1300. Although in no instance did the government claim that these property taxes were a substitute for military service, Strayer is unquestionably correct in concluding that most people assumed that commutation was the underlying basis for this new form of taxation.[4]

These hundredths and fiftieths proved wildly unpopular. Chroniclers complained about them more than any other tax during Philip's reign,[5] so it is hardly surprising to find that in 1302, when taxation again became necessary after a two-year interval, the French government adopted a different approach. All males over fifteen were summarily called out for military service throughout the kingdom, and those unwilling to appear were encouraged to purchase exemption through a system of fines in which payment was initially set, perhaps unsurprisingly, at one-fiftieth of each person's propertied worth. In this way the connection between taxes and military service was made explicit, and those choosing to pay the fine were ipso facto deemed to have given their individual consent.[6]

Because the new approach met with considerably more acceptance, the French continued to use it through 1305, the last year in which a general tax was levied before 1313–14, at the very end of Philip's reign. In those two years, however, when the government relied again on this technique, the results were less fortunate, and collections had to be suspended, though for reasons having nothing to do with the procedure itself. Rather, the Flemings, against whom military campaigns were envisaged, decided in both instances to negotiate, and in the absence of hostilities Philip appears to have felt duty-bound to observe the legal maxim, *cessante causa, cessat effectus:* the threat of war having ended, he suspended the tax and ordered the monies collected to be returned.[7] In short, there is nothing in the record to indicate that the French had found the procedures devised in 1302 anything but eminently satisfactory, for, as Strayer puts it, they were rooted in principles that all but the most recalcitrant had to accept, however reluctantly:

> The new tax was based on the theory that all subjects could be summoned to defend the realm in case of emergency. Once summoned they would be glad to buy exemption from actual service. This theory had no stronger historical foundation than the earlier claim that all subjects could be taxed for defense. Yet a demand for military service was less shocking to the medieval mind than a demand for money. . . . [T]o take money instead of service was an undoubted prerogative of any ruler by 1300. Once the right to demand universal service was admitted the king could raise an army and obtain the money needed to support it by a single act of summons.[8]

This interpretation of French tactics raises serious doubts about the validity of traditional views on the English crisis of 1297. Insofar as that crisis is supposed to have started when Edward I called out all £20 landholders for service in the army, and then attempted to transform their supposed military obligations into an equally dubious right to tax, his basic approach bears a striking resemblance to that employed by Philip the Fair only five years later, one that the French king was again to use at least five more times in the course of his reign. It does not follow from the parallel that Philip was consciously trying to follow the English precedent; on the contrary, everything suggests that the background of his thinking was entirely French.[9] Still, if 1297 had been anything like the disaster for Edward that historians allege, it seems highly improbable that the French would have so blithely embarked on such a similar course so soon thereafter. After all, English and French alike have always had a fairly accurate knowledge of developments on the other side of the Channel—especially of the relative successes and failures experienced by each other's governments—so a royal defeat in

England would hardly have encouraged Philip to employ the approach he used in 1302. Quite the contrary, one would expect that a defeat on Edward's part would have led Philip to adopt a different strategy.

Nevertheless, in terms of the issue here being raised, it must be stressed that the question whether Philip the Fair even knew of, let alone acted upon, Edward's experience in 1297 is of no importance. It is sufficient simply to pose a purely hypothetical problem, whether the apparent success of the French in employing these methods should lead to a re-evaluation of the traditional story of Edward's defeat. In other words, it makes no real difference whether a causal relationship can in fact be established, for it is enough to ask: If Philip the Fair *had* reviewed his knowledge of 1297 while deciding upon his own best course of action, is it at all likely that he would have seen anything in the English events of five years before that would in any way have led him to reconsider, or even to abandon, the new military and financial policies he was so successfully to introduce?

Strikingly, to give the question this new frame of reference is also markedly to change the nature of the answer received, for to move from an emphasis on long-term constitutional significance to one simply seeking to measure more immediate success or failure is to begin to see the extent to which Edward, far from being defeated in 1297, actually achieved most of his goals, and at a price he was clearly willing to pay. His tactics displayed considerable political acumen and therefore are of no small interest insofar as they suggest how, in practice, the successful English ruler made his monarchy work. But more fully to grasp the point one must review events as Philip the Fair might have seen and interpreted them.

The story begins on January 5, when Archbishop Winchelsey ordered *Clericis laicos* read throughout the archdiocese of Canterbury. In that bull, since Boniface VIII had forbidden laymen to tax the clergy—or the clergy to pay if those laymen persisted—the effect of this declaration was to deprive the king of all ecclesiastical sources of revenue.[10] Nothing daunted, Edward responded by outlawing the clergy on January 30, which was also the day (as he later learned) on which French troops had disastrously defeated the earl of Lincoln in Gascony, and only four days after the government had summoned the magnates to a parliament that was supposed to open at Salisbury on February 24. With the clergy outlawed, royal officials could simply confiscate their goods in lieu of taxes, and with no fear of legal reprisal since, in the eyes of the law, the clergy no longer existed. But when the magnates met at Salisbury, a new problem developed: They refused to go to Gascony unless the king accompanied them, something the latter was loath to do because his own plans called for an independent royal expedition to come to the aid of his new ally, the count of Flanders.[11] As Edward envisioned it, Philip the Fair was to be caught on the horns of a two-pronged offensive.

In no way did this baronial reluctance impede the royal preparations. On April 23, the king ordered all wool and wool fells seized in the kingdom, and he also began to levy heavy prises on beef and pork.[12] Come what may, he was determined to be well supplied and financed. One cannot say whether, at this point, he was also considering the possibility of accompanying his marshal and constable, Bigod and Bohun, as a means of ending his differences with them, but if he were, that option disappeared toward the end of April when Edward became convinced that Philip the Fair was planning to invade Flanders.[13] That meant that its count would need assistance, so any thought of a royal expedition to Gascony went glimmering.

Edward's response to this turn of events showed considerable political insight. On May 15, he "commanded and firmly enjoined" all £20 landholders to be at London on July 7, suitably armed and "ready to cross with us to . . . foreign parts." Simultaneously, however, he sent letters to the magnates, informing them of this action and then only "requiring affectionately and asking" that they, too, be in London on the same day for the same purpose.[14]

These letters placed the barons in an awkward position. Edward had merely asked, not ordered, that they serve, but the magnates had little reason to believe that the £20 landholders would refuse to obey the royal command, and if they were to come while the barons did not, the latter would run considerable risk of becoming the objects of scorn and ridicule, with all honor lost. Moreover, even if they were not to appear, in the £20 landholders the king had discovered the resources needed to carry out his plans. And this was true whether these so-called knights served in person or whether they commuted their service, thereby providing the money with which mercenaries could be hired. One assumes that Edward would have preferred money, given what must have been the landholders' near-total lack of training, but at the same time this was scarcely a decision he had to make in May. Far better simply to leave his options open. To the magnates, though, it was abundantly clear that continued opposition on their part was unlikely to sway or check the king.

Nevertheless, fully to understand the nature of the evolving situation, and of the documents to which it gave rise, one must appreciate the extent to which both barons and knights saw the king's strategy initially not as a shrewd Hobson's choice, but only as a direct means of raising troops. In the 1290s, formal taxation remained a recent innovation, and insofar as taxes had hitherto been rarely sought, subjects had yet to learn the imaginative skill with which rulers could seek them. Whatever justification Edward had for his summons clearly lay in distraint of knighthood.[15] and since those thus distrained had never before been asked to commute their military obligations, it seems to have occurred to no one other than the king that such service could be transformed into cash contributions. But neither did it occur to anyone not to appear. The morning of July 7 saw barons and knights alike assembled in London, all the while protesting that lesser knights had no obligation to serve overseas. Edward remained deaf to all complaints, and on July 8, when the marshal and constable refused to muster the troops, he simply appointed new men who would.[16]

On July 11, Edward began the process of calming his subjects, moving first to heal the breach with the Church. This he did by restoring all confiscated land to Winchelsey.[17] In turn, that gesture made possible the affecting scene three days later when, on a platform erected in front of Westminster Hall, the archbishop joined the king in painting a grim picture of the dangers Edward was about to undergo. Both men then appealed for oaths of fealty to the young Edward of Carnarvon, who was being left behind as regent, but whose station, it was stressed, might be suddenly and tradically elevated by the fortunes of war. Tears were shed by all, and two days later, on July 16, even the constable and marshal swore the required oath.[18] At the same time, Winchelsey summoned a convocation of the Church for August 10, at which meeting it was anticipated that a subsidy would at last be voted for the king's war. Further, in this letter the archbishop expressed for the first time his belief that, in return for financial assistance, the king might prove willing to confirm the charters. Three days later, on July 19, he and other bishops volunteered to help Edward negotiate his differences with his barons.[19]

Now, if one is reviewing these events from the hypothetical perspective of Philip the Fair some five years later, their most striking feature down to this point is that, as they say in New England, Edward hadn't moved a damned inch. He had, it is true, displayed a remarkable flexibility since January, abandoning one course of action and trying another when the first seemed unlikely to work; but the hard fact of the matter is that both barons and knights had appeared in London contrary to their every instinct, and by the middle of July it seemed likely that the clergy would soon approve a subsidy. Thus far, then, Philip would have been hard put to find a royal defeat.

Moreover, when looked at this way, the rest of the story suggests the same conclusion. In late July, the £20 landholders bought off their military service with a tax of an eighth on the laity (a fifth on the towns), and the government moved swiftly to raise it, appointing collectors on the 30th.[20] When the clergy met on August 10, it agreed to ask Boniface VIII for permission to tax itself, but since their response remained filled with rhetorical references to the binding nature of *Clericis laicos,* Edward showed his contempt and increased the pressure by ordering the seizure of all clerical property on the 12th. Graciously, though, he offered these outlaws a choice: Each cleric was permitted to surrender either one-third of his temporalities or one-fifth of his assessed revenues, whichever he preferred.[21]

After justifying his actions in a masterly and statesmanlike letter of August 12,[22] the king sailed for Flanders on the 22nd, leaving the rest of the affair in the hands of his council of regency. And the need for its involvement was quick to arise since, almost as soon as Edward had left, his thoroughly confused and far-from-heroic barons stormed into the Exchequer, furious about the tax authorized by the distrained knights. Receiving no satisfaction, they retired to sulk and to prepare their position for the parliament that, in an attempt to mollify them, the council had called for September 30.[23]

But the interim was to bring yet another unexpected development: On September 11, Wallace won a stunning victory at Stirling, thus raising once more the specter of renewed Scottish invasion and devastation.[24] Isolated already, the magnates could scarcely afford to prove intractable in the face of this threat to the security of the realm, for its defense required their full cooperation. As a result, the council was able to arrange the denouement of October 10: In return for Edward of Carnarvon's confirmation of the charters, an action ratified by his father at Ghent on November 5, parliament voted a subsidy of a ninth to replace the eighth that had earlier been authorized by the £20 landholders.[25]

Later in November, reassured both by the confirmation and by Boniface VIII's increasing moderation, the clergy voted a tenth and a fifth.[26]

Once again, and to return to our hypothetical Philip the Fair, if the French king had studied these events and their outcome, he could have reached but one conclusion, that despite all obstacles, Edward had in the end obtained his money. Indeed, he had also been able to conduct his double continental campaign very much as he had originally planned it, though surely with less happy results than he had anticipated. Given these facts, it may not be even unreasonable to ask whether Philip would have seen Edward's difficulties as obstacles at all, for they were nothing compared to the frustrations that more real French kings had experienced, and would continue to experience, in their endless rounds of individual and local negotiations over troops and taxes.[27] Clergy, barons, and knights had been outmaneuvered at every turn; most of the time, they, and especially the baronage as led by Bigod and Bohun, appear not to have had the slightest understanding of what was happening or of how they were being manipulated. In fact, much of the subsequent confusion and debate over the exact significance of this crisis— whether it was primarily military or financial, whether the confirmation of the charters really guaranteed for all times to come parliament's exclusive right to levy taxation—appears to have arisen precisely because all of the leading protagonists, except the king, were themselves confused, and reflected that confusion in the documents they produced. In short, there is absolutely nothing in the English experience of 1297 as the French would have seen it that would in any way have caused them to hesitate about adopting a similar strategy in 1302.

What, then, is to become of the traditional story of Edward's defeat and of the capital constitutional significance to be found in his confirmation of the charters? Of course, one could argue that the old interpretation also remains valid, testimony to the fact that Frenchmen, medieval or modern, real or fictive, have never adequately grasped the subtleties of English constitutionalism. Furthermore, since the thirteenth and fourteenth centuries were fully familiar with the doctrine of the twofold truth, it may be, perhaps, that the crisis of 1297 should be viewed as little more than a secular example of it. Yet, for all that solution's potential attractiveness, one is (as the French say) permitted to doubt it.

For the constitutional historian, possibly the most difficult aspect of the crisis to explain is why nothing in the surviving evidence suggests

that Edward himself ever thought that he had anything to lose in confirming the charters. If, as is so frequently asserted, that step imposed
significant constitutional restraints on his freedom of action, one would
have supposed that he would have resisted it with all of the not-incon-
siderable means at his disposal. Quite the contrary, Edward appears to
have originated the idea himself, as a meaningless sop to Winchelsey at
a time, mid-July, when the king's campaign to outflank his reluctant
baronage was proceeding extremely well.[28] Moreover, with respect to
whatever military and financial restrictions the confirmation is supposed
to have placed on the hitherto unfettered royal will, it is a striking fact
that not once did Edward seek to remove them, not even in 1305 when
he finally appealed to Clement V to absolve him from the reconfirma-
tion of 1299. These points are exceedingly hard to reconcile with the
traditional story of Edward's concessions, indeed of his outright defeat.

Nevertheless, because the barons soon proved dissatisfied with the
settlement of November 5, 1297, and because the king so stoutly resisted their attempts to enlarge the specifics of his original confirmation,
historians have usually and unthinkingly assumed both that Edward's
attitude in the late 1290s and early 1300s could be taken as an accurate
reflection of his outlook in 1297; and, further, that the struggles of those
later years represented merely a continuation of the first quarrel, one in
which an already successful baronage sought additional victories over a
weak and increasingly senescent king.[29]

This view is mistaken. Even Stubbs recognized—and documented—
the extent to which the disputes of 1298–99 involved a fundamentally
different, though equally ancient issue: the right of the king to enjoy,
impose justice on, and derive revenues from, those portions of the realm
that he and his ancestors had designated as royal forests. As always, the
barons sought to break their sovereign's monopoly, in this case through
further concessions embodied in Edward's wording of a new confirmation of the Forest Charter.[30] This quarrel had little to do with the matters
disputed in 1297; rather, if there was any connection at all, it is to be
found only in the magnates' apparent assumption that in the confirmation at Ghent they had discovered a useful model and precedent for
solving their seemingly endless differences with the king over their
rights in his forests.

In this view, they, too, were mistaken. After all, the forests formed
part of the royal demesne and, as such, they were a part of that "estate
of the crown" that Edward II's Statute of York was later and flatly to

place beyond the power of mere subjects to review, amend, or re-dress.[31] His father agreed completely, and it is in that context that Edward I's appeal to the pope should at last be seen. In seeking to infringe on the estate of the crown, his subjects had finally gone too far. They had to be taught a lesson, and the appeal provided the appropriate vehicle for doing it.

As Clement V's bull of absolution made abundantly clear, the confir-mation of 1297 found a place in Edward's concerns of 1305 only insofar as it, too, contained "harmful concessions" on "the forests and other rights belonging of old to the crown and the honor of your royalty." Thus, contrary to received opinion, the bull in fact absolved Edward only of any vows he might have made to observe those "harmful concessions," ones which, as the pope observed, ran counter to the oath that Edward had taken at his coronation "to preserve the honor and rights of the crown." More practically, and in still further explanation of the king's decision to appeal, Clement also quashed all royal letters, largely from 1299, that had commanded excommunication for "all who infringed the said concessions," and in conclusion he further lifted any "sentences of excommunication which were perhaps promulgated . . . to ensure their observation."[32] In short, the point at issue was not troops and taxes, but, rather, a much more important one: the preserva-tion of estate, both of the crown and, even more strikingly, of Edward's immortal soul. In all other respects, the confirmation of the charters in its 1297 version continued to be observed.[33]

That being the case, perhaps only one other matter needs modest review, the standard assumption that the crisis of 1297 had a twofold constitutional significance because it showed, first, that the barons and knights had the political skills and common interests to form an alliance strong enough to check the king; and, second, that their tactics, by forcing the king to seek taxes only in parliament, insured the ultimate supremacy of that body. Here again one is permitted to have some doubts.

With regard to the first point, to adopt a French perspective is to underscore the extent to which Edward I was not checked. He won, and he did so by running circles around a political opposition that in its confusion was never able to block him or to keep him from achieving his basic objectives. With regard to the second, to argue that, because parliaments in future times would prove more successful in devising techniques with which to restrain the king, the events of 1297 represent a victory for those parliamentary forces is, philosophically speaking, to argue that history has a closed future and hence that, in this case, Edward's "concessions" in 1297 made the later victories of parliament inevitable. There were no concessions, and like all philosophical propositions, this one is at best debatable.

First and foremost, Edward I himself would doubtless have disagreed with it strongly. If he showed a willingness to seek approval for taxes in parliament, that was because everything in his experience suggested that such approval would be swiftly forthcoming—as, indeed, it was in the end even during the crisis of 1297 itself. Parliament was, after all, very largely Edward's invention, and if he used it with frequency, that was because he had found in practice that it could be an efficient organ of government. Because he and his subjects accepted its meetings as times when the full political community was either present or came into being, such occasions provided an attractive opportunity for the hearing of petitions, the declaration of statutes, and, occasionally, even the granting of taxes.[34] In turn, though, none of these activities would have been possible without a significant amount of cooperation between and among the various parties involved. Moreover, this ability to work together, to produce mutually acceptable results, seems itself to have been the product not just of the king's political skills, so apparent in 1297, but also of a basic consensus about the nature of England's government, its needs and goals. In the absence of some kind of fundamental accord, conflict would have been the inevitable result, and if parliaments had produced nothing but strife, one assumes that Edward and his successors would no longer have summoned them.

To put the case a bit differently, to assert blindly that Edward's willingness to use parliament in 1297 should be seen as a royal defeat is to contradict everything that Richardson and Sayles attempted so impatiently to teach the ignorant about parliament as the creation and instrument of strong, politically effective kings.[35] For "the first Edward," as Stubbs would have put it, *was* a strong king. Though surely not "the English Justinian" in the sense that the bishop of Oxford intended that phrase, nevertheless he conducted his affairs with a kind of consistently strong-minded authority that inevitably calls to mind not so much the Byzantine autocrat, but more that equally forceful monarch across the Channel, Edward's future brother-in-law Philip the Fair. For in their tactics and goals, if not always in their accomplishments, these two rulers had much in common.

If historians are ever to understand the motives and actions of people in times past, they must assume that their field has an open future, one in which the later consequences of actions taken are far from being known, inevitable, or certain. In the present instance, for example, it may well be that the crisis of 1297 and its outcome strengthened the precedents suggesting that requests for subsidy were best made in parliament, but in no way does that mean either that Edward was defeated or that subsequent parliaments would of necessity develop the authority, or gain the skills, with which to check the king; overthrow his ministers; or reverse his policies. After all, in France, Philip the Fair's creation, the estates-general, was never to gain such powers, and if the experience of its English counterpart proved different, a large part of the explanation lies in developments that only an unknown future would decide, doing so with as great an uncertainty, as great an ignorance of long-term consequences, as characterized the thought and actions of those involved in the crisis of 1297 itself. In that struggle, Edward I appears to have seen little more than the clear immediate benefits of his policies and, in pursuing them, he was doubtless confident that both he and his successors would be able easily to overcome any of the contingent threats to royal supremacy that those policies may have contained. At least that is how Philip the Fair might have viewed the matter, and since his appearance here is entirely a figment of the historical imagination, who is to say he was wrong?

5

Richard II and the
Wilton Diptych

Although art historians have long admired the Wilton Diptych, universally praising it as a masterpiece of medieval art, until recently they
displayed no such confidence when discussing its date, provenance, or
specific meaning. Now, however, a large measure of agreement has
emerged, a general consensus best expressed in the statement of the
owner, London's National Gallery, that "the Diptych cannot have been
painted earlier than about 1395"; that it is somewhat ambiguously to be
classified as belonging to the "French (?) School"; and that "Richard
II may have commissioned it."[1] Disagreements on overall interpretation remain, but insofar as Richard is deemed to have been its probable
patron, selecting himself as its principal subject, a better understanding
of its themes may well lead to deeper insights into the views of that
troubled monarch not just about himself, but about what he thought
kingship should be. In a sense, then, the Wilton Diptych has evidentiary
value not unlike that possessed by Louis IX's Mise of Amiens and
Edward I's Confirmation of the Charters.

Complex as the Diptych undoubtedly is, description of its principal
features is relatively easy. The work itself consists of two wooden
panels, hinged together, and painted on both sides. The front of the left
panel emphasizes a kneeling Richard in the right foreground. He is of
indeterminate age, but young. Ornately crowned, he wears a broom-cod
collar around his neck as well as a badge on his breast that carries an

75

image of his personal emblem, a white hart lodged. His gown, orange-red cloth embroidered in gold, is also patterned with a series of similar harts, each enclosed in a circle of broom cods. Though kneeling, he is not at prayer, for his hands, while extended, are separated, their fingers slightly spread.

To Richard's left, which is the near background as the viewer sees it, stand three saints, all with haloes and two of them crowned. Thanks to the symbols they bear, no doubts about their identity exist: On the right stands John the Baptist, barefoot, emaciated, and clad in the rough brown garb of the desert. His left arm is crooked, the better to hold the Lamb of his preaching. Most prominent, because at the center, is King Edward the Confessor, robed entirely in white except for an undergarment of blue that shows at the wrist. In his left hand, he holds a ring set with a large blue gem, presumably a sapphire. To his right, our left, stands King Edmund Martyr, his left hand touching the shaft of one of the arrows of his martyrdom. He is shod in red buskins and his undergarment, again visible only at the wrist, is blue. His gown is of the same color, embroidered with gold peacocks so arranged that they face each other in pairs. The heads of each pair are obscured, however, by a single crown that encircles them. Edmund's outer robe is green, though lined and trimmed at the shoulders with ermine, in that respect resembling the robe of the Confessor. All three saints extend their right hands toward Richard, as though to present him, and in the Baptist's case, since he stands immediately beside the kneeling king, his right arm almost embraces Richard, while his hand actually touches the back of that monarch's shoulders.

To the right of John's legs, at the panel's edge, there appears a small but seemingly natural rock formation shaped to resemble four ascending steps. Above the rocks comes a small patch of indeterminate vegetation, possibly woods from the Baptist's wilderness. Yet, whatever the case, both features are apparently designed to show that the scene takes place on earth, in the temporal world of nature. Nevertheless, sky is replaced by a gold background, all of which is incised with circles of inwardly turning trefoils so arranged that each circle contains four trefoils or twelve distinct segments.

If the left panel shows earth, the right shows heaven, its ground filled with the flowers of paradise. And if Richard dominates the left, the right gives prominence to the Virgin, standing serenely, gazing to the left, and holding the Christ Child in her arms. She wears her traditional blue, and she holds the Babe's right foot gently between the thumb and index finger of her left hand. In so doing, she appears to prepare it for Richard's kiss, a possibility made more likely both by the direction of her gaze and by the way in which he holds out his hands, as if to receive some proffered object. Christ's hips and legs are wrapped in a blanket of gold, with only His feet showing; He looks and leans to the left, again toward the kneeling king; and as He does so, He extends His arms, with right hand beginning to form the sign of benediction. Both mother and Child have haloes, but whereas hers is quite simply radiated, His is delicately incised with the nails and thorny crown of His future Passion.[2]

Eleven angels surround this central grouping, their gowns also blue, though seemingly of a slightly lighter shade than the Virgin's.[3] Their heads are garlanded with pink roses and, like Richard, each wears a broom-cod collar and his white-hart badge. Unlike his, however, theirs lack an ornamentation of inset pearls. The angel immediately to the left of Christ holds the staff of the banner of St. George in both hands, left index finger extended to point at Richard. The gesture implies that he is about to receive the banner, and again the position of his hands allows that possibility. In the foreground, three other angels repeat their colleague's pointing gesture, each with extended arm (one with pointing finger also). Nine of the eleven look to the left, in an earthly direction. Only the angel holding the banner gazes at Mary and Jesus, apparently either awaiting orders or simply finding out whether the holy pair realizes who is waiting below, expectantly. The remaining angel, view blocked by a position just to the right of the Virgin, contemplatively watches the gesturing activities of companions to the lower right. The top background of the panel is again of gold, in this case decorated with fleurs-de-lis. Because the design consists of a repeating pattern of four such lilies joined at their stems, the result is an endless series of X's, each X having one fleur-de-lis at the end of each arm, thus emphasizing the number twelve as much as the left panel's pattern of trefoiled circles.

The back of the Diptych has lesser interest except for purposes of dating and sponsorship. On the rear right—that is, the back of Richard's panel—a large white hart lodged is depicted, its golden antlers barely visible against the gold background. Its collar, also of gold, is shaped like a crown, though much simpler in design than any of those shown on the front. From it hangs a chain that falls down and then loops over the animal's tucked left foreleg. On the left—the Virgin's side on the front—appears a shield on the right side of which the lions of England are quartered with the lilies of France. These, the arms of Richard II, are then halved or, to use the technical heraldic term, "impaled" with the traditional ones of Edward the Confessor on the left, a gold cross surrounded by five footless birds, the legendary martlet, all against an azure background. Above the shield stands a crowned lion on top of a chapeau, crown, and mantle that are now so badly damaged that their presence has to be reconstructed largely on the basis of a similar design that appears on seals of the Black Prince, Richard's father.

As far as dating is concerned, although Richard adopted the white hart as his personal emblem in 1390, his followers were not allowed its use before 1394–95, during his next-to-last expedition to Ireland.[4] Similarly, the king's devotion to Edward the Confessor first took heraldic form only around 1395, when he introduced a new signet on which Edward's arms were impaled with his. This he called "our own personal signet of St. Edward," and he continued to use it for the rest of the reign.[5] In other words, external evidence demonstrates that the Diptych's Ricardian imagery gained general use only in the mid-nineties, thus making that period the terminus *ab quo* for its composition. Since, when the panels are closed, the Diptych displays only symbols that were unique to Richard, ones that he regarded as personal, it seems overwhelmingly likely that he alone commissioned it. In particular, this use of his symbols on what amount to its outside covers makes it improbable in the extreme that it was created only after his death on the instructions of faithful followers who wanted to portray and memorialize his entry into heaven, an interpretation that the National Gallery also accepts as possible.[6]

In bare outline, then, such are the basic features of the Wilton Diptych, and while the meaning of many of its specific details remains disputed, some points have received general assent. For example, insofar as the front shows three crowned kings in conjunction with Virgin and Child, all agree that its type is that of Epiphany scenes. Further, since Epiphany, January 6, was also Richard II's birthday, it would appear that this dating reference was not fortuitous. If not, then the point should not be dropped, for the feast days of the three saints depicted bear a close relationship to the various steps by which Richard achieved the crown, and those feasts were the ones used for dating purposes at the time.

Edward, the Black Prince and Richard's father, died on the Trinity,

June 8, 1376. Until his death, of course, he had been heir to Edward III, his father, but with his passing the succession entered a brief period of uncertainty. His son Richard of Bordeaux was only nine, and if woe came to the land whose king was a child, England's rules of succession were also far from certain. Did Richard automatically succeed to the rights enjoyed by his father, or should the crown pass to John of Gaunt, eldest of the king's surviving sons? No one doubted that Gaunt might want it, and it was even rumored that he was seeking to challenge his nephew's eligibility. Specifically, he believed that upon the death of Henry III the kingship had wrongly passed to Edward I, it being Gaunt's contention that Edmund Crouchback, the founder of his House of Lancaster, had been Edward's older brother, passed over because of his deformity. And that wasn't all, for the rumors also told of how Gaunt, in league with Charles V of France, was planning to seek a papal declaration of Richard's illegitimacy, the alleged grounds being the "notorious" adulteries of Richard's mother, the Black Prince's wife, Joan of Kent.[7]

To put such uncertainties to rest, on June 25, 1376, "Wednesday the day after the St. John,"[8] Richard was presented to parliament, the commons having earlier

> prayed humbly to our lord the king in parliament that it would please their lord our king, as a great comfort to the whole realm, to have the noble child, Richard of Bordeaux, the son and heir of the lord Edward, lately the eldest son of our lord and king and Prince of Wales (whom God save), come before parliament, so that the lords and commons might see and honor Richard as true heir apparent to the realm.[9]

The implications of this presentation were then made concrete on November 20, the feast of St. Edmund Martyr, when Richard was formally invested as Prince of Wales.[10] A month and a half later, he celebrated his tenth birthday on January 6, that day of Epiphany on which, in 1066, Edward the Confessor had been buried at Westminster, and in the January parliament that followed soon thereafter, he served as president, replacing his ailing grandfather.[11] Adam Houghton, chancellor and bishop of St. David's, gave the opening sermon, and in it he quickly underscored the significance of all that had recently transpired:

> My lords, you can see that our said lord the king loves you, for . . . the king has fulfilled your desires, by ordaining and granting to [Richard] fully, as the king may, the said principality of Wales, the

duchy of Cornwall, and the earldom of Chester, and has sent him as his deputy to this parliament before you, to comfort you and to rejoice him, in the very manner Scripture speaks of: "This is my beloved son. This is the desired of all nations." To him you should, and are every one obliged to, do honor and reverence as to your lord and the heir apparent of the kingdom. And do him honor in the same manner as the pagans, that is the three kings of Cologne, did to the Son of God.[12]

Edward III died on June 21 or, as the official announcement had it, "the Sunday preceding the feast of St. John the Baptist"; the reign of Richard II began on the following day.[13] And if the chancellor had earlier compared the new king none too subtly to Christ, even using the words of the voice that had spoken at the time of His baptism by John,[14] Simon Sudbury, the archbishop of Canterbury, continued the theme at Richard's first parliament, which opened on October 13, the feast of St. Edward the Confessor. For on that day he preached on the text, "Behold thy king cometh to thee," the prophecy of Zechariah that had been fulfilled by Christ's entry into Jerusalem.[15] Not content with that, however, Sudbury also returned to other themes stressed by Houghton, presumably in response to the rumors about Joan of Kent's sexual indiscretions:

> Now is it thus that our lord the king here present, whom God preserve, has come into your presence as your . . . natural and legitimate liege lord, as has been said, not by election or any other collateral way, but by lawful succession of inheritance: for which you are the more bound by nature to love him perfectly, and humbly to obey him; and furthermore to thank God, from whom all grace and good proceed, especially because He has given you such a noble lord as your king and governor.[16]

In short, if the Wilton Diptych presents its viewers (and initially Richard himself) with an Epiphany, at the same time the dates suggested by its saints serve to underscore the significance of crucial events involved in that king's reception of his title, events during which he had more than once been likened to Christ. Nevertheless, this interpretation still remains incomplete insofar as it fails to take into account the stress placed at the time on Richard's legitimacy, on the fact that he had succeeded "not by election or any other collateral way, but by lawful . . . inheritance." Yet that element, too, finds its place in the Diptych, again in the persons of its attending saints.

As portrayed, these saints bear a strong resemblance not just to each other, but to Richard himself: Their long, aquiline noses combine with similar eyes, eyebrows, and foreheads to suggest an attempt both at specific portraiture and close family relationships. Seeing this fact, art historians have often speculated about the identity of the people involved,[17] but the challenge to Richard's legitimacy makes their identities clear: On the left stands Edward II, a king as martyred as St. Edmund himself and the royal great-grandfather for whose canonization Richard II began to press in 1387, going so far in 1390 as to visit his tomb at Gloucester, there personally to gather the stories of his miracles.[18] In the center comes Edward III, whose own death had led to the succession of his grandson. Indeed, because an inventory taken by Westminster Abbey in 1388 lists the Confessor's sapphire-set ring as among its most precious possessions, there is every reason to believe that the creator of the Diptych wants its viewers to understand that it was this ring that the new king had received from both Edwards at the time of his coronation.[19]

Finally, in this reading the John the Baptist of the Diptych becomes none other than Edward, the Black Prince, the uncrowned precursor and Richard's father. He stands closest to the kneeling king, and if, in a sense, all three saints present Richard to the Virgin and her Son, it is above all the Baptist/father who does so, directly touching him and taking him under his protective wing, seeming to say: "This is my beloved son, in whom I am well pleased." So much, then, for the stories about his mother Joan of Kent: Richard is his father's son, and his line stretches back in unbroken succession to that new martyr, his great-grandfather, the recognition of whose own sanctity is being sought. In sum, Richard's descent proceeds from Edward II, and that its glories become ever greater, culminating in Richard himself, is implied both by the steadily increasing richness of the crowns that each king wears and, perhaps, by the four natural steps on the rocky formation to the right. For if, as it seems, these are steps on which each generation should stand, then there can be little doubt about the identity of the person who should occupy the highest place, the one closest to Mary, her Son, and heaven. It was, after all, the only logical spot for a king who had dedicated his realm to the Virgin.[20]

Because the Diptych so stresses dates, all of which refer to events related to Richard's accession, it is frequently assumed that the scene depicted somehow involves his coronation. Yet to that interpretation two obvious objections arise, the more troubling of which is that Richard is shown already crowned. Second, even though he is portrayed as young and unbearded, he appears significantly older than the true age of the boy who received his chrism in 1377. Medieval artists may often have had difficulty in capturing the look of youth with any fidelity, but the skill with which the Diptych presents a Christ who is genuinely a baby demonstrates that its artist, at least, could easily have painted a youth of ten, if ten had been the age desired.

Here the banner of St. George takes on added significance since, as Joan Evans was among the first persuasively to demonstrate,[21] it stands for the sovereignty of England. That being the case, the Diptych's temporal frame of reference begins to expand far beyond the immediate events of 1376–77. Richard may have received the crown in July of the latter year, but with it he failed to receive full rule of his kingdom. On the contrary, others ruled in his name and continued to do so at least down to 1389, the year in which he declared his majority.[22] Indeed, when Robert de Vere, earl of Oxford, carried the banner at Radcot Bridge, his losing battle against the king's enemies in 1387, both he and Richard were to be harshly cóndemned for the impropriety of this display, de Vere at the time and Richard twelve years later, in the charges brought against him in the Lancastrian depositional activities of 1399.[23]

This line of reasoning shows the extent to which the Diptych involves not just the specific events of 1376–77, but an extended meditation on the nature of kingship, the sources of its power, and the reality of their reception. If, in Richard's case, one source lies in his direct legitimate descent from those ancestors who had earlier been England's kings, another—much more profound—derives not from his birth, but from heaven's gift, a gift bestowed in the Diptych's imagery by the angel holding the banner of St. George, who will pass it to Richard only when so ordered by the Virgin and her Son. At that point, and not before, he will at last become fully king, God's anointed and lieutenant on earth, a king who will rule thanks to an office directly and immediately received from the Creator of all being. To put it mildly, this vision of divinity represents a highly unusual view of English kingship.[24]

Nevertheless, the vision does not end there, with reception of the banner. The one feature of the Diptych that has attracted most puzzlement over the years is undoubtedly the group of eleven angels who surround the Virgin, all wearing the collar and badge of Richard II. Because eleven is a number with no symbolic meaning, commentators have tried to explain its use here with a host of ingenious theories. Some have held, for example, that the number refers to the fact that Richard was in his eleventh year at the time of his coronation, while at least one believes that the angels symbolize "an esoteric counterpart of the Order of the Garter," a group of loyal followers to which Richard must have given secret but formal organization late in the reign.[25]

Yet such hypotheses overlook the obvious, that in medieval art the Christ of the Resurrection is frequently shown with just eleven disciples, Judas not being replaced.[26] That the Diptych has the apostles constantly in mind is suggested by the insistence with which its gold backgrounds stress the number twelve in their patterns, and since, in 1377, at least two bishops had openly likened Richard to Christ, it seems unremarkable to find such an identification repeated here. What needs stressing, though, is that the Diptych's reference is not just to any Christ, but quite specifically to the One who had risen from the tomb, the resurgent Christ, the triumphant Christ. It is He whom Richard will become from the moment of the banner's reception, and in so becoming, he, too, will be transfigured into the One who will come again not with meekness and mercy, but with a sword, to visit death and destruction upon all His enemies. And that surely suggests the Richard who first emerged in 1397, on the Epiphany of which year he also became thirty, the age when Christ had begun His ministry.[27] Richard's, however, was to prove of shorter duration.

Although no one can ever know Richard's thoughts concerning his Diptych, a few speculative conclusions are clearly in order. First and foremost, kingship for him was a family affair. If he wore broomcods—that is, *plantae genestae*—on robe and collar, that was because he was a Plantagenet,[28] and if, by his day, that family had ruled England for over two centuries, his membership and rights as legitimate heir were demonstrated by the sponsoring line of ancestors, two kings and one prince, who presented him for heaven's blessing and final investiture. So much, then, for John of Gaunt's aspersions on his birth, aspersions repeated as recently as 1394.[29] For only he, Richard, was "descended by right line of the blood" (as Gaunt's son would later and wrongly phrase his own claims), and that meant, in turn, that he alone was worthy of a sovereignty that only God, not man, could bestow. Thanks overwhelmingly to his lineage, he would become the Christ-figure who would rule in His stead.

Beyond that, however, the manner in which the three saints of Richard's panel also stand for his immediate forbears suggests that the man who commissioned and presumably specified the details of the Diptych must have long pondered both his own experiences and those of his line. If not, the extent of the continuing parallels would defy explanation. Still, while the doubling was undoubtedly conscious, it remains uncertain just how far Richard himself had thought through all the possible implications seemingly involved. Take John the Baptist, for example. As the uncrowned precursor he was the perfect type to represent Edward, the Black Prince, and his emaciated body further recalled the wasted father whom the son would have remembered. But did Richard as worshipper also meditate on two lives spent in the desert, one in the wilderness of the Holy Land, the other in the wilderness he himself had made out of France? Were the father's campaign rations compared with John's locusts and honey, or did the boy whom the father touched with one hand become in his adult mind the Lamb that the Baptist held with his other, the one the fulfillment of a prince's political dreams, the other the fulfillment of prophecy? It seems likely, but we shall never know.

With Edward the Confessor and Edward III the possibilities become even richer. It was in Westminster, which the Confessor had built, that this saint had been laid to rest in 1066, and on Richard's birthday. It was there, too, that Richard had been crowned, swearing in his coronation oath to uphold the Confessor's laws. Even more strikingly, perhaps, the Abbey had been consecrated on Holy Innocents' Day in 1065, and the whiteness of the Confessor's Diptych vestments must have served to remind Richard of the white with which John of Gaunt had similarly clothed him at his coronation, the better to emphasize the new king's own innocence.[30] Edward's blue cuffs linked him to the blue of heaven, the mandate of which he—or was it they?—had enjoyed, and the sapphire ring he held—possibly that of the coronation, possibly that which the Confessor had in legend given to a beggar who turned out to be St. John the Evangelist, and possibly that which the abbot of Westminster had removed from Edward's sainted finger during the translation of 1163[31]—was in some mystic way the one that Richard himself had received from both men in 1377. It was, then, wholly unlike those lesser rings that Alice Perrers, Edward III's mistress, was reputed to have brazenly stripped from the fingers of a dying king.[32]

But with the associations called forth by Edmund Martyr and Edward II—the one a saint, the other a man for whose acknowledged sainthood Richard yearned—possible thoughts become truly obsessive. Like the two Edwards, blue cuffs tie this Diptych figure to Mary and heaven, and if he is presented in an outer robe richly embroidered with peacocks, the explanation seems equally clear: The legendary incorruptibility of the peacock's flesh had long made it a symbol of the immortality that both kings had achieved. Furthermore, that both men were explicitly intended is nowhere better demonstrated than by the way in which the peacocks are paired, heads hidden by the crown they share, a crown that in their case was less one of kingship than of martyrdom. Such associations must have given Richard much to ponder, especially since he himself was no stranger to martyrdom, either his own (as he would have viewed it) or that of the most devoted of his followers.

Simon Sudbury, the archbishop who had compared him to Christ, had been the first to go, brutally beheaded by rebels in the Peasants' Revolt of 1381,[33] but he had been followed by many more—though not at the hands of peasants. Moreover, that such thoughts were ever present in Richard's mind finds proof in the red buskins that Edmund /Edward wears, *sotularia* of the same imperial color that Richard himself had worn for his coronation by Sudbury. At the end of the ceremony, because crowds were as thick as the boy-king was tired, he had been carried out of Edward the Confessor's Westminster Abbey on the shoulders of Simon Burley, among the most redoubtable of the knights who had served the Black Prince, but in the surrounding turmoil one of the buskins had slipped from Richard's foot, never to be recovered.[34] He had revered Burley, among other things making him a Knight of the Garter, and in 1389, in the aftermath of his own declared majority, he had even ordered the buskins replaced.[35] By that time, however, Burley himself was beyond replacement, struck down in the previous year by those Lords Appellant who had arrogated to themselves that rule of the realm that belonged, of right, solely to Richard—and all supposedly so that they could effect reforms on his still-too-youthful behalf. Anne of Bohemia, England's queen, had pled for Burley's life on bended knee, but the most she had been able to obtain was mitigation of the savage punishment usually meted out to traitors: In his case, the Appellants agreed, hanging, drawing, and quartering could be replaced by simple beheading, a grace they had accorded to precious few others, Richard's supporters every one. Of the five men initially appealed of treason that year, Sir Nicholas Brembre, former mayor of London, and Sir Robert Tresilian, former chief justice of king's bench, had suffered treason's full penalties at Tyburn; Michael de la Pole, earl of Suffolk, and Robert

de Vere, earl of Oxford, had fled, subsequently to die in exile; and
Alexander Neville, archbishop of York, while saved from death by his
clerical condition, had been humiliatingly demoted and transferred to
the see of St. Andrew's. And all of this Richard remembered. In 1395,
for example, when de Vere's body had been brought home from Louvain for interment in Essex, the king had ordered his coffin opened,
after which he had silently held the earl's now-lifeless hand even as he
looked long and longingly at the face of this friend whose principal
crime had been to carry the banner of St. George loyally but unsuc-
cessfully at Radcot Bridge.[36] Yet it was Burley whom he treasured most
of all, with a love that found expression in the seeming tranquillity of a
martyr's red shoes.

How much, too, the life of St. Edmund called forth these events,
serving to foster the sense of Richard's own martyrdom even as it
focused his attention on the villainy of the Appellants, notably that of
their chief. As the English version of *The Golden Legend* told the story,
Edmund had been a king "of the noble and ancient lineage of the
Saxons." He was, moreover, "from the beginning of his first age a
blessed man, soft, virtuous, and full of meekness," a man who "kept
truly the very religion of Christian faith, and governed his kingdom full
well to the pleasure of Almighty God." Disaster struck, however, when
a pagan duke, Hingvar by name,

> came out of Denmark and . . . came into the country where this most
> Christian St. Edmund reigned. . . . Now the Danes had always
> custom that they would never fight battle set nor appointed, but ever
> lie in wait how they might by sleight and deceit prevented, fall on
> good Christian men, and so slay and destroy them, like as thieves lie
> in await to rob and slay good true men. Wherefore, when he knew
> where this holy king was, he . . . himself followed with all his host to
> the end that suddenly he should fall upon this king unadvised, and that
> he might subdue him unto his laws and commandments. Then [he
> had] his legation and message [made] . . . to this holy king St. Ed-
> mund . . . in this wise: "Our most dread lord by land and sea,
> Hingvar, . . . sendeth to thee his commandment that thou incontinent
> come and make alliance and friendship with him. And that thou depart
> to him thy paternal treasures and riches in such wise that thou mayest
> reign under him, or certainly thou shalt die by cruel death." And
> when the blessed king, St. Edmund, had heard this message, . . . the
> king a while said nothing but remembered him well, and after many
> devout words at the last, he answered to the messenger in this wise

and said: "This shalt thou say to thy lord: Know that for truth, that for the love of temporal life, the Christian king Edmund shall not subdue him to a paynim duke."

Edmund's death followed soon thereafter, but in the monastery where his body took its final rest, "Almighty God hath showed many miracles for the holy king and martyr."[37]

Although England in the fourteenth century suffered no longer from pagan dukes, in 1385 Thomas of Woodstock, youngest of the king's uncles, had become duke of Gloucester, and in his ducal career he was to do much in which Richard II would have discerned Hingvar's model. In the very next year, for example, Gloucester had hotly opposed his nephew in parliament, going so far as to remind the young king that "by ancient statute and recent precedent" subjects had the right to seek his deposition.[38] This was, of course, a threat based on the fate of Edward II, whose miracles from the tomb so starkly resembled those of St. Edmund Martyr, and after Radcot Bridge, Gloucester and his allies had added to the insult, cornering Richard in the Tower where (or so it was reported) for three days they had declared him deposed, *de-coronatus*. And even in less zealous moods they had continued to point out that since he had "an heir of full age"—that is, Gloucester—he himself was expendable. All in all, then, it was an ordeal that had left Richard understandably stunned, *stupefactus*.[39] Moreover, if Gloucester as leader of the Appellants had subsequently assured the merciless parliament of 1388 that he had no usurping intent, his actions at its sittings had made it clear that like Hingvar he wanted a king who would no more than "reign under him," responsive to his every whim or fancy.[40] For that, surely, was the message of his wrath as experienced by Richard's friends, above all by the former chief justice, Tresilian, whose counsel had led the royal judges to proclaim in the previous year that the king alone had the right to rule and, in particular, that anyone who cited "ancient statute and recent precedent" to argue the contrary had, by that very assertion, transgressed the laws of treason.[41]

Given these facts, it seems likely that when Richard turned his attention to the heavenly side of his Diptych, he would have spent no little time meditating on the nails and thorns so faintly visible on his Saviour's halo. In them he would doubtless have seen the instruments of his own passion, one endured not in the years of maturity, but during those of childhood. Like Christ, he, too, had avoided the Massacre of the

Innocents, but whereas the Holy Child had escaped through flight into Egypt, in the Peasants' Revolt of 1381 he, though also a child, had remained in London while his elders fled. In fact, he had not just stayed on, but had actually saved the situation with his quick-witted offer to become the rebels' captain after the murder of Wat Tyler. He had showed the world that he was fully a king that day, and he had further exercised his royal authority by immediately knighting Nicholas Brembre for critical service and loyal support.[42] Yet what had it availed either of them? Brembre had been slaughtered in 1388, while the Appellants continued to deny their sovereign the very essence of his kingship. If vengence was the Lord's, then what lies at the heart of the Diptych is a simple statement, that Richard II, the new Christ of the new resurrection, was longing to visit it upon all his enemies.

Some contemporaries, future Lancastrians, thought that Richard had gone mad in his later years, and there is much in the record, if true, that sustains their judgment. Frenzied by memories of past wrongs and present injuries, he dreamed increasingly of a sovereignty that sometimes involved possession of the imperial title,[43] sometimes the full acceptance by others of his Christ-like status. All kings insist on their majesty, of course, but Richard alone is reported to have ordered a throne constructed of enormous proportions, one from the heights of which he could unblinkingly survey his subjects on feast days. And when any of them caught his eye, they were required not just to kneel or to bow, but to genuflect.[44] This insistence on such an all-encompassing obeisance would appear to have about as much to do with sanity as does the way in which Richard finally struck out at the former Appellants in 1397, after attaining his thirtieth birthday.

In the beginning, his scheme seemed harmless enough, no more than an invitation to dinner. With the wisdom of hindsight, though, Walsingham was later to claim that it had been a feast not unlike that at which Salome's dance had earned for her the head of John the Baptist.[45] Of the leading Appellants, only Warwick attended, with Arundel simply refusing to come and Gloucester citing ill-health to cover his absence. But such caution did none of them any good: At the end of the meal Warwick was summarily led off to the Tower; Arundel and Gloucester were seized soon thereafter. And when Gloucester pleaded for mercy, the king assured him coldly that he would receive as much as he had showed to Simon Burley.[46] Then, at a meeting of the council held at Nottingham, Richard discussed his strategy for the September session of parliament. There, eight of his most devoted kinsmen and followers were to play the role once played by the Appellants, for they themselves were to be appealed of treason exactly as they had earlier appealed their monarch's friends. Although Warwick and Arundel were both found guilty, Arundel was immediately beheaded at Tower Hill, whereas Warwick was merely exiled in perpetuity to the Isle of Man. As for Gloucester, it was announced that he had already died at Calais, undoubtedly murdered, but after parliament had heard what was alleged to be his full confession, it had no difficulty in declaring that he, too, had been guilty of treason, with all property forfeit. Richard was now near the edge of total victory, and he underscored its basis by insisting, via his new Appellants, that the 1387 opinions of his judges on the necessity of an unfettered royal rule be affirmed and the acts of the merciless parliament quashed.[47] When parliament agreed, to most observers Richard's triumph must have seemed complete.

As he himself would have viewed it, though, there would have been one last loose end still remaining, one to which the Wilton Diptych speaks. For who was Judas, the missing angel? Villainous and disloyal though Gloucester may have been, he had never been Richard's disciple, and nothing suggests that the king had ever so regarded him. Warwick and Arundel make equally unpromising candidates, but when the Diptych is reviewed for additional clues, one that begins to emerge is the right panel's second most prominent feature, the banner of St. George. It may often serve as a symbol of England's sovereignty, the one for which de Vere had died in exile, but insofar as the saints of the left panel sometimes function as dating references to crucial events in 1376–77, it seems not unreasonable to ask whether anything of importance had happened on St. George's Day, April 23, in either year. Unsurprisingly too, at least by now, in 1377 it turns out that on that day, and in St. George's Chapel at Windsor, Richard of Bordeaux had become a knight. More specifically, he had been invested with one of the blue robes of the Order of the Garter. Furthermore, with his entry into his father's place in the Order's first stall, he had also succeeded him as the commander of an equally blue-robed twelve-knight team, the principal function of which was to joust with their twelve chivalrous companions, the Garter team of Edward III.[48] Even though we in the modern world may frequently smile at such activities, in Richard's day the obligations they entailed were taken with the utmost seriousness, especially the loyalty owed by all members to each other and, above all, to their chief. For to betray that loyalty was to violate any order's most sacred trust.[49]

In 1377, however, another stall had also been vacant, the one previously occupied by Jean de Grailly, Captal de Buch and, of all the Black Prince's comrades in arms, probably the most esteemed. So, on St. George's Day that stall, too, was filled: by Richard's identically ten-year-old cousin, John of Gaunt's son, Henry Bolingbroke, earl of Derby, Leicester, and Lincoln.[50] Yet in 1387 he had served to his eternal discredit in Richard's eyes as the youngest of the Lords Appellant and leader of their forces at Radcot Bridge. By 1397, he had become duke of Hereford and, with his father's death imminently expected, presumed heir to the duchy of Lancaster. He, then, is the missing blue-robed angel in the Diptych, for by breaking his sacred Garter trust he had become a second Judas, to be punished as such. And punished he was, first with temporary exile, then with perpetual banishment, and finally with the loss of his Lancastrian inheritance.[51] How Richard must have loved it!

Be that as it may, Henry was to prove a Judas who won. Moreover, whether he himself wanted it or not, his very triumph restored to England a view of kingship much more traditional than Richard's. In 1399, for example, the new king's coronation may well have taken place on October 13, the feast of St. Edward the Confessor, but in the events preceding it, Henry like Edward I before him, was to rely less on claims of divine authority than on his own political abilities. In so doing, he was also to gain the approval of those people, his future subjects, who had deposed Richard by appealing solely to that authority that they found vested in their own persons as "the estates and the people" of England. That is, however, another story, far different from the one told by the Wilton Diptych. A masterpiece of medieval art it doubtless remains, but its true message was meant for Richard II alone.

PART III

THE ROLE OF PARLIAMENT

IF THE Wilton Diptych expresses the political views of Richard II, his fate demonstrates the extent to which others disagreed. For them, government involved more than an unfettered kingship, and the form of English monarchy would remain incomprehensible unless linked to the gradual emergence of parliament as a body that came to believe that it had sufficient authority in times of crisis to challenge, limit, and possibly even to select, the king. Moreover, since governments tend to reflect the experience of a society, and especially since parliament claimed that its decisions represented nothing less than the considered judgments of the community—or, later, the three estates—of the realm, the story of parliament's changing role would be incomplete unless placed in the context of all the vicissitudes experienced by English society in the later Middle Ages.

Historians have discerned almost as many origins for parliament as there have been scholars of the subject.[1] Nineteenth-century romantics, mystically inclined, thought they had found them in the forests of Germany, dark places where the "Germanic idea of freedom" arose. Others, more pragmatic and recent, argued that parliament came into being as an assembly in which the king sought consent for taxes—and then gained in authority thereafter as it learned how to grant money only in return for political concessions. Still others have urged the importance of so-called military feudalism and of its need for some kind of body where the reciprocal duties of the lord-vassal contract, especially those of aid and counsel, could most easily be performed. Lastly, though most reflective of views today, Richardson and Sayles held that parliament had begun as a court, the highest form of the king's council, a place where cases could be heard, petitions decided, and political matters of the highest importance discussed.

Disparate as these theories may be, none of them is really wrong, only incomplete. Significant evidence favors each approach, and to dismiss even one of them would be to distort what was, in fact, a very complicated development. The interpretive difficulties that the problem involves resemble nothing so much as the story of the blind men and the proverbial elephant, for while each theory conveys a partial truth, its

A SESSION OF PARLIAMENT   Flanked by King Alexander III of Scotland, Prince Llewelyn of Wales, and assorted prelates and clerks, Edward I presides over parliament in the first known picture of one of its meetings. (*The Bettmann Archive*)

93

proponents claim that it represents a total explanation. In the present instance, however, a further difficulty arises from a failing all too often found in history, the conscious or unconscious assumption that modern concepts and categories can be usefully applied even to the study of times and places that were ignorant of their meaning. Such is seldom the case, unfortunately, and parliament provides the perfect illustration, an institution the origins and growth of which were intimately connected to the changing nature of law.

In the early Middle Ages, legislation gave way to a law that was overwhelmingly customary. In theory, custom was God's law, His earthly arrangements for a humanity that He Himself had created. In practice, though, because God does not deign to speak to mere mortals on a daily basis, knowledge of His law depended on recollection of precedents; on the memory of what people had done in the past; or, in short, on knowledge of a law that earlier generations had by their actions made. As a result, the source of law appeared both divine and human, and its content was equally ambiguous. In the most general sense, laws are those universally recognized rules that bind members of a community, but insofar as custom depended on the memory of precedent, discovery of such rules proved far from easy. For memory is unique to the individual, not to the group, and since its accuracy varies enormously from person to person, a community could know its binding precedents, and hence the content of its enforceable law, only if its individual members had some way of coming together to see whether their memories agreed so that thev could express what, in discussion, they had found to be their collective judgment and will.

Potentially more confusing still, custom was all-embracing. Modern societies would find it difficult to function in the absence of certain basic distinctions: among the various branches of government, for example, or between public and private, political and social, habit and law. Nevertheless, for much of the Middle Ages people carried on their affairs unaided by these distinctions, a situation that makes it difficult in medieval writings to tell just where one subject leaves off and another begins. Indeed, given the failure to develop an adequate vocabulary for expressing such concepts and categories, it is misleading even to talk about them before their verbal appearance. Silence provides the presumptive proof that they did not, as yet, exist.

Because early medieval law was little more than custom based on precedent, the whole of life took on a legal character. In the twentieth century, always to do something in a particular way is merely a habit, not binding on others. But in the tenth century, if many people had the same habit, it could form a precedent that was at least potentially applicable to the whole community. Similarly, if kings were to govern with consistency as custom required, then knowledge of precedent became crucial in their every policy decision: Rulers both had to know the past and were condemned to repeat it if they wanted their actions accepted as legal.

These realities help to explain why nineteenth-century historians were so often inclined to find the roots of parliament in the forests of Germany. The nature of customary law in early medieval society dictated that people would frequently have to consult with each other in quasi-judicial fashion. In this regard, kings appeared little different from their subjects, for if a ruler could decide important political questions only after receiving the advice and counsel of his leading men, the whole process took place in the *curia regis,* the royal *court.* Although that term has now acquired varied meanings, in pre-twelfth-century Europe it had but one. In effect, even matters that the present-day observer would regard as purely administrative were then seen as essentially legal, an attitude that may shed some light on the manner in which the wide range of later parliamentary activities could have arisen from a single source, the outlook so pervasively engendered by the rule of undifferentiated customary law.[2]

During the reign of Henry III, people began using the word "parliament" for the first time to describe meetings of the king with his magnates. Just why they did so remains unclear, but it seems likely that no more was involved than a new term for an old practice. No new institution had suddenly come into being; rather, Henry's intentions appear to have been little different from those of his ancestors. At most they took on a more formal character, but this quality merely reflected the increased formalism of the age and the need, thanks to the unfortunate experiences of John, to reassure the mighty that their views were at all times being given proper weight.

Nevertheless, over the course of the reign there were signs that the political community thought increasingly of parliament not just as a new word for a traditional gathering, but more concretely as an especially solemn occasion at which grievances could be aired and settled. Here, of course, Henry's disputes with his barons were of crucial importance, as in 1258 when the Provisions of Oxford stipulated that parliaments were to meet three times a year "in order to examine the state of the kingdom and to consider the common needs of the kingdom and likewise of the king."[3] Even more striking were Simon de Montfort's two parliaments of 1264 and 1265, gatherings clearly intended to rally popular support for the baronial cause, but also ones that were, in words put into Henry's mouth, "to deliberate with our prelates, magnates, and other faithful men concerning our affairs and those of our kingdom" (1264)[4] or to "hold a deliberation with our prelates and magnates to make salutary provision for [the Lord Edward's] release, . . . and to consider certain other affairs of our kingdom which we are unwilling to settle without your counsel" (1265).[5] Without a doubt, then, parliaments were gaining in stature, at least with the barons if not the king, but the principles upon which they were assumed to operate appear to have undergone little significant change.

Most important, those principles rested on the belief that there existed at the national level a community that was the apex of those local ones so essential to the discovery and declaration of customary law. As early as Magna Carta the barons had claimed to be "the community of the entire country," and in the Provisions of Oxford the oath of the baronial party carried the explanatory rubric: "Thus swore the community of England at Oxford."[6] Further, and even more crucially, the law deemed that this rather mystical group was always present at meetings of parliament. As the Statute of York put it in 1322, its provisions had legal force because they had been "agreed and established . . . by our lord the king, by the said prelates, earls, and barons, and by the whole community of the realm assembled in this parliament."[7] With the entire national community thus present, parliaments found themselves potentially vested with the kind of omnicompetent authority so characteristic of earlier, typically more local, assemblies and courts.

It was this potential, one assumes, that first led Henry III's barons to see parliament as a forum for redress of grievances, for their complaints were almost entirely legal within the medieval understanding of that term. If God and the community were the source of all law, that view made the king less a sovereign than a judge, one whose highest duty, to uphold justice, meant that his principal function was simply to carry out the intent of the law, not to make or amend it. As an aphorism of the times phrased it: *Lex regem facit, non rex legem,* "The law makes the king, not the king the law." Therefore, if the barons believed that Henry had violated this highly judicial conception of office, it followed that parliaments were the logical place for the community to render its judgment.

Nevertheless, there is another side to the story, one that explains why Edward I should have chosen to place his growing reliance on a nascent institution that had so recently displayed such antiroyalist proclivities, and against his father at that. Parliaments were in large measure a court, and if modern courts need both judges and juries, in analogous terms the king in parliament was the judge, all others the jury. Subjects were summoned solely to declare the facts and thereby, with royal instruction and final assent, to transform history into law by granting community recognition to what was taken to be, like guilt or innocence, a preexisting truth. If so, parliament could function only with the presence and full participation of the king. It was his court; its members were his representatives; and, as Edward's tactics in 1297 had shown, a king gifted with political skills had little trouble in managing its decisions.[8]

To put the point another way, Edward I was no Henry III. Able, forceful, and domineering, he inherited few of the failings that had brought his father so often to grief. Moreover, insofar as he was an anointed monarch, a ruler by grace as well as blood, he enjoyed a station in life far above that of his subjects. As a result, he soon learned that, when endowed with his abilities, a king could use his status to seize the initiative, for it gave his opinions such a presumption of truth that, in the absence of overwhelming evidence to the contrary, his subjects were apt to accept them. Thus, far from being limited by parliaments, Edward was usually able to dominate their meetings and, as in 1297, to achieve his objectives.

Still, those objectives were not just the king's alone. For England was changing, and much of the parliamentary activity in his reign arose out of a need to address the problems that accompanied economic expansion, a demographic explosion, and rapid urbanization. Exciting though these changes were, they also confronted English society with a host of vexing new problems for which its customary law provided no remedies. Magnates saw themselves losing both revenues and personal services as lands were increasingly mortgaged, sold, or, in return for prayers, simply deeded to the Church. Bankers found no rules to guide their debt collections, and the customs of an agricultural society were of little use to merchants in their contract disputes.

When viewed in this context, the principal activities of Edward I's parliaments begin to make sense. Because the law of the land could not by its nature respond to these unprecedented developments, each session of parliament received a flood of petitions, statements from individuals that set forth the peculiar circumstances in which they found themselves; explained how the common law either did not apply or would lead to pernicious results, if observed; and then requested parliamentary relief. If, after investigation, a petition was found to have merit, those hearing it would approve the desired relief in either of two forms. When circumstances seemed truly unique—the usual case— then the remedy came in the form of an individual exception to existing law. Not infrequently, however, a number of petitions might raise the same issue, or the government itself might recognize without prodding that a more general problem existed for which accepted custom suggested no answers.[9]

To deal with such instances—for example, the difficulties created by the developments just cited—individual exceptions were patently insufficient. For such cases a different and more universal solution was needed, and though the one devised, statutes, carried with it intimations of a new form of sovereignty that, when realized, would bring the Middle Ages to an end,[10] that was far from Edward I's original intent. Rather, he, his contemporaries, and centuries of their successors saw the question in another, and fundamentally nonlegislative, light. To their minds, the issue involved was complexly simple: how to discover and continue to implement God's eternal plan, His legal arrangements, under conditions of societal change the very novelty of which denied humanity that knowledge of precedent that had hitherto served as its guide. The challenge, then, was not to innovate, but merely to preserve and realize divine intentions even as society broke free from the constraints of the past. Briefly put, that is why statute law was at first so profoundly conservative in intent, why it was framed less as legislation, as new law, than as a declaration of what had always been true, though previously unknown to Englishmen whose earlier circumstances had obviated the need to know such truths.

Here, of course, the real presence of the community of the realm was of crucial importance to parliamentary success. From a practical point of view, that presence made possible all the political negotiations on which the formulation and broad acceptance of law so frequently depend, but at a more theoretical level it also insured that those declaring the law were doing so by means of an authority and process remarkably similar to those long used in their discovery of custom. Moreover, insofar as statutes claimed to declare, and hence to recognize, only those truths that had always been true, they were enforceable not only without prior publicity, but even, in some instances, retroactively. As Chief Justice Thorpe explained in 1365, once the king had assented to a statute,

> everyone is immediately held to know it when it is made in parliament, for as soon as it has concluded anything, the law understands that each person has knowledge thereof; for the parliament represents the body of the whole realm; and thus it is not necessary to have a proclamation [about it] before the statute takes its effect.[11]

In short, Edward I took what had been a meeting, an occasional event, and through frequent use began its transformation into a regular institution of government, the highest court in the realm. By the opening years of the fourteenth century, it had become the recognized place for addressing problems of law and, in particular, for making whatever adjustments in England's legal system that the new needs of society appeared to require. At the same time, cooperative though members generally proved, at least under effective leadership, it seems unlikely that many of them would have grasped these advantages from the very beginning. Instead, because meetings of parliament were time-consuming, and because they were expensive for those who attended, as well as for anyone else on whom a tax might be levied, one assumes that under most circumstances few subjects would willingly have attended without vigorous royal encouragement. Stubbs may well have been right in deeming one of Edward's parliaments the very model of medieval representation, but if so, it was doubtless a reluctant one.

By the end of the reign no one claimed, as rebels had done under Henry III, that the community of the realm had an independent existence, possibly an independent authority. Edward's more royalist views had come to prevail, one consequence of which was that parliaments were fast turning into what was purely the king's court; and their members, into his representatives. Yet over time parliament came on occasion to play a role vastly more complicated than that, and its transformation into something not definable as a mere tool of the king is often regarded as one of history's greater mysteries. That may well be, and perhaps the mystery will never be fully solved, but what follows appears to be at least part of the explanation.

6

Celestine V, Boniface VIII, and the Authority of Parliament

Pope Nicholas IV died on April 4, 1292, but the choice of a successor proved frustratingly difficult. The law of the conclave then in force required unanimity among the cardinals, and they were badly split by national rivalries, family antagonisms, and pure personal differences. Twenty-seven months had therefore passed without an election when, on July 4, 1294, the college received a letter from Peter of Morrone, a cave-dwelling hermit of almost eighty. Apocalyptic in tone, the letter foretold of coming doom if the cardinals did not rapidly move to heal the Church's wounds by restoring its head. Response to Peter's predictions was immediate: On the very next day, July 5, the college elected this hermit pope.

Taking the name Celestine V, Peter quickly turned into a pious disaster. As Clement V's bull of canonization put it in 1313, he was a man "of marvelous simplicity and inexperienced in everything belonging to the rule of the Church Universal, . . . a man who from his earliest years down to extreme old age had shaped his heart to divine and not worldly matters."[1] For example, he was reputed to have happily signed blank charters of papal donation for others to fill in, but even more familiar is the story of the hut he caused to be built inside the great hall of the royal palace at Naples. As he envisaged it, this was to be a rude place of solitude to which he would retire for the Advent season, and he proposed in the interim to delegate governance of the Church to three cardinals markedly more practical than he. Finally, of course, even he was brought to recognize the impossibility of the situation, and fearing, again in Clement V's words, "lest . . . some catastrophe might come upon the Church Universal from his government of it,"[2] on December 12, 1294, he issued a bull affirming his right to resign, a step he then took on the following day.[3]

If Celestine's had seemed an unfortunate reign, that of his successor Boniface VIII proved scarcely better, just longer and strikingly different in the range of problems it raised.[4] Elected on December 24, 1294, he found his pontificate quickly embroiled in controversies that included quarrels with Edward I and Philip the Fair over taxes; revolution in Florence; conflict with the Aragonese over suzerainty of Sicily; retention of benefit of clergy; and a quasi-crusade that he preached against two members of his own college of cardinals. By June 1303, the French were loudly calling him a heretic, and on September 7, Italian troops stormed the papal palace at Anagni so that William of Nogaret, an Occitan lawyer of Philip the Fair, could issue the captured pope a personal summons to appear before a general council of the Church, there to answer the charges of heresy against him.[5]

If the highly legal intent of this plan was frustrated—first by violent Colonna intervention at Anagni, then by Boniface's escape and subsequent death on October 11—over the next ten years the French did everything within their power to insure that even his memory would not go gentle into that good night. Through 1311 they continued to demand a posthumous heresy trial, and as proof of further unspeakable crimes they were rumored to possess a skull, purportedly Celestine's, the brutally pierced cranium of which was the presumed result of a nail driven in at his successor's command. Finally, to underscore the moral differences between these two popes, not to mention what the French saw as Boniface's usurpation of office, they pressed unceasingly for Celestine's canonization, the political purpose of which was only partially thwarted by Clement V's declaratory bull, one that vested the sanctity solely in Peter of Morrone, the private person, and not in Celestine, the pope.

Memorable as these events undoubtedly were, they would have little interest for English history if Queen Isabella had not decided to rid the realm of her husband Edward II.[6] Given that poor man's well-documented incompetence, she and her lover Mortimer found it none too difficult in 1326 to invade England successfully, but removing the king from office proved rather more difficult. Above all, it had to be done in such a way as to retain the support of those prelates and magnates whose allegiance they needed in order to establish, and maintain, their own regime. Custom had long permitted aggrieved vassals to defy their lord, of course, and formal diffidation clearly broke all bonds of allegiance. Nevertheless, it seemed far from certain that such an approach could be persuasively extended to cover the actual deposition of God's anointed, the king. None had, in fact, been removed since the Conquest, and if some, like John, had had violent differences with their barons, even chapter 61 of the original Magna Carta had exempted the persons of the king, the queen, and their children from the direct consequences of the right of revolution it sought to enshrine. In short, although Isabella's supporters sometimes used the procedures and vocabulary of diffidation in their campaign to convince the doubtful that their actions conformed to law, in the end they were forced to look elsewhere for ultimate justification.[7]

Here the entwined stories of Celestine V and Boniface VIII began to take on unexpected significance. The events were recent, and that they were especially well known in England is suggested by the extent to which modern knowledge of them depends on English sources.[8] What gave these papal crises their importance in 1326–27 was the fact that they had engendered a lively theoretical debate about the circumstances under which a pope could either renounce his office or be deposed. The debate owed not a little to earlier canonist thought,[9] but the pressing realities of the 1290s and early 1300s had given that thought an unusual immediacy, a potential applicability that encouraged men to transform what had once been the purely speculative into something both practical and concrete. Moreover, because the papal cases raised questions analogous to those facing Isabella and Mortimer; and because several of their chief advisers were bishops well versed in canon law,[10] the answers advanced in the first instance became models for those used in the second.

Before deciding on renunciation, Celestine V had sought the advice of his cardinals, among them Benedict Gaetani, the future Boniface VIII. As his later editing of *The Sext* demonstrates, Gaetani was an expert on the legal arguments needed to validate Celestine's desires, and in words put into the pope's mouth, he was quick to express them: "My age, my manners, the grossness of my language, my lack of intelligence, my want of prudence and experience make me feel the peril to which I am exposed by the Holy See."[11] Edward II confessed to no such shortcomings himself, but chroniclers were quick to make up the deficiency or, rather, his deficiencies:

[F]rom childhood he gave himself up in private to the art of rowing and of driving horses, to digging ditches and thatching roofs, as it is commonly said; to working at blacksmithing at night with his associates, and to other mechanical occupations with which it was not fitting that a son of a king should be occupied.[12]

In this account, hardly unique, Edward's plebeian grossness begins to match Celestine's, and even as one doubts the specifics involved, one should recognize that in both cases the source of the ineptitude, the unfitness for office, was undoubtedly the same, a desire to make the "facts" conform to the requirements set forth in canon law for either forced or voluntary removal from office. Of particular relevance was the concept of the *rex inutilis* or "worthless king," the formulation of which in the mid-thirteenth century had allowed canonists to explain how Pope Stephen II had licitly sanctioned Pepin the Short's decision to overthrow and supplant the last of the Merovingians—or how, by extension, the unfailing incompetence of any ruler qualified him for regency or coadjutorship at best, deposition at worst.[13] Such thinking had clearly animated the views of Cardinal Gaetani in 1294, so it seems unsurprising that they should have reappeared in 1327 as well.

In fact, further parallels abound. If, for example, the French joined the most extreme of the Spiritual Franciscans in charging that Boniface VIII had become pope through fraud,[14] almost inevitably it was reported that Edward had been no king's son at all, but a changeling, the child of a carter whom a nurse had hastily substituted for the infant prince after a boar had wandered into the royal nursery and goared him.[15] Similarly, if William of Plaisians accused Boniface of sodomy,[16] the Chronica de Melsa claims that Edward "especially delighted" in the practice,[17] a charge the frequent recurrence of which in depositional literature is best explained by the medieval tendency to associate heresy with sexually deviant practices. The very term "buggery" derives, after all, from the medieval French for Bogomil or Albigensian.[18] Lastly, in the event that still another parallel is needed, if the cardinals observed the law of the conclave's ten-day mourning period after Celestine's abdication and before they turned to the election of a successor,[19] so, too, did the English find it expedient to pretend that Edward had died: The royal household was dissolved; its steward Sir Thomas de Blount broke his staff of office as was more typically done over a dead king's grave; and throughout these events Edward himself was portrayed as dressed in black, fainting, weeping, and wailing, altogether the perfect though somewhat unusual mourner at his own funeral.[20]

These and other similarities were soon to become such commonplaces that later instances in which they recur can have little evidentiary value for demonstrating the influence of one event on another. At the opening of the fourteenth century, however, these shared specifics were as new and unusual as was the whole process of deposition itself. As a result, the extent of the parallels makes clear the extent to which England's managers had found imitation of papal precedent an attractive way to increase the likelihood that Edward II's downfall would be seen, understood, and above all accepted within a context that included much more than formal diffidation. Further, those managers did not limit their borrowings to concrete deeds and suggestive symbolism. Rather, these similarities merely reflect a more profound debt that extended even into the realm of ideas and theory.

Although canonists and publicists had often differed among themselves about the kinds of charges that were grave enough to warrant the removal of a pope, certain crimes appeared in their writings with monotonous regularity, especially obdurate heresy and personal insufficiency. Others almost equally popular included murder, gross moral turpitude, dissipation of the goods of the Church, and the taking of doctrinal positions contrary to the fundamental laws of the Church, these last usually defined as the teachings of Scripture and the decrees of the early councils. In the opinion of most writers, any pope found guilty of such sins would cease to be pope.[21]

Perhaps needless to say, the charges brought against Edward II bore a remarkable resemblance to those stressed by the canonists. Insofar as one may judge, no one spoke to the heresy demonstrated by his alleged sodomy, at least not for the public record, but on January 13, 1327, when Archbishop Reynolds of Canterbury presented six "reasons" for ending his reign, they included the following: The king's "person . . . was not sufficient to govern. . . . He has destroyed Holy Church and imprisoned some of the persons of Holy Church and brought duress upon others and also many great and noble men of his land he has put to a shameful death, imprisoned, exiled and disinherited." Not only had he lost all of Scotland as well as lands in Gascony and Ireland, but "he has stripped his realm and done all that he could to ruin his realm and his people." As far as breaking the fundamental law was concerned, like the crime against nature a transgression tantamount to heresy, he has consistently failed to do right to his subjects and has equally failed to keep "the other points of the oath that he took at his coronation."[22] In short, the English pattern again repeated that of the canonists, and because the charges also repeated ones brought by the French against Boniface VIII,[23] that pope would have had little difficulty in recognizing the pattern and divining its intent. Besides, he had used much of it himself when advising his predecessor.

Still, striking as these similarities may be, they fail to address some crucial issues, notably the nature and source of the authority needed to depose a reigning monarch, not to mention the vexing question of who may be said to enjoy it and why. Here again, though, the arguments of the canonists and publicists provide some intriguing possibilities. Ecclesiastical thinkers had long shared a vague sense that the Church as a whole had both the right and the duty to limit a wayward pope, but the actual scope of that sense began to take a precise and legal form only during the twelfth and thirteenth centuries. Thus, for example, in wording later incorporated into the *Glossa ordinaria* Johannes Teutonnicus found: "Where matters of faith are concerned . . . a general council is greater than a pope."[24] In turn, that position created its own difficulties, not the least of which lay in the problem of conflict between the two and its proper mode of resolution.

At one extreme, Huguccio held that a council lacked the authority to depose an erring pope, but added that a heretical one really deposed himself and that a council was fully capable of recognizing that reality.[25] In a sense, then, Huguccio's councils possessed powers not unlike those of the modern jury, a body without sovereignty, and yet one having the capacity needed to determine and to declare which of many competing "facts" are legally true. If so, a council would also resemble the parliaments of Edward I insofar as they, too, made statute law merely by giving their formal recognition to a pre-existing truth.[26] As a consequence, Huguccio may help to explain how, in theory, even a court without ultimate sovereignty can on occasion take positions on which definitive sovereign action can be based.

At the other and more conciliar extreme stood Alanus, perhaps significantly an Englishman, who argued that "for the one crime of heresy a pope can be judged even against his will. It is so in this crime because, in matters that pertain to the faith, he is less than the college of cardinals or a general council of bishops.''[27] Unlike Hugguccio, Alanus thus believed that in this one instance a council possessed authority independent of the pope, but whatever the differences between their two theories, and whatever new crimes others might add to the judgeable list, there was little dispute over the practical outcome—a pope who was no longer a pope. In the equally practical word of politics, that was possibly the one thing that mattered, whether that world was the one of Boniface VIII and the French, or that of Edward II and his French wife.

If these theories enjoyed popularity among Isabella's supporters, that was largely because they helped to conceptualize a justification for the desired end, a fully legal deposition that would be accepted as such. Yet the ideas involved were hardly new, especially in England. Rather, their importance lay in their use of abstract language and juridical categories that gave fresh life to the long-held, though frequently inchoate and unverbalized view that in the declaration of legal truths, the community had greater claims to an independent and binding decision-making authority than did the king.[28] In other words, the adaptation of canon-law theories to the English circumstances of 1326–27 did not represent a new departure as much as it simply reanimated and gave practical application to dimly sensed, deeply held, and previously unrationalized notions about the proper relationship between the monarch and that community over which he normally ruled.

It seems likely, though, that those moving for the deposition of Edward II failed adequately to consider what were apt to prove some of the long-term consequences of their course of action. For the canonists had not remained silent on the question of ultimate authority and its source, on why it was that a council could at times judge a pope, and their answers as transmitted by publicists at the time of Boniface VIII had seldom been of a variety congenial to those who favored strictly monarchical rule.[29] Nevertheless, of all the explanations advanced only two need discussion here, the mystical and the corporative, since only they were to have a significant impact in England.

In Matthew 18:20, Christ is reported to have assured his followers: ''For where two or three are gathered together in my name, there am I in the midst of them.'' Not surprisingly, this text had quickly become the key for understanding how any group of normally fallible men could, with the aid of the Holy Spirit, arrive at inerrant decisions. Thus, to cite a typical instance, when John XV sought to defend the decisions of a Lateran synod in 993, he did so by arguing that this biblical passage guaranteed the participation of the Holy Spirit in that council, something that proved in turn that its findings were true. For, he wrote, it was impossible to lie in any gathering where that sanctifying Spirit was present.[30] Moreover, this theory had already played a modest if occasional role in the political affairs of England, as in 1199 when the archbishop of Canterbury had proclaimed John's legitimacy as king because, as he pointed out, "after invoking the grace of the Holy Spirit, we are unanimous in electing him."[31] When combined with what was taken to be Christ's promise in Luke 22:23 that the faith of the Church would never fail, the assurances in Matthew provided canonists with the texts needed to explain how it was that a council could lawfully judge an erring pope. In the simplest terms, they held that because such a group was a *corpus mysticum,* a "mystical body" or corporation, it always spoke with an authority divine.[32] And that these ideas had a leading part to play in the deposition of Edward II is nowhere more fully demonstrated than in the archbishop of Canterbury's sermon of January 15, 1327, a sermon preached on the old Carolingian text, *Vox populi, vox Dei,* "The voice of the people is the voice of God." Reynolds had much more in mind than is ever conveyed by the modern cliché, for it was through use of this text that he sought to justify the sermon's announcement that "by the unanimous consent of all the earls and barons, and of the archbishops and bishops, and of the whole clergy and people, King Edward was deposed from his pristine dignity, never more to reign nor to govern the people of England."[33]

Still, because most canonists like most Englishmen were not much given to mystical notions, in their analyses they tended to stress the practical reasoning of Roman corporate law much more than the miraculous interventions of the Holy Spirit. Thirteenth-century decretalists could readily accept the opinion of Johannes Teutonnicus that the unity of the Church derived from "the Holy Spirit in us that makes us one body,"[34] but they much preferred the earlier view of theologians like Hugh of St. Victor that the *corpus mysticum* of the Church was in a very real way no more than the *universitas* or *congregatio fidelium,* the "corporate body" or "congregation of the faithful." As a result and with great regularity, their emphasis fell just on the purely legal implications they saw flowing from the technical composition of that body.

To simplify a bit, though not overmuch, Gratian's *Decretum* had several times repeated the law of the early Church that bishops were to be elected by the clergy and people of their dioceses, but to these corporate-minded lawyers this terminology meant only that, by a process analogous to the imperial *lex regia,* a corporation known as the bishop-and-chapter had come into being; a corporation the primary purpose of which was, in legal terms, to guard, maintain, and to exercise the rights of that congregation of the faithful known as their church. Bishop-and-chapter thus represented all Christians of the diocese, and the principal challenge as seen by the canonists was to determine the proper spheres of authority for both constituent parts of the greater corporate whole, the precise legal capacities of those who were usually termed, in the anthropomorphic imagery of the times, the head and the members.[35]

The solution most widely accepted was that of Hostiensis, a leading thirteenth-century expert who held that head and members each possessed authority that varied in relationship to the nature of the question involved. The bishop transacted all business, but if it concerned the chapter alone, he acted solely in his capacity as one of the canons, *ut canonicus.* On the other hand, if the business pertained to the bishop alone, he acted in his capacity as a prelate, *ut prelatus.* And in matters involving both head and members, notably decisions about the property of the whole church, bishop and chapter had to act jointly; in such instances, by far the most common, the authority of the bishop was legally no more than that of a proctor empowered to represent the entire corporation that alone possessed lordship or *dominium.*[36]

Because this approach had an obvious applicability to the Church Universal and not just to a diocese, canonists were quick to explore the possibilities. Moreover, with the renunciation of Celestine V and the attempted removal of Boniface VIII, their purely speculative conclusions began to take on a quite practical significance. One has only to read the works of John of Paris, by far the best known of the publicists caught up in these controversies, to see the extent to which he fashioned his case out of the earlier conclusions of others. He argued, in brief, that even though the pope was the head of the Church, true lordship rested with the congregation of the faithful alone. This view then entailed the further conclusion that the bishop of Rome was merely the proctor or trustee (*dispensator*) of agency law, a man who could exercise his authority not as supreme lord, but only on behalf of the Church itself, *propter ecclesiam.* Furthermore, in spite of the fact that his power of orders, his sacramental authority, came "immediately from God," that of jurisdiction came directly "from the people electing or consenting." In turn, though, because in this case the pope would be acting as no more than the agent of others, and because either the college of cardinals or a general council could act "in the place of the Church" or "in the place of the whole clergy and people," John concluded that both bodies had the divine authority needed to depose a pope, their normal head, for causes ranging from heresy and notorious crimes to "mere incompetence."[37]

When, on January 14, 1327, the bishop of Winchester preached to those gathered in Westminster Hall to hear the charges against Edward II, he used as his text the words, "My head pains me," explaining "with sorrow what a feeble head England had had for many years." Then, on the following day and after announcing that the voice of the people was the voice of God, the archbishop of Canterbury reported the deposition, adding "that all . . . both laity and clergy, unanimously agreed that my lord Edward, his first-born son, should succeed."[38] Yet in some measure the deposition was still incomplete, for on January 20, a representative committee met with the royal prisoner at Kenilworth where Sir William Trussell, "proctor of all in the land of England and of the whole parliament,"[39] performed a final ceremony in words variously recorded, but the essence of which went as follows:

> I, William Trussell, procurator of prelates, earls, and barons and other people named in my procuration, . . . retract the homage and fealty due to you Edward, king of England, as you were king before these hours. . . . And I declare in their name and in the name of every one of them, that they will not henceforth be in your fealty nor your liege, nor claim to hold anything from you as king. And thus they deem you a private person, with no matter of royal dignity.[40]

It may seem odd that the deposition had not earlier reached its final stage, but the explanation is again to be found in canon law. Under its terms, a trial could proceed with the defendant absent, but if so, he had to receive a personal summons before it could begin. Similarly, no judgment was allowed to take effect until the court had informed him in person of its decision.[41] Since both procedures were followed in Edward's case, it becomes clear why his reign came to an end here, with these formal words of diffidation and not five days earlier, when Archbishop Reynolds had announced in his absence the fact of his deposition to those assembled in Westminster Hall. Only with Trussell's committee did he cease to be king, and only then was it possible for Sir Thomas de Blount to break his staff of office.

Nevertheless, in 1327 the precise nature of the body that had judged its king defied easy legal definition. If some found it a true parliament, others did not. Because Edward himself had participated in none of its meetings, more cautious observers saw his absence as something that had denied this assembly the kind of royal presence and sanction needed for full parliamentary status.[42] Yet no one then used this seemingly crucial point to argue that the deposers had acted illegally, without proper judicial authority. On the contrary, the general silence suggests the extent to which factors both expedient and persuasive had convinced even people of consequence to accept the legitimacy of what had been done. And if fear played a role in this seeming acquiescence, so did reasoning similar to that of the chroniclers of Lanercost and Lichfield, men whose accounts echoed the vocabulary and thought of John of Paris in their insistence that those judging the king had been nothing less than "the whole clergy and people" or "a general council of the whole clergy and people" of England.[43] In this way, more of the ideas first given clear conceptual form by the canonists began to influence the form of English political assumptions, and while the point would be difficult to prove, it seems likely that these views, a natural extension of the importance long accorded to the community of the realm, had not a little to do with the stress that all sources place on the representational character of all the various groups that had participated in the depositional process.[44]

At the purely political level, 1327 thus marked a potential turning point, one in which men of politics and law had discovered a theoretical justification for the view that, in times of crisis, parliament had the independent authority to become more "the people's" court than the king's, a body in which the community could use God's sanction and its own to arrive at judgments legally binding on all Englishmen including the one who normally ruled. Still, even to make the point is to overstate it, for Isabella and Mortimer were thoroughly practical people faced with a strikingly practical problem, how best to depose Edward II. As a result, and because this action was in English terms wholly unprecedented, there is no reason to suppose that their conduct was in any significant way limited or guided by the ideas they and their followers claimed to profess. Insofar as they seem to have been willing to take any position, the general acceptance of which might help them to achieve their goal, their borrowings from the canonists were doubtless little more than rationalizations of the moment, positions they were fully prepared to abandon if different ones appeared more promising.[45]

And so it proved in the aftermath. In spite of the constitutional implications of their depositional justifications, the new regime attempted no radical transformation in the bases of its authority. Indeed, one was never to occur, at least not completely. It was, after all, a fearful thing to remove one of those whom God had anointed, and just as the government found it desirable to stress that the sources of Edward III's kingship were little different from those of his father's, so, too, did it return to, and make more explicit, the earlier view of parliament as the king's high court.[46]

When studied in isolation, then, the deposition of Edward II would seem to demonstrate little more than the fact that the world of practical politics is normally open and fluid, seldom guided or channeled by overly great concern with past precedents and future consequences. Success usually goes not to the rigidly principled or firmly committed, but mainly to those who have the tactical flexibility needed to accept compromises, to form coalitions, and in all possible ways to manipulate the immediate situation to gain their own political advantage. Moreover, the process typically involves neither strategy nor strategic planning since, as the careers of Isabella and Mortimer suggest, the challenge is to meet today's problems, with the devil taking the morrow.

On the other hand, from time to time crises arise that prove impossible to resolve purely on the basis of short-term political manipulation. They rarely occur, but when they do, participants are forced to change their approach, even their modes of discourse. Formerly flexible politicians find events unexpectedly compelling them to take stands based on solemn adherence to principle; newly minted statesmen express a deep if recently discovered concern for "the lessons of history"; and resolution of the conflict at hand comes to depend less on the usual forms of political behavior than on ringing appeals to those fundamental ideas, rooted in precedent, the function of which is to create quasi-religious fervor for the cause, and the consequence of which, if the cause is victorious, is to prove just how fundamental those ideas are. In short, during moments of crisis the purely political can rapidly turn into the strikingly constitutional. The politicians involved may well remain manipulators at heart, but because circumstances deny them the chance to practice their accustomed arts, the observer is offered a rare opportunity to see which historical incidents are so frequently and successfully cited that their supposed lessons may be said to have become principles of the constitution, precedents that so limit present choices that they channel the future as well.[47]

If the events of 1326–27 provide no such opportunity, the reprise of 1399 does, for in deposing Richard II, Henry Bolingbroke first tried to use the flexible approach of politics. In the beginning, when he returned from exile, he claimed that he sought no more than restoration of the duchy of Lancaster, the inheritance of which the king had wrongfully denied him, and this tactic gained him immediate support, notably from the Percys. Furthermore, when he decided that his difficulties would remain unresolved unless and until he himself had assumed the crown, he continued his attempt to keep the struggle at the low level of problem-solving, not at that of principle. The prospect of bringing Richard to formal trial had little appeal, for it would raise all the basic issues about the nature and source of ruling authority best avoided by one who wished truly to be king. Much better, then, as far as possible, to keep the dispute within the royal family by arguing that his own descent from Henry III was superior to Richard's and hence that he deserved the title by hereditary right alone.[48]

In the end, though, Henry's maneuvers, his attempts to avoid matters of potentially divisive principle, proved unavailing. As a result, when his hereditary claims were rejected by the very commission he had appointed to review them, he was forced to fall back on the precedents created seventy-two years before. He found, therefore, that justification for his own actions had to be modeled on the course pursued in 1327; and because 1399 became the model for the endless depositions of the fifteenth century, the fall of Edward II began to take on constitutional significance. And understandably so, for once again a quasi-parliamentary body, "the estates and the people," had deposed a king.[49]

It should be noted, though, that these events did not take place in isolation. On the contrary, the very fact that Henry's *coup* had occurred within the context of a Europe seeking desperately to end the Great Schism doubtless contributed not just to Lancastrian success, but also to growing acceptance of the ideas that had legitimated his seizure of power. For, starting in 1378, the Schism had caused a crisis that served to revive and amplify all the theories that had earlier justified the renunciation of Celestine V and the attempts to remove Boniface VIII.[50] In an age that so vigorously debated how best to restore the seamless garment of Christ—whether by councils, withdrawal of obedience, or by way of cession—the ideas of the conciliar movement tended almost inevitably to merge with, and reinforce, the Edwardian precedents. Together they provided the needed cultural, political, and constitutional context for grasping how the partisans of Lancaster could use the authority of both God and the realm to replace Richard II with Henry IV.[51]

If the consequences of 1399 were to prove more durable than those of 1327, a major cause lay in the fact that, unlike Edward III, Henry IV was not the deposed king's son. Because men could reasonably doubt whether he or any of those who came to the throne in the fifteenth century was God's chosen instrument, the crown's true heir,[52] it is scarcely surprising to find that during those troubled times kings and subjects alike should have decided to give parliament increased prominence as the one body through which God and the realm inerrantly spoke. Thus, for example, statutes and petitions began to specify the correct procedures needed for lawful election to the commons; similarly, greater attention was paid to the question of who, as of right, could sit with the lords.[53] By such means greater proof was offered that the members of parliament were at all times proper representatives of the estates or the community and hence that their decisions carried with them the full authority of the realm.

Moreover, this change made itself manifest in a multitude of other ways. Whereas the official record of sessions under Edward III had often started with speeches from war heroes or the lord chief justice,[54] in the fifteenth century it began almost invariably with a sermon by the chancellor, himself always a prelate and whose preaching was seemingly designed to show that if parliament were to follow the cited biblical precedent, it would thereby be acting on the basis of God's authority and command.[55] Last, that the idea of collegial bodies as a *corpus mysticum* contributed substantially to these developments is nowhere better illustrated than in 1401 when the speaker of the commons found parliament's tripartite form—king, lords, and commons—to be analogous to the Trinity itself. Not content with that, he then went on to compare the various aspects of parliamentary process with what he claimed were the corresponding parts of the mass.[56]

To look at the matter in a different and more pragmatic light, insofar as the powers of parliament had, by 1399, come increasingly to depend on the view that at its every meeting the entire community of the realm had somehow participated, it follows that the shapers of Richard II's deposition had been almost forced to demonstrate that what they called "the estates and the people," that group which had judged the king, had in fact been the same men who had been summoned to parliament under Richard and had then actually served under Henry—and hence that these deposers had represented the kingdom and enjoyed its Godly powers just as fully as did a regular parliament, the absence of valid writs and royal presence to the contrary notwithstanding.[57] That being the case, an entirely unlooked-for but eminently logical result was that parliament itself soon began to claim as its own that capacity for ultimate judgment that had previously belonged solely to God and the realm. Precisely because Henry had found it necessary to argue that the legitimacy of his title derived in large measure from the kinds of representation his subjects found present in parliament, people came rapidly to believe that at least during moments of conflict and crisis, it alone had the right to speak with this, the highest possible authority.

Although phraseology to that potential effect had first appeared as early as 1398,[58] it took on constitutional significance only in the October parliament of 1460 when, to prevent civil war and after exploring every conceivable alternative that politics could offer, Henry VI's reluctant lords made Duke Richard of York the royal heir, silently disinheriting young Edward of Lancaster in the process. For they did so not by appeals to the alleged wishes of God or the kingdom; rather, they rested their decision entirely on what they called, with deceptive simplicity, "the authority of parliament."[59] By 1484, Richard III and his advisers so well understood the legal implications and possibilities of all these developments that they showed themselves perfectly prepared to ask parliament, not in the past an ecclesiastical court, to declare the "pretensed marriage" of his brother Edward IV invalid. When it did so, again using no more than that same authority, it demonstrated that the range of its spiritual competence now covered not just the jurisdictional issues of earlier statutes, but sacramental ones as well.[60]

By the end of the Middle Ages, then, the role and place of parliament had changed enormously since the days of Edward I. What had once been uniquely a royal court, the king's parliament of England, surely remained that when times were good and the political leadership of the king, effective. For parliament was a collegial body and its survival depended on its continuing usefulness. In turn, though, that usefulness further depended on cooperation among all the parties to its meetings, the most important of whom was clearly the king. Nevertheless, the fourteenth and fifteenth centuries, especially the latter, were a time of troubles in which normal assumptions frequently broke down. And when they did, parliament was forced to acquire a new role. No one intended the result. Rather, what appears to have happened is that crisis in 1326–27 encouraged the tentative acceptance of better defined and protoconciliar theories of government. Then, when crisis recurred at the time of the Great Schism, and in remarkably similar form, repeated use of these theories had the effect of building them into the fabric of English political life, thereby vesting parliament with enhanced powers and a potentially independent authority such as it had not earlier possessed. This is not to say that these changes transformed political behavior under normal circumstances: England remained a monarchy, after all, and behaved as such. But it is to say that these ideas lurked in the background, a ready resource upon which to draw whenever need arose.

These facts serve to place the achievements of Henry VIII in fresh perspective. To have broken with Rome may well have been to break with much of the medieval past, but to have done so entirely on the basis of parliament's sovereign authority seems far less revolutionary. For if the statutory foundations of that Reformation were legally based on new claims of imperial status, the medieval context within which these claims should be seen gives those foundations a reassuringly familiar and divine aura. For example, if Henry's subjects came to accept this change with surprising equanimity, significant numbers appear to have done so both because they shared Dr. Nicholas Hawkins' abiding faith that it was impossible to believe that "a parliament would err in a manifest truth,"[61] and because, in words of John Mores spoken to Thomas Cromwell, they held that

> an act of parliament made in the realm for the common wealth of the same ought rather to be observed within the same realm than any general council. And I think that the Holy Ghost is as verily present at such an act as it ever was at any general council.[62]

In 1543, when Henry VIII boasted that "we be informed by our judges that we at no time stand so highly in our estate royal as in the time of parliament, wherein we as head and you as members are conjoined and knit together into one body politic,"[63] anyone with a knowledge of medieval precedent can surely doubt whether those judges had dared to inform the royal majesty on some of the sources of his imagery. To Henry the proposition doubtless seemed harmless enough, little more than testimony to his own greatness and power, but to men more versed in the past than he, those same words must have called forth the memory of a world in which kings, ever the servants of their people, were held fully accountable for the propriety of their acts. The meaning of this difference was one that no Tudor ever had to learn, but in the following century crowned heads would do so to their regret, thereby giving silent witness both to the fruitfulness of the Middle Ages and to the enduring legacy of two unfortunate popes.

PART IV

JOAN OF ARC AND RICHARD III

In the twelfth century, the English justiciar Ranulf Glanvill observed that "only God can make an heir,"[1] surely a medieval commonplace. By the end of the fifteenth, however, He had managed to do so in remarkably varied ways. When Henry VII received the victor's crown at Bosworth, he became nineteenth in a line of kings that stretched back to Hastings, but of that line, eight—over 42 percent—had been neither the son nor grandson of his immediate predecessor, Henry first among them. In France, on the other hand, God had favored a more procreative approach. In 1461, when Louis XI replaced his father Charles VII, he stood twenty-first in the line that had originated with Hugh Capet, and of that twenty-one (here including John the Posthumous as Louis would have), only three—well under 15 percent—had come to the throne as someone other than the eldest son of the departed king. Moreover, the continuity of English father-to-son succession had been interrupted at regular intervals throughout the period, whereas French discontinuity had occurred but once, in the short twelve-year interval between 1316 and 1328.[2]

Modern medicine has made this French experience seem not unusual, but in medieval terms it was extraordinary. Sixteenth-century historians have calculated that "ruling families could expect to die out, or suffer a minority or female succession, on average every second generation,"[3] and while the appearance of syphilis doubtless lowered the chances for reproductive success, improvements in housing, diet, sanitation, and climate went far toward counterbalancing whatever negative impact this new disease may have had. In the Middle Ages as in the sixteenth century, discontinuity would thus appear to have been the statistical norm, so if French kings produced direct male heirs without interruption from 987 to 1316, and then again from 1328 to 1498, this record of successful fecundity flew in the face of actuarial expectation.

At first glance, though, the two kingdoms seem more alike in terms of the number of times each was forced to devise some sort of regency government to deal with the youth, mental incapacity, or mere absence of their kings. From the accession of Philip Augustus to the death of Charles VII, from 1180 to 1461, France had to create regencies for five

RICHARD III In 1980 the Richard III Society unveiled this statue at Leicester, but the frequency with which vandals saw off its sword suggests that the Society's enthusiasms are not universally shared. (*Photograph by Geoffrey Wheeler, London*)

of its rulers: Philip Augustus (youth and crusade); Louis IX (again youth and crusades); John I (youth preceded and followed by uncertainty of succession); John II (captivity); and Charles VI (youth followed by madness). In England the number was scarcely higher since, from the accession of Richard I to the death of Richard III, from 1189 to 1485, only seven reigns had experienced regencies for comparable reasons: those of Richard I (crusade and captivity); Henry III (youth); Edward I (crusade); Edward III (youth); Richard II (youth); Henry VI (youth followed by madness); and Edward V (youth). Nevertheless, this comparability is a bit misleading insofar as English continental commitments meant that there were many additional occasions on which a king would find it necessary to be out of the realm, sometimes for years on end. The difference is important because regencies forced men to ponder the sources of government at times when royal rule was not directly personal, and if one were to total the sheer number of times and years in which England had had to do without the services—or even the presence—of its king, it would become immediately apparent just how different its experience had been from that of France.

Put these facts together and one sees more clearly why, in France, dynasticism shaped its political culture in ways unthinkable in England. It accorded with reality as only the French knew that reality. Moreover, if only God could make an heir, the regularity with which He used primogeniture to do so for Capetian and Valois alike helps to explain the ease with which subjects came to accept the sacred character of the family that ruled them, a family that counted Louis IX as only the first among its several saints. To contemporaries of John of Warenne, on the other hand, Edward I was no more than a descendant of William the Bastard,[4] and if Henry III had picked his heir's name to underscore ties with the Confessor, the relationship was collateral at best and further marred by a series of successions in which the right to rule had been far from seminally transmitted. Small wonder, then, that Edward's achievements were in large measure the product of political skills imaginatively applied. For his successes differed substantially from those of St. Louis, a king who could act as the font of justice, using not politics as the English understood them, but precise legalism and his reputation for sanctity to ride roughshod over the contrary advice that even he sometimes received. Yet when Richard II tried similar methods in England, the result was disaster. In the present context, however, it seems likely that his fall was less the consequence of personal insufficiency, of

shortcomings in the approach itself, than it was of the sheer un-
suitability of such a conception of kingship in a realm the attitudes of
which had been shaped by something other than centuries of sacred
dynasticism.

Here regencies take on added significance, for if neither land proved
fully capable of solving the problems they raised, it is also true that
insofar as government without a king forced each country to create
variant forms of rule, albeit of limited duration, the choices they made
were strikingly different, strikingly shaped by their different histories.
In France, the very success of dynasticism ensured that regencies would
turn into family affairs, whereas the broader participation of English
practice demonstrates the extent to which even the royal family accepted—or lacked the power to deny—the earl of Warenne's supposed
proposition that the partnership of the Conquest entailed the right of
continuing partnership in government. In other words, the form of
English regencies proves that this belief was not one that at all times had
to be forced on a king, like Henry III in 1258, at the point of a sword.

The long-term survival of parliament suggests a similar conclusion.
Edward I found the parliamentary participation of his barons—and
sometimes of others—exceedingly useful in the practical administration
of his realm, and the record of parliaments in the fourteenth and fifteenth centuries testifies to the soundness of his judgment. For under
most circumstances they willingly processed petitions, made political
and judicial decisions, declared laws, and levied taxes with an efficien-
cy far beyond that attainable through other means. From the royal point
of view, exceptions to this generally favorable experience, big exceptions, came primarily at those times of depositional crisis when men
who wished to replace their king discovered that theories drawn from
the canon law could be used to legitimate their actions. Over time, this
borrowing was to give parliament a new source from which to derive its
authority, but this was a discovery the full meaning of which remained
incompletely explored until well after the end of the Middle Ages. It
was, however, never to be forgotten, though it is equally true that God
and the realm wholly supplanted the king as the ultimate source of
authority only during the brief interim of Puritan supremacy.

In France, too, the composition of regency governments reflects
broader patterns of thought, ones in which the royal family—its princes
of the blood—not infrequently assumed the role played by the magnates
in England. In the 1280s, Beaumanoir had observed that the king had

the right to make establishments, the French equivalent of statutes, to which he added the following operational qualifications:

> Albeit the king can make new establishments, he must take care that he makes them for a reasonable cause and for the common profit and by great counsel, and especially so that they be not made against God nor against good customs; for if he did so (which, God willing, will never happen) his subjects would not have to suffer it because each one above all else must love and fear God with all his heart and for the honor of Holy Church, and, after, his earthly lord.[5]

The views of Beaumanoir would thus seem to agree with those of English contemporaries insofar as legal thinkers on both sides of the Channel emphasized that the creation and declaration of law could occur only through a process of wide consultation in order to insure, among other things, that this law was of benefit to the community and consistent with the intent of arrangements already established by God and previous custom. Nevertheless, French practice differed substantially from the English. In France's great territorial fiefs, for example, responsibility for the enforcement of law remained the fief-holder's alone, and only in his default was royal intervention possible.[6] Further, if the king sought "great counsel" when devising ordinances, proof of that fact tended to be framed in highly familial terms, as when Philip V assured his subjects that before issuing his ordinance on alienations he had "many times at many places had great and full deliberation with our brother, our uncles and those of our lineage, and with many other prelates and barons of our kingdom."[7]

Such tendencies help to explain why the estates-general should have developed in ways profoundly different from English parliaments. Consultative assemblies had long been known in France, and at the local level they had often enjoyed a wide range of responsibilities.[8] On the other hand, when Philip the Fair summoned central assemblies—first to rally support against Boniface VIII; then to condemn the Templars; and finally to gain consent for taxation—they and their successors displayed features understandably at variance with their English counterparts. Parliament emerged out of the *curia regis* and retained many of that court's omnicompetent characteristics, whereas the estates-general could pretend to no such origins. The French *curia regis* may have similarly evolved into a series of more specialized bodies, but it was to be parlement that acquired its judicial functions, and apart from the estates. As a result, it alone became the king's high court, and if edicts and ordinances took on legal force only when "not made against God nor against good customs," it fell to parlement, not the estates, to make that determination through its right to refuse registration to all law that failed to meet the test.

In fact, though, kings seldom used the estates to declare new law, though for reasons having little to do with that body itself. Because France remained relatively fragmented, few saw the need for much national law, and even the kings who did lacked the resources needed to achieve it. For the royal successes of the early thirteenth century had been purchased at the price of continuing provincial autonomy: Philip Augustus and Louis VIII may have greatly increased the royal domain and thereby made good their claim to be the true rulers of France, but in so doing, they failed to suppress provincial custom, though it is doubtful that they had ever seen this as a desirable objective. A major consequence of their policy was that no sense of national community developed except when it centered on the person of the king and his family.[9] Each province retained its own customs. its own narrow outlook, and all were prepared to defend what they regarded as their ancient liberties. For example, when Louis X confronted widespread revolt in 1314–15, he was forced to issue a series of provincial charters and not just one great charter of liberties as John had done a century earlier. Similarly, when Philip V attempted to standardize weights and measures in 1321, the Parisian proctors at one of his assemblies responded that "their own measures sufficed rather well for them before,"[10] and if proctors from Amiens and other northern towns apologized for *leur petit conseil* when rejecting the royal plans,[11] it seems not unfair to translate that phrase as "their small-mindedness."

Still, this is not to say that the estates were indifferent to the national interest, only that their own divisions made it difficult to claim that they spoke for, and could carry out the will of, the French equivalent to the English community of the realm. There was no equivalent. After the capture of John the Good in 1356, Étienne Marcel may well have tried to use the estates to reform the government and to increase its strength so that it could at last defeat the English, but even as his attempt shows the extent to which all agreed that the king or his regent deserved support as the one person who could act for France, so, too, does his failure demonstrate the extent to which others, in this case the estates, lacked the experience, common interests, and political acceptability needed to assume the burdens of rule.[12] Indeed, these difficulties typically appeared in more prosaic ways, notably in the variant forms that estates could take. In theory, one estates-general should have sufficed for the kingdom, but in practice problems of distance, language, and law often made it preferable to hold separate meetings for the estates of Languedoïl and those of Languedoc. In the end, not infrequently kings were to find that the most effective estates, the ones that could act because they represented a genuine community, were those of the single provinces.[13]

Historians used to expend great amounts of intellectual capital pondering the failure of French estates, but in large part their efforts were based on little more than a misapplication of the parliamentary model followed by endless ruminations about the reasons why the French weren't more like the English.[14] They just weren't. Moreover, to stress failure is to run the risk of overlooking the regularity with which estates met and played a significant role in the conduct of governmental affairs both during the Middle Ages and long thereafter. Besides, that the authority of parliament came to embody something more than the authority of the king was largely an accident, and that the French estates in any form never acquired similar powers seems to have been equally a fluke, one that started as the chance product of provincial differences in a large kingdom coming face to face with monarchs whose own caution, capacities, and continuing dynastic success gave subjects few reasons for ever wanting to explore other alternatives.

Nevertheless, if the fifteenth century brought a series of crises to England, crises that were to culminate in the trying reign of Richard III, it brought disasters to France that likewise threatened to overturn all previous experience. These difficulties began with the intermittent insanity of Charles VI, but they gathered tidal force during the civil wars of Burgundy and Armagnac and then swept over the land in the form of Henry V's invasion and victories. Flood stage arrived with the dauphin's murder of John the Fearless, the Treaty of Troyes, and, after 1422, the resulting circumstances in which supporters of Henry VI and Charles VII alike had plausible grounds for believing that only their candidate had the right to wear the crown of France. Such was the world into which Joan of Arc would venture, and because that world was overwhelmed with doubts, her life, like that of Richard III, would test the very foundations of all those assumptions on which the political life of each of their lands had long been differently based.

7

Joan of Arc

In 1415, when Joan of Arc turned three, she was far too young to understand the world into which she had been born. Nevertheless, events in that year did much to shape her role in history as well as the way in which her contemporaries would view her. First and foremost, 1415 saw Henry V's stunning victory at Agincourt, that unexpected miracle of St. Crispin's Day that made possible English reconquest of Normandy and, after Charles the dauphin's murder of Duke John of Burgundy at Montereau, the Treaty of Troyes in 1420. In it, England's king was given Charles VI's daughter Catherine of France in marriage, and all rights to the French throne were transferred from a discredited dauphin to Henry and the heirs of his body.

A second event was less noticed, at least within the context of French history, but it was to have near-equal importance: the opening of the Council of Constance, the assembly which had been called to end the Great Schism that had divided Christendom for more than a generation. In April of 1415, the council took its first and most important step, declaring that insofar as it was itself "lawfully assembled in the Holy Spirit, . . . it ha[d] its authority immediately from Christ; and that all men, of every rank and condition, including the pope himself, [were] bound to obey it."[1] Next, quickly using this authority, the council first deposed all those who claimed to be pope and then, though only two years later, elected Martin V in their stead. In so doing, the council was clearly basing its actions on theories of ultimate authority remarkably similar to those that the English had so successfully used in their depositions of Edward II and Richard II.[2]

Unfortunately, however, not all of the deposed accepted the judgment of Constance. Their resistance received no support from the significant powers of Europe, but it did attract the sympathy of other lords, men less confident of the powers by which the council had acted. In France, for example, John IV, from 1418 the count of Armagnac, was among those who refused to acknowledge the pontificate of Martin V. Instead, he first recognized Benedict XIII and then later switched his allegiance to Clement VIII. In the face of this intransigence, Martin responded appropriately and on March 4, 1429, placed John under interdict, declaring him both a schismatic and an apostate. As a result, if the count wrote Joan of Arc in August of that year of her greatest triumphs, he did so as a complete and utter outcast:

> My very dear lady, I commend myself humbly to you and beseech you for God's sake, seeing the division that now exists in the holy church universal, concerning the question of the pope (for there are three contending for the papacy: . . . The first, who is called Pope Martin [V, dwells at Rome and] was elected at Constance by the consent of all the Christian nations; he who is called Pope Clement [VIII] was elected at Peñiscola, after the death of Benedict XIII, by three of his cardinals; the third, called Pope Benedict XIV, was secretly elected at Peñiscola . . . by the cardinal of St. Étienne), I beseech you to entreat our Lord Jesus Christ that in His infinite mercy He declare unto us through you which of the three aforesaid is the true pope, and which He would have us henceforth obey, him who is called Martin, or him who is called Clement, or him who is called Benedict; . . . for we are all ready to do the will and pleasure of our Lord Jesus Christ.
>
> Entirely your count of Armagnac.[3]

Modern assumptions can make this a puzzling letter. Why, after all, should the count of Armagnac have assumed that Joan, a peasant maid, would inerrantly know which of three men was God's true pope? On the other hand, to Christine de Pizan, one of medieval France's greatest poets, the answer was not just abundantly clear but a principal theme of the last poem she ever wrote, the *Ditié de Jehanne d'Arc*. Finished on July 31, 1429, just two weeks after Charles VII's triumphant coronation, the work celebrates Joan by placing her firmly within the traditions both of French history and of religious prophecy. Before developing her themes, though, Christine is content to stress to the king the simple wonder of what has occurred:

> And you, Charles, King of France, . . . now see your honor exalted by the Maid who has laid low your enemies beneath your standard (and this *is* new) in a short time; for it was believed quite impossible that you should ever recover your country which you were on the point of losing. Now it is manifestly yours . . . And all this has been brought about by the intelligence of the Maid who, God be thanked, has played her part in this matter![4]

Nevertheless, the poem quickly makes it clear that intelligence was but a part of the story since, as Christine expresses the point in a direct apostrophe to Joan, the source of her powers transcends mere human capacities:

> And you, blessed Maid, . . . God honored you so much that you untied the rope which held France tightly bound. . . . You, Joan, born in a propitious hour, blessed be He who created you! Maiden sent from God, into whom the Holy Spirit poured His great grace.[5]

With these words, so reminiscent of Mary in their content, Christine transforms Joan into a chosen instrument through which the Holy Spirit both speaks and operates. To the poet, then, this "blessed Maid" becomes in her own being a mystical body not unlike the "holy Council of Constance" or all those English parliamentary gatherings that had claimed to be "lawfully assembled in the Holy Spirit" and to have had their "authority immediately from Christ." The principal difference, a striking one, is that, whereas the divine authority of councils had long been recognized, Joan was a simple country girl, largely untutored, and lacking all proof of divine mission other than the purity of her own being. Still, if Christine de Pizan had no doubts about that mission or in proclaiming that it was through the Holy Spirit that Joan had been able to know the true king and to crown him, it becomes clear just why the count of Armagnac should have assumed that, by using the same grace, she would easily be able to tell him which of three men was the true pope, the one whom Christ "would have us henceforth obey."

In spite of such confidence in her capacities, matters appear to have seemed rather less clear to Joan herself. As she was later to testify at her trial, she had received the count's letter at Compiègne, but because it had arrived while she was mounting her horse, she did not believe that

she had answered it. On the other hand, when a response was introduced in evidence, one on which she had placed her sign manual, she
acknowledged that "she thought she had made that answer in part, but
not all of it."[6] Nevertheless—and Joan's caution here appears to be
based more on fear than on doubt—the reply reads as follows:

Jhesus ✠ Maria

> Count of Armagnac, my good and very dear friend, Joan the Maid
> informs you that your message has reached her, wherein you declare
> that you have sent to her to discover which of the three popes . . . you
> should believe. In truth I cannot well for the present tell, . . . for I am
> now too pressed by the business of war: but when you hear that I am
> in Paris, send me a message and I will tell you in whom you should
> rightly believe, and what I shall know by the counsel of my just and
> sovereign Lord, the King of all the world, and as far as I can, what
> you should do. I commend you to God: May He keep you. Written at
> Compiègne the 22nd day of August [1429].[7]

That Joan proved unable to help the count seems scarcely surprising,
for there is little in the record to suggest a person who knew much either
about the politics of France or headship in the Church. A year and a half
after sending her letter, though in Rouen rather than Paris, she may have
testified that "as for herself, she held and believed that one ought to
obey our lord the pope at Rome,"[8] but nothing about her response
suggests that she then knew what his name was, or if she even knew
whether he were still Martin V, whom John of Armagnac had named as
Roman pontiff. In fact, Martin had died only nine days before, but the
count's concerns were by then so far removed from her own that when,
earlier in the same session, that of March 1, 1431, she was
"[a]sked . . . whom she believed to be the true pope, she answered by
asking if there were two of them."[9] It seems likely, too, that she had
heard of no council other than Constance, and it only obliquely, in John
IV's one passing reference. Thus, for example, when Brother Ysam-
bard de la Pierre advised her to submit to the impending Council of
Basel, the first session of which would take place within two months of
her martyrdom, she "asked what a General Council was."[10] In other
words, Joan's own confidence in the divine origins of her mission
appears to have rested on something other than a detailed knowledge of
contemporary realities.

In a strictly temporal sense, the mission arose in the context of Henry

V's victories, Charles VI's intermittent insanity, and the dauphin's murder of the duke of Burgundy. After John the Fearless' assassination, the new duke Philip the Good was understandably eager for revenge, and he chose to seek it through an English alliance that led in the following year, 1420, to the Treaty of Troyes and formal peace between England and France. In accord with the treaty's provisions, Henry V married Charles VI's daughter Catherine, and these same provisions then used the dictates of canon law to argue that because consummation of the marriage had made Henry the flesh of Catherine's flesh, he had also become the true son of Charles VI, one obligated to "love and honor" the French king and his queen, Isabeau of Bavaria, "as father and mother." Next, Troyes denounced unspecified but "horrible and heinous crimes" of Catherine's brother Charles the dauphin, and, because of them, his right of succession was firmly denied, a judgment in which the parlement of Paris concurred the following December, when it found him responsible for Burgundy's murder. The Treaty of Troyes, having disinherited the dauphin and having transformed Henry into a true son of Isabeau and Charles VI, then ended by proclaiming that England's king was henceforth to be known as "heir of France," with succession to rest in his line.[11] As a result, when Henry V and Charles VI both died in 1422, it was the infant Henry VI, not Charles VII, who became the formally recognized king of France, all the dictates of that realm's purely male succession to the contrary notwithstanding.[12]

It seems unlikely that Joan of Arc knew much more of Troyes than of popes and councils. The extent of her knowledge would have been limited not just by her station in life and youth at the time, but also by the poor communications between Paris and the land of her birth, the frontier region between Champagne and Lorraine. On the other hand, it is equally clear that she knew something, however vague, about the circumstances that had led to the disinheritance of the man who was to become her "gentle dauphin":

> Asked whether she thinks and firmly believes that her king did right in killing or causing to be killed my lord of Burgundy,
> She answered that this was a great tragedy for the kingdom of France; and whatever there had been between them, God had sent her to the help of the king of France.[13]

As for why God had so sent her, she remained suggestively vague, referring the matter back "to the King of Heaven, Who sent her to

Charles, son of Charles king of France, who should himself be king of France.''[14]

If great patriots often come from border areas, the explanation is not so much that the contested life of the frontier forces them to choose sides, usually with great ardor. Rather, it is more typically the case that their very distance from the centers of power serves also to protect them from all knowledge of the frequently nasty realities of politics as experienced by those who are much more directly involved than they themselves. Moreover, because outsiders have a marked tendency to view political clashes not as limited quarrels between and among the self-interested, but as struggles of near-mythic proportions over the true nature of national identity and purpose, they bear a marked resemblance to those who, in times of crisis, transform the purely political into the inalterably constitutional by introducing elements of principle into the debate.[15] Finally, because such people see high ideals as central to clashes that had previously lacked them, they and their views will often gain favor with those at the center who find their own aims ennobled by them.

Joan of Arc was unquestionably this kind of person. In her testimony above, for example, the dauphin's obvious duplicity in the assassination of John the Fearless appears never to occur to her; instead, she sees only a more general point, that whatever the cause of Burgundy's death, it had been "a great tragedy for the kingdom of France." Even more strikingly, it is equally apparent that for her, human judgment of Charles, any attempt to disinherit him for his part in the murder, is wholly irrelevant. If "God had sent her to the help of the king of France," the fact was that because her dauphin was "son of Charles king of France," it followed that he "should himself be king of France," and this regardless of what mere mortals might say about his moral stature. Since only God could make an heir, only He, not men, could unmake one. With artless symplicity, then, did Joan confirm that sacred dynasticism had become a central part of France's political culture.

To extend the point, much of the fascination to be found in the record of Joan's trial arises not just from the glimpses it offers of a remarkable human being, but more particularly from the insights it gives into the process by which a young girl was transformed into the saviour of her land. For Joan had not always been the Maid with a mission. On the contrary, though as she herself was the first to admit, God's purposes had become known to her only in stages, beginning roughly at the onset of puberty:

[S]he said that . . . she received revelation from Our Lord by a voice which taught her how to behave. And the first time she was greatly afraid. And she said that the voice came that time at noon, on a summer's day, a fast day, when she was in her father's garden, and that . . . after she had heard it three times, she knew that it was the voice of an angel. . . .

She said that firstly he told her that she was a good child, and that God would help her. . . . She said also that this voice had always taken good care of her [and] . . . that it taught her how to behave. And it said to her that she ought to go often to church. . . .

She said also that the first time she heard her voice, she vowed her virginity as long as it should be pleasing to God. She was then of the age of thirteen or thereabouts.[16]

As this testimony demonstrates, Joan's initial voice appears to have come to her less as a result of France's difficulties than in response to the turmoil through which she herself was then moving, in the transition from childhood to maturity. It seems, too, that her response was not so very different from those of other girls over the centuries. Suddenly faced by the responsibilities of adulthood, their own awkwardness and lack of self-esteem frequently intensified by parental assurances that they will prove unequal to the challenge, many are those who have sought relief in the consoling counsel of dolls, pets, and inner voices. Similarly, when disturbed and confused by the realities of a newly discovered sexuality, many are those who have also vowed themselves to perpetual virginity, thereby seeking a return to childlike innocence. In most cases, however, this stage soon passes, whereas in Joan's it was to prove but the first step in a long and complex development.[17]

Despite the frequent vagueness of Joan's trial evidence, it remains remarkably easy to follow the human dimensions of the process by which her voices came to stress the plight of France more than the comfort they could provide for the anxieties of her own development. For example, even though she testified initially that only "later" had the voice that first spoke to her at thirteen "said to her that it was necessary that she should go into France," almost immediately she provides needed precision to this chronology by adding that "with this, it said to her that she must hurry and go and raise the siege of Orleans."[18] Since the English did not begin that siege until October 1428,

in turn that means that the idea for Joan's French mission could have
begun to take shape no earlier than three months before she set off, in
January 1429, for Vaucouleurs and, ultimately, the court of Charles VII
at Chinon, a destination she reached on February 23.

It seems clear, too, that events as Joan experienced them in 1428
provided an unusually fertile ground in which new ideas could take
root. For the siege of Orleans was no more than the capstone to a series
of incidents and crises that brought France's predicament vividly to her
attention. Not, of course, that the dangers of the Anglo-Burgundian
alliance were ever far from mind:

> Asked if the people of Domremy sided with the Burgundians or the
> Armagnacs,
>   She answered that she only knew one Burgundian, whose head she
> would like to see chopped off, that is if it had pleased God.
>   Asked whether at [the neighboring village of] Maxey they were
> Burgundians or Armagnacs,
>   She said they were Burgundians. . . .
>   Asked if the voice told her in her childhood that the English should
> come into France,
>   She said they were already in France when the voice first spoke to
> her.
>   Asked if she were ever with the other children when they played at
> fights between English and French,
>   She said no, as far as she could remember. But she had often seen
> those of her village fighting against those of Maxey, and sometimes
> coming back wounded and bleeding.[19]

Still, if some of the consequences of a divided land had always been
part of Joan's experience, those consequences took on greater immediacy during the early summer of 1428 when Antoine de Vergy, the pro-
Burgundian governor of Champagne, led a marauding expedition
against Vaucouleurs, the administrative center of the bailiwick of Chau-
mont, of which Domremy formed a modest part. Domremy and a few
neighboring villages were burned, but not before their inhabitants had
had a chance to flee. Joan herself went to Neufchâteau where, as she
reported at her trial, she stayed for two weeks with a woman named La
Rousse, doing the household chores but none of that tending of cattle or
sheep with which her modern admirers have so often associated her—
but that she herself was always at such pains to deny.[20] Even more
troubling, at least personally, it was at this point, too, that she appeared

before the court of the bishop of Toul to answer the charge of an unknown plaintiff that she had failed to marry him, and this contrary to the arrangements made by her parents and, apparently, also to her own sworn word.[21]

It would appear, then, that the start of the siege of Orleans was less the cause of Joan's mission than the occasion that suggested a course of action to her which might address the problems, both personal and national, that had so recently become the dominant elements in her life. Hesitantly to put the case into the more psychoanalytic framework of Erik Erikson, it looks as though Joan's adolescence had involved a series of identity crises and that the siege of Orleans was but the last such crisis, the one out of which a strong new sense of identity began to emerge(Her mission to raise the siege of Orleans was central to what would quickly become her mature personality, but even more crucial, one suspects, was her recognition of, and identification with, the specific saints who had for so long been speaking to her.)

Nevertheless, this recognition was far from immediate. At age thirteen, after all, Joan had had no idea of her first voice's identity. Rather, it merely frightened her, and only after hearing it three times did she recognize "that it was the voice of an angel." Her subsequent identification of the speaker as St. Michael then led to the following exchange with her inquisitors:

> Asked how she knew that it was Saint Michael,
>   She replied: By the speech and language of angels. . . .
>   Asked how she knew that it was the language of angels,
>   She answered that she believed it immediately; and desired to believe it.
>   She also said that Saint Michael, when he came to her, told her that Saint Catherine and Saint Margaret would come to her, and that she should follow their counsel; for they were ordered to lead and counsel her as to what she should do; and that she should believe what they told her, for it was by Our Lord's command.[22]

Now, if Joan's mission began to take shape only during the fall of 1428 and in response to a series of crises that had begun with her flight to Neufchâteau, it seems far from coincidental that the feast days of these three saints are celebrated in autumn or that they follow each other in suggestive sequence: Michael on September 29, Margaret on October 8, and Catherine on November 25. For in that sequence, and in the saintly attributes that would have been stressed in sermons and homilies, there emerge a host of problems with which Joan would have strongly identified as well as tales of success in surmounting them that suggested personal qualities which would prove central to her own maturing sense of being. Thus, insofar as God wished to enlist her as the agent of His intentions, it becomes difficult to conceive of more suitable intermediaries.

In *The Song of Roland,* St. Michael is portrayed less as the archangel of the Judgment Day than as that guardian and patron who will save the Franks even from the worst of their adversities. In the even more popular *Golden Legend,* he assures victory to the people of Sipontus over the still-pagan invaders from Naples, after which the Neapolitans not killed, "acknowledging the power of the archangel, abandoned the cult of the idols, and submitted to the yoke of the Christian faith." In addition,

> when Lucifer sought to be the equal of God, the Archangel Michael, standard-bearer of the heavenly host, came forward, and cast the rebels out of Heaven, imprisoning them in the dark regions of the air until the day of judgement. They are not permitted to dwell in Heaven, which is . . . bright and pleasant; nor with us on earth, lest they molest us excessively. They abide therefore between Heaven and earth, that they may suffer when they look upward to the glory which they have lost.[23]

This was suggestive imagery, surely, for a daughter of the holy kingdom of France, but such suggestiveness must have taken on greater personal immediacy nine days later, with the celebration of the feast of St. Margaret:

> Margaret the virgin, who was also known as Pelagius, was most fair, rich and noble. She was guarded by her parents with zealous care, and taught to live virtuously; and so great were her probity and modesty that she refused to appear before the eyes of men. Finally she was bespoken in marriage by a noble youth, and both her parents gave their consent; whereupon the most lavish and delightful preparations were made for her nuptials. . . . But suddenly, God inspiring her, the virgin gave thought to the loss of her virginity, and to the sinful riotings with which it was celebrated; and prostrating herself upon the ground, . . . in the middle of the night she cut off her hair, garbed herself in the habit of a man, and recommending herself to God, secretly took flight.[24]

Taken in by a monastery where she passed herself off as the monk Pelagius, Margaret was soon recommended to serve as the brother in charge of a convent of nuns where, alas, disaster struck: Responsibility for the pregnant condition of one of the nuns having been imputed to Pelagius, the only "man" around, she was therefore immured in a cave for the rest of her days. Only at death were the mistake—and the probity of her life—discovered.[25]

Nine weeks later, on the feast of St. Catherine, all these themes found their fullest expression in the legends associated with this daughter of King Costus of Alexandria. One day "at the age of eighteen," so the story went, Catherine heard the roaring of beasts and, upon inquiry, discovered that the emperor Maxentius had brought them to the city to turn loose on all Christians who refused to sacrifice to the gods:

> Stricken to the heart with grief, she made her way boldly to the emperor, and spoke as follows: "I offer thee greeting, Emperor, not only out of deference for thy rank, but also that I may reason with thee, and persuade thee to acknowledge the Creator of the heavens, and to renounce the worship of false gods!"[26]

Moreover, since the princess "was instructed in all the liberal arts," she first argued "according to the divers modes of the syllogisms, by allegory and metaphor, by logic and mystic," but not content with that, she then reverted to "common speech," and with a brilliance that left the emperor "dumfounded."

Indeed, when she remained obdurate, he responded: "If it be as thou sayest, then the whole world is in error, and thou alone hast the truth." Furthermore, though remarkably like the uncrowned Charles who was to send Joan to Poitiers for clerical examination after her arrival at Chinon, Maxentius thereupon summoned fifty orators and philosophers to refute her, but they had even less success than he: The maid refuted them instead, after which their master proclaimed their conversion to Christ. Furious, the emperor now had all fifty burned alive, but in a spirit of concupiscent generosity offered Catherine a place in his palace second only to that of the queen. Imprisonment followed her refusal, and during it she converted the captain of the guard, two hundred troops, and the queen herself. When Maxentius discovered this turn of events, not to mention the failure of his attempts to starve Catherine to death (she having been fed on "celestial food" by a dove sent from heaven), in a rage he ordered the troops and their commander to be tortured and beheaded. The queen, too, was similarly decapitated after having had her breasts cut off. As for Catherine herself, the emperor

ordered four knived wheels to be constructed, under the turnings of
which the poor girl would meet her doom; but at the crucial moment
God intervened to overturn this fearsome contraption, the net result of
which was that four thousand pagans were crushed to death.

Maxentius having thus become a widower, he now offered Catherine
an improved set of options: marriage or death. She, of course, chose
eternity, but "when her head was cut off, milk gushed forth from her
body instead of blood." Angels buried her on Mount Sinai, where her
bones continue to yield an oil "which strengthens the limbs of the
weak." In terms of Joan's own story, though, and especially in possible
explanation of her increasing stress on St. Catherine in the course of her
trial, one last detail from *The Golden Legend* is perhaps worth mentioning:

> It is said that a certain monk of Rouen betook himself to Mount Sinai,
> and there abode for seven years, devoting himself to the service of
> Saint Catherine. When this monk prayed earnestly that he might be
> made worthy to possess a relic of her body, suddenly one of the
> fingers broke off from her hand. The monk received the gift of God
> with joy, and carried it away to his monastery.[27]

Joan's recent experiences make it clear why, in the fall of 1428, these
saints' lives should have had such an enormous impact on her thinking.
If St. Michael's associations both with the Franks and with victory led
inevitably to thoughts of defeating the English at Orleans, the examples
offered by Sts. Margaret and Catherine spoke even more directly to her
condition. Like Margaret's parents, Joan's "mother and father took
great care to keep her safely," and if they, too, "were very strict with
her, . . . she was always obedient to them save in the incident at Toul,
the action for [breach of promise of] marriage."[28] Yet in this response
Joan was not being entirely accurate since, of course, she had gone on
to engage in an even more crucial act of disobedience in January of
1429 when, in the words of Margaret's life, she "secretly took flight"
from Domremy without telling her parents because, as she herself put it,
she feared that "her father . . . might hinder the journey":

> Asked if she believed that she had done well in leaving without the
> permission of her father and mother, seeing that it is said that one
> should honor one's father and mother, . . .
>   She answered: Since God so commanded, I had to obey.
>   She added that since God so commanded, if she had had a hundred

fathers and mothers, and if she had been a king's daughter, she would still have gone.[29]

Moreover, even though Joan assured her judges that her parents had forgiven her later, her testimony makes it apparent just how terrified their presumed reactions had made her feel at the time. In fact, when she was queried on the subject—and especially on the extent to which her voices had counselled this secret departure for Vaucouleurs—her response conveys an inner turmoil that is so intensely imagined that it seems likely that the specifics surrounding her decisions to leave involved more than a little autosuggestion:

> [A]s for her father and mother, the voices were well enough pleased that she should tell them, had it not been for the trouble that they would have caused if she did tell them. For herself, she would not tell them for anything. . . .
>
> [W]hen she was still with her father and mother, she was often told by her mother that her father had said that he dreamed his daughter Joan would go off with the soldiers. . . .
>
> She said further that she had heard her mother say that her father had said to her brothers: If I thought that such a thing could happen as I have dreamed, I should want you to drown her; and if you did not, I would drown her myself. And that she greatly feared that they would lose their minds when she left to go to Vaucouleurs.[30]

In turn, this fear helps to explain the centrality of Sts. Margaret and Catherine in Joan's thinking. Nevertheless, of the two, St. Catherine was clearly the more important, for if Margaret's flight dressed as a man suggested how effectively Joan herself could avoid marriage and break free of her parents' domination, the example thus presented remained limited in its applicability. Joan was not, after all, a person for whom the life of a transvestite monk would hold much appeal, and Margaret's experiences suffered from the further limitation that they spoke only to Joan's personal problems, not to those of France. In that regard, Catherine's story offered much richer possibilities since she, unlike Margaret, was a woman who had not just rejected marriage, but one who had also spoken as confidently to her sovereign as Joan was going to have to speak to hers. This duality thereby brought together all Joan's concerns, both public and private. Just as Catherine, ever the virgin, had cogently argued the true way even to the mightiest in her land, so, too, could Joan, who lacked all knowledge of philosophy and the liberal arts. For in her rural simplicity all she had to do was to imitate the example of the urban princess who had once resorted to "common speech" to dumfound Maxentius, and in so doing she could always, as she later put it, join her hands together at times of uncertainty in order to beg and pray that her voices would "help and advise her in what she had to do." The advice then given seems always to have been frustratingly vague—usually no more than that she should speak or act "boldly"—but it was enough for Joan, who appears never to have worried about this lack of specifics. On the contrary, with her departure from Domremy she was rapidly to develop a stunning capacity for acting with confidence and remarkable vigor.[31]

If, moreover, the crisis provoked by the siege of Orleans had become so acute by late 1428 that the clergy of France began calling for weekly processions to increase "the prosperity of the king's arms,"[32] and if Joan's own mission then took shape within the context of those autumnal saints' days that helped to define the role she should play, her confidence in the specifics of that mission owed not a little to her growing knowledge of the so-called Merlin prophecies. These prophecies, long known and widely believed, were variously attributed: some to Merlin, others to Bede, and still others to Charlemagne, St. Louis, and the Sibylline oracle.[33] In varying forms they foretold that just as France had been lost by a woman, so would it be saved by a maid, one who, in some versions, would come from an oaken wood, the Bois Chenu. Given the uncertain nature of the evidence, though, it is impossible to say just how much she knew of them prior to her arrival at Vaucouleurs and Chinon. At her trial, for example, she remained cautiously evasive when the subject was raised, and for understandable reasons:

> Questioned concerning the tree,
> She answered that quite close to Domremy there was a tree which was called the Ladies' tree; others called it the Fairies' tree; and near it there was a spring. . . . She had heard several old folks say, not of her family, that the fairies frequented it; and she had heard her godmother Jeanne . . . say that she had seen them there. . . .
> She said further that she had seen garlands hung on the branches of the tree by the girls; and she herself had hung them there with the other girls. . . . She also said that ever since she learned that she must come into France, she played [there] very little, the least that she could. . . .

She also said that there was a wood called the Bois Chenu that one could see from her father's house, not more than a league away. . . . She said further that when she came before the king, many people asked whether in her country there was not a wood called the *Bois Chenu*, for there was a prophecy saying that from the *Bois Chenu* should come a maiden who would perform marvellous acts; but she put no faith in it.[34]

Still, whatever Joan's cautions were when confronted by an inquisition anxious to prove diabolical conspiracy, after the event people were more than eager to impute to her full knowledge of these prophecies from the very beginning. At her rehabilitation trial, her cousin Durand Laxart, the man who had taken her to Vaucouleurs, testified that she herself had asked him in explanation of her intentions, "Was it not said that France would be ruined through a woman, and afterwards restored by a virgin?"[35] Similarly, Catherine Royer, the woman with whom she had stayed while at Vaucouleurs, then confirmed this testimony, adding the detail that Joan had further specified that this virgin saviour was specifically to be "a maiden from the marches of Lorraine."[36] A bit more convincingly, perhaps, Jean Barbin then added substance to Joan's own statement that "many people" had asked her about her role in prophecy "when she came before the king," and specifically during the three weeks in March and April when Charles had had his parlement investigate her purity and probity at Poitiers. As Barbin told it (and his testimony was hearsay only), Joan had been questioned there about Master Jean Erault's recollection that Marie d'Avignon had predicted to Charles VI that a virgin warrior, not Marie, would soon appear to save his kingdom, at the end of which questioning Erault had proclaimed that he himself was convinced that Joan was indeed the long-sought saviour.[37]

Fragmentary and uncertain though the evidence is, it begins to present a suggestive scenario. In it, the extent of Joan's knowledge of the Merlin prophecies before leaving Domremy seems relatively unimportant. Rather, the crucial facts as she would have seen them were only three: that Orleans had to be relieved; that Charles was truly king; and that she herself was to have a leading role in helping to make her first two "facts" into lasting realities. On the other hand, precisely because her assumptions accorded so well with the prophecies then current among Charles' supporters, she was almost guaranteed a warm reception, at least from those whose own views coincided with hers. Men who had already been urging aid for Orleans could use her appearance to achieve it, and once the siege had been lifted, those who preferred an immediate coronation to any other course of action found that they, too, could rely on her beliefs for support. After Orleans and its attendant victories, for example, when some of the military commanders joined princes of the blood in arguing that the next step should be the liberation of Normandy, others appealed to Joan's view that, in Dunois' words, it was better first "to go to Reims" because she believed that "if once the king were consecrated and crowned, the power of his adversaries would decline, and that in the end they would be past the power of doing any injury, either to him or to his kingdom."[38]

Although events were ultimately to prove her right, what remains unclear is just why coronation made such a difference in her mind—and why, in fact, it seems genuinely to have made a difference in transforming Charles into a man who was accepted as king, a man who was ultimately able to drive the English out of France. The view that his crowning explains all is surely common enough, and it may well be accurate within certain limits, but at the same time it fails to address a whole host of troubling issues. After all, kings of France had long assumed the powers and title of king immediately upon the death and burial of their fathers, so why should Joan have believed that Charles remained mere dauphin until the moment of his coronation? Similarly, if the issue in her mind was that the Treaty of Troyes and the parlement of Paris had wrongly denied Charles' rights of inheritance, then on what basis did she assume that investiture at Reims would demonstrate that they had been in error? The answers to such questions would appear to lie in the ways in which Joan herself came to conceive of her mission.

By the end of her life, Joan had arrived at a remarkably clear understanding of her basic goals, testifying on March 27, 1431 that

> she brought news from God to her king; and that our Lord would restore his kingdom to him, have him crowned at Reims, and drive out his enemies. And that she was God's messenger in telling him that he must put her boldly to work, and that she would raise the siege of Orleans.[39]

What becomes clear from such evidence, and from Joan's ways of expression, is the extent to which she herself seems to have seen the nub of Charles' difficulties as lying not in his lack of coronation, but in his supposed disinheritance. As she appears to have understood the situation, no human being had the authority to deny him his right to rule; that right came only from God.

If so, it follows that Joan conceived of the utility of the coronation within that context. Its object would not have been coronation for its own sake, a regally capacitating ceremony analogous to the sacrament of ordination, one through which Charles would acquire possession of the kingly office. Instead, what she expected Charles to undergo— what, on July 17, 1429, he in fact underwent—was in her eyes an entirely different kind of quasi-sacrament, one in which the divine sanction for his kingship would be not ordained, but confirmed. And in this ceremony of confirmation, Joan with her banner would (and did) stand close to her king, slightly in front and just to the left of the altar, which is precisely where sponsors at baptisms and confirmations are supposed to stand. Moreover, since the oil of confirmation "symbolizes . . . the sweet but penetrating sway of the Holy Spirit," whereas the sacrament itself is a "Gift of Fortitude" that renders the recipient "capable of struggling against the enemies of faith even unto martyrdom," the sponsor's duty being to "help and guide him in the struggles of the Christian militia in which he is enrolled," to accept this view of the coronation is perhaps better to see both the Charles and the Joan whom we have always known, but never quite fully comprehended. At the very least, since canon law further requires that "the sponsor must physically touch the candidate in the very act of confirmation,"[40] it is surely to understand why, at the moment of Charles' anointing, Joan should have thrown herself at his feet, clasped his legs, and exclaimed:

> Noble king, now God's will is fulfilled, that I should raise the siege of Orleans, and that I should bring you to your city of Reims, there to receive the holy chrism, thus proving that you are true king, and that the kingdom of France should rightly be yours.[41]

In short, Joan may have left Domremy filled with the lives of Sts. Margaret and Catherine, but as she came to know the Merlin prophecies more completely—possibly before she reached Chinon and certainly in the course of her interrogation at Poitiers—she began to conceive of her role within their terms, as God's agent who would serve as a kind of second Mary, confirming Charles' kingship and repairing the damage wrought by Isabeau of Bavaria in her guise as the disinheriting Eve.

That being the case, even the increasingly prophetic certainty of her language becomes comprehensible, most familiar in a letter she dispatched during Holy Week of 1429:

✠ Jhesus Maria ✠

King of England, and you, duke of Bedford, calling yourself regent of France, . . . do right in the King of Heaven's sight. Surrender to the Maid sent hither by God. . . . She comes in God's name to establish the Blood Royal, ready to make peace if you agree to abandon France. . . . [Y]ou will not withhold the kingdom of France from God, King of kings, blessed Mary's Son. King Charles, the true inheritor, will possess it, for God wills it and has revealed it through the Maid.[42]

Significantly, too, others accepted these claims and in accepting them doubtless expanded the specifics of Joan's mission as she herself was increasingly coming to understand it. Thus, in the very process of welcoming Joan as France's saviour, Christine de Pizan can excitedly heap new burdens on her:

Her achievement is no illusion for she was carefully put to the test in council . . . and well examined, before people were prepared to believe her. . . But it was found in history-records that she was destined to accomplish her mission; for more than 500 years ago, Merlin, the Sibyl and Bede foresaw her coming, entered her in their writings as someone who would put an end to France's troubles. . . . She was miraculously sent by divine command and conducted by an angel of the Lord to the king, in order to help him. . . . Oh how clear this was at the siege of Orleans where her power was first made manifest! . . . Oh! What an honor for the female sex! It is perfectly obvious that God has special regard for it when all these wretched people who destroyed the whole kingdom—now recovered and made safe by a woman, something that 5000 *men* could not have done—and the traitors [have been] exterminated. . . . Has she not led the king with her own hand to his coronation? . . . As they return [now] through the country, neither city nor castle nor small town can hold out against them. . . . No matter how strong the resistance offered, it collapses beneath the Maid's assault. . . . Before the event they would scarcely have believed this possible.[43]

Although Christine's assessment is a high one, it no more than parallels what came to be Joan's own views in the end. If Christine saw a girl sent by God and filled with the grace of the Holy Spirit, Joan herself saw to it that her army left Blois for Orleans led by priests, carrying the banner of Mary and Jesus, and singing the *Veni Creator Spiritus*.[44] Moreover, the poet's faith in the divine origins of the Maid's mission sheds light on what appears to have been Joan's own beliefs, for when one asks how Christine "knows" that Joan was God's agent, sent to aid the king, her knowledge depends very clearly on proofs "made manifest" by success: in the relief of Orleans, the coronation of the king, and the collapse of all resistance "beneath the Maid's assault." In much the same way, the very nature of Joan's voices suggests a similar pattern, one in which each of her actions became, for her, nothing less than a judicial ordeal, a test in which the legitimacy of those voices— indeed, the reality of their presence—was validated only by her success in achieving the goals they had set for her.

Nevertheless, the point can never be proved conclusively, largely because Joan's own testimony on the subject is frequently vague, ambiguous, and contradictory. In addition, the question is further complicated by the difficulties inherent in trying to explain in purely human terms phenomena that many have long believed to have been divine. Despite such obstacles, though, some facts are clear. First and most suggestively, Joan's voices appear never to have recommended a course of action that had not previously been suggested by some more human agent, and this whether the issue at stake was merely her proper conduct at the time of puberty or the steps she should take in aid of her king. Moreover, with the notable exception of the time during her early captivity when the voices failed to prevent her leap from the tower at Beaurevoir, they appear never to have given her advice that proved unavailing—and even in that incident they later forgave her. Yet in this action they again showed themselves to be not unlike her human companions, in this case the parents who had earlier forgiven her for leaving home, also against their wishes.[45]

On the other hand, when human expectations far exceeded Joan's capacity to deliver, her voices fell silent, but nowhere more poignantly than in response to the kind of quasi-millenary program that her supporters in France saw as the ineluctable consequence of the coronation at Reims. Christine de Pizan was again only the most eloquent of those who gave it expression:

I don't know if Paris will hold out (for they have not reached there
yet) or if it will resist the Maid. But if it decides to see her as an
enemy, I fear that . . . things will go badly for them, for [the king]
will enter Paris, no matter who may grumble about it, for the Maid
has promised him. . . . She will restore harmony in Christendom and
the Church. She will destroy the unbelievers people talk about, and
the heretics and their vile ways, for this is the substance of a prophecy
that has been made. . . . She will destroy the Saracens, by conquering the Holy Land. She will lead Charles there, whom God preserve!
Before he dies he will make such a journey. He is the one who is to
conquer it. It is there that she is to end her days and that both of them
are to win glory. It is there that the whole enterprise will be brought to
completion.[46]

When, in fact, Paris and other places failed to fall as predicted, Joan
was quick to deny that her voices had had anything to do with her
defeats. Rather, she told her judges that she had attacked Paris not "by
revelation of her voices . . . [but] at the request of certain nobles who
were desirous of having a skirmish or an assault at arms." As she later
explained, "It seemed to her that they did well in attacking their enemies."[47] Similarly, when pressed about her failure at La Charité, she
added that she had gone there only "at the desire of the captains" or,
somewhat contradictorily, "at her king's request."[48] In both instances,
however, even though the saints had failed to guide her, she remained
confident that her actions had been "neither against nor according to the
command of her voices."[49] In this way, apparently, she avoided the
possible implications of her belief that, "if she were in mortal sin, the
voice would not come to her,"[50] while at the same time consoling
herself with a logical explanation for the silences she had disastrously
experienced.

Christine's final predictions go well beyond the themes of the Merlin
prophecies. Instead, they find their source in her application to Joan of
the so-called Second Charlemagne Prophecy, one that foretold that
"Charles, son of Charles" would expel all enemies from his kingdom
and, eventually, become the emperor of all Christendom.[51] Although
these rather mystical expectations had been known in French literary
circles for nearly half a century, the extent to which Joan herself had
been introduced to them remains uncertain. When she testified that God
had "sent her to Charles, son of Charles king of France, who should
himself be King of France," she employed the fomulaic interconnection

so stressed in the prophecy itself, but apart from that one instance, the evidence from her trial reflects no sign that she knew either of Charlemagne or of the expectations associated with a later king who would bear his name.[52] In fact, just as she remained ignorant of all specifics regarding popes, councils, and the fragmenting schism, so, too, does she appear to have known little about the particularities that lay at the heart of French royal mythology. Thus, to illustrate, Dunois swore at the rehabilitation proceedings that she herself had explained to him that God had sent her to relieve Orleans ''on the petition of Saint Louis and Saint Charlemagne,''[53] but in the records of her own trial, strikingly, she is represented as mentioning neither man. In short, albeit that Joan's life and ultimate significance may have been strongly shaped and influenced by the mystical strands of the prophetic tradition, she herself was far from knowing the whole of it. Even more tellingly, perhaps, in her own person she was far from being either a prophet or a mystic.

That said, however, it still remains true that what she believed—and what she did—remained extraordinarily useful to Charles' cause and, over time, to that of the French monarchy. Incomplete as Joan's mission in life was to prove, its impact on the political culture of France was immense, confirming and strengthening as it did the assumptions that had long shaped its governmental practices. First and foremost, insofar as she emphasized again and again that ''she brought news from God to her king . . . that Our Lord would restore his kingdom to him, have him crowned at Reims, and drive out his enemies,''[54] she reinforced the belief that in France, at least, God alone could create a king—and that those whom He had created could not be denied by such human instruments as state treaties or the judgments of parlement. ''Blood Royal'' was also needed, as she elsewhere insisted, but even in that she was underscoring the same point since, as in Glanvill's similar thinking, ''Only God can make an heir.''[55] Moreover, she made it equally clear that the rule of God's king must cover ''[a]ll the kingdom [a]nd that if my lord of Burgundy and the other subjects of the realm did not come to obedience, the king would make them do so by force.'' She was, Joan added, ''God's messenger in telling'' Charles these things and in insisting ''that he must put her boldly to work . . . [to] raise the siege of Orleans.''[56]

In so saying, Joan envisaged—and was helping to create—a France profoundly different from the realm of England. There, while its king continued to rule by the grace of God, his subjects in parliament could lay claim to a parallel authority, one in which they, too, could speak as a mystical body with the voice of the Holy Spirit. By way of contrast, in Joan's France only the king himself enjoyed such an intimate relationship with the divine, for God's messenger herself affirmed it. If, as it appears, the potentially autonomous authority of medieval representative institutions depended on their being representative not just of the king, his subjects, or his kingdom, but, rather, of God, then it becomes clear that widespread acceptance of Joan's assumptions would put all such French bodies at a serious disadvantage in comparison to their seeming English counterparts. Such French institutions, notably the parlements, may have frequently laid claim to a mystical authority, but within the framework created by the implications of Joan's views it followed that any divine powers they exercised were enjoyed not autonomously, but merely by virtue of delegation from the king. And, as conciliarists were to discover within the Church when confronted by Eugenius IV's opposition at the Council of Basel, what he who was acknowledged as God's vicar had delegated, he could also take away.[57]

Doubtless, though, these thoughts far exceed Joan's capacity to have understood them, for she lived in a concrete, immediate world, whereas they depend on a kind of abstract reasoning and modern view of history wholly foreign to her experience. On the other hand, if she was to have an impact on French history, that impact was not entirely of her own creation. She was not, in Anouilh's image, "a lark in the skies of France, high over the heads of her soldiers," one who had appeared suddenly out of nowhere, "singing a joyous, crazy song of courage."[58] Rather, the acceptance of her mission, and hence its importance, depended from the very beginning on the remarkable extent to which everything she did or said was strikingly consistent with French political assumptions as they had existed long before her coming. In other words, what was crucial to her long-term success was not her addition of anything significantly new to those beliefs, but more her insistent urging of their reality, something that breathed new life into a French kingship, the divine nature of which had come increasingly into doubt thanks to English victories, the dauphin's murder of John of Burgundy, and the devastating Treaty of Troyes. Thus if that doubted kingship had earlier become highly sacralized, when Joan argued that "He who makes war on the holy kingdom of France makes war on King Jesus," the words may have been uniquely hers, but the sentiments they expressed were not.[59] Quite to the contrary, they merely reanimated the past and, in so doing, further defined and confirmed the way in which the future would go.

Moreover, that is far from the whole of the story. After Joan's death, the tide began to turn in Charles VII's favor, but in ways that made it increasingly undesirable to present an accurate portrayal of who she had been or what she had attempted to do. From a purely practical point of view, the crucial change came in 1435, when Philip the Good of Burgundy returned to French allegiance and, in so doing, abandoned his quest for vengeance against the man who had murdered his father. The Church then quickly granted the king its absolution also, and Luigi *de Gariis,* a Bolognese jurist, was prevailed upon to write an opinion in which he held that, whatever the then-dauphin's responsibility for Montereau, neither Charles VI nor those acting on his behalf had enjoyed the authority needed to disinherit him.[60] With the feud within the French royal family thus momentarily ended, and with the legal basis for Charles VII's title no longer in doubt, his coronation, the acme of Joan's achievement, began to lose its importance as that rite through which his claim to the crown had been divinely confirmed.

Nevertheless, because Burgundy's changed allegiance had negated the Treaty of Troyes, supporters of Henry VI were forced to devise new grounds on which to deny the legitimacy of Charles' kingship. These they found in the political career of Isabeau of Bavaria, and especially in her earlier support of Louis of Orleans. With Isabeau near death and no longer able to defend her reputation, dark rumors began to circulate that her progeny's ineligibility for office had resulted not from his murder of John the Fearless, but from the "fact" that he was not his father's son. Instead, it was claimed that he had been the unfortunate product of an alleged love affair between Louis and Isabeau, an adulterous liaison that was also used to explain why the duke of Burgundy had seen fit to have the duke of Orleans assassinated. With acceptance of these rumors, then, the English could hope that Isabeau as quean would undercut Charles' legitimacy as king, thereby strengthening the claims of his Lancastrian rival.[61]

These developments shed considerable light on the new focus of Joan's rehabilitation during the 1450s. In as much as Charles VII could scarcely allow the person responsible for his coronation to remain a relapsed heretic, a retrial was doubtless inevitable under any circumstances. Nevertheless, the context created by the changed grounds on which his enemies were attempting to deny his right to the crown insured that the evidence presented would contain new emphases, all of them designed to prove yet again that he alone was God's elect, the chosen ruler of holy France.

In the testimony, of course, many reassuringly familiar features remained. Joan's relatives reported that she had known from before her departure that she was to be the fulfillment of the Merlin prophecies, while Dunois solemnly related how, after the French victory at Jargeau, the captured earl of Suffolk had been shown "four verses about a Maid who would come from Bois Chenu and ride against them on the back of archers."[62] Not content with that, he also rephrased his earlier evidence, now saying that "this young girl swore that she had had a vision in which Saint Louis and Charlemagne prayed God for the safety of the king and this city [of Orleans]."[63]

Still, if the basic components of Joan's mission stayed much the same—relief for Orleans, coronation for the king—witnesses tended to suggest that only the latter had initially concerned her. Durand Laxart testified that at the time that he had taken her to Vaucouleurs, her sole purpose in wanting to go to France was, in Michel Lebuin's confirming phrase, to get the dauphin "anointed at Reims." Orleans had become part of her agenda somewhat later, when the plight of the city was brought to her attention.[64] Joan herself appears to have arrived at these goals in quite the opposite order, but to reverse them in 1455–56 was obviously to give pride of place to the only one that continued to matter. Moreover, if the coronation was thus underscored as Joan's quintessential accomplishment, its true significance was reshaped to meet the challenge posed by the implications of Isabeau's supposed adultery. For Joan, chrism and crown had confirmed her belief that mere mortals lacked the authority needed to disinherit her dauphin, that he had, in fact, become the successor to his father from the moment of that father's death. Within the context stressed at her rehabilitation, however, while the coronation remains a kind of confirmation, it confirms something quite different, the legitimacy of Charles' birth and hence the kingly source of his royal blood.

It need hardly be added that this development was fully consistent with that monarch's own wishes. Toward the end of his life, for example, he "confessed" that when he had had his first private interview with Joan, the evidence that had most persuaded him of her role as God's agent was her knowledge of the secret prayer in which he had made three requests, the most important of which expressed the hope that his own doubts over the legitimacy of his birth might soon be ended.[65] Suspiciously, the same point had earlier emerged at the retrial, notably in the testimony of Jean Pasqueral, an Augustinian friar who claimed long to have been Joan's confessor. He asserted that she herself had told him of that interview at Chinon, but under the circumstances and given her own statements on the subject, his version of her words sounds too good to be true:

> Gentle dauphin, . . . I am called Joan the Maid; and the King of Heaven sends you word by me that you will be consecrated and crowned at Reims, and that you will be the lieutenant of the King of Heaven. . . . On the part of my Lord, I tell thee thou art true heir of France and son of the king; and He sends me to lead thee to Reims to the end thou mayst receive thy crowning and thy consecration, if thou wilt.[66]

In one respect, though, Pasqueral was here being entirely accurate in reporting Joan's views or, more probably, her views as those who wrote in her name found it best to express them. He may link knowledge that Charles was "true heir of France and son of the king" to his capacity successfully to undergo the confirming ordeal of consecration and crowning at Reims, but in so doing, Pasqueral insists that Charles would become no more than "lieutenant of the King of Heaven." Joan's letter to Henry VI, Bedford, and the other English captains in France makes the same point, protesting that they "do not hold the realm of France from God" and proclaiming that "he who will thus hold it is Charles, the true heir, for God the King of Heaven so desires."[67] Yet the letter's phrasing is muted, whereas Pasqueral's is not—and his stress was to be endlessly repeated by other witnesses. John, Joan's gentle duke of Alençon, reported that at Chinon she had told the dauphin "that he should give his kingdom to the Lord of Heaven; and when he had made this gift, . . . the King of Heaven would do to him as He had done to his predecessors and restore him to his former state."[68] For Bertrand de Poulengy, Joan's squire, the picture was even clearer. In his version of her interview with Robert de Baudricourt at Vaucouleurs, she argued "that the kingdom belonged not to him, the dauphin, but to her Lord; that her Lord would have the dauphin king and hold the kingdom in trust; that she would make him king, in spite of his enemies."[69]

All agreed, then, that a good part of Joan's message lay in her insistence that Charles VII would—and did—hold France only as the regent of God, His lieutenant for the kingdom. Indeed, the point was further made in the transformation experienced in descriptions of her banner over the course of her rehabilitation. In 1431, when Joan's judges asked her "whether, when she was before the city of Orleans, she had a standard, and of what color it was,"

> She replied that it had a field sown with fleurs-de-lis, and showed a world with an angel on either side, white in color, of linen or *boucassin;* and she thought that the names JESUS MARIA were written on it; and it had a silk fringe.
> Asked if these names JESUS MARIA were written at the top or the bottom, or along the side,
> She answered that she thought they were along the side.[70]

Twenty-five years later, memories were suspiciously better and betrayed a different emphasis. Dunois swore that the standard at Orleans had been white and had showed "the figure of Our Lord holding some fleurs-de-lis in His Hand";[71] Pasqueral differed on minor details, but offered much the same picture, describing a banner "with the image of Our Saviour painted on it, sitting in judgment among the clouds of Heaven, and with Him a painted angel holding a fleur-de-lis in his hand, which Our Lord was blessing.[72] In either case, though, the symbolism was clear: France remained ever in the protective custody of God; He blessed it always; and since He judged all men, no earthly king could achieve success unless and until he acted as God's appointed agent, one who ruled his realm in trust. In such ways did Joan's rehabilitation bring together and give final medieval form to those elements—sacred blood, strict dynasticism, and a king who served as the sole representative of both God and the realm—that were later to form the underpinnings of that seventeenth-century theory of absolutism that is known as the divine right of kings.

Still, what Joan herself would have thought of these developments remains an open question. On the one hand, her own views in life appear to have been so much more cautious, so much more restrained, that one is led to wonder whether their later transformation does not explain the disappearance of all records from her interrogation at Poitiers. For if what she said there differed significantly from what was later claimed, their continuing existence would have proved awkward indeed. On the other hand, insofar as her voices served to ratify the knowledge that she first acquired from more human sources, knowledge that had proved its worth in the ordeal of reality, it could well be that Sts. Margaret and Catherine would have approved the changes wrought by Charles, the victorious king. Joan had fought hard, after all, to ensure that his would be the winning side.

That said, however, it remains to confront the reality of her death, the horror of that final ordeal through which she was made to pass. And of that ordeal, as well as of the mystery of Joan's being, no one spoke more tellingly than Martin Ladvenu, the Dominican who was described in the early stages of her rehabilitation as "especial confessor and adviser of the said Joan in her last days."[73] Because Ladvenu had served at her trial, his own hands were far from clean, but more than most, he had an appreciation of just who she had been, just what she had endured. His testimony was given in 1450, and in it he first lamented the bias of his former colleagues, men like Pierre Cauchon, the bishop of Beauvais, who had "ordered that Joan should be kept in a secular prison and in the hands of her mortal enemies . . . permitted her to be tormented and ill-treated." As he then summed up the enormity of the result:

> They put questions to her which were too difficult in order to catch her out by her own words and opinions. For she was a poor, rather simple woman who scarcely knew her Pater Noster and Ave Maria.[74]

If there are those who can only grieve over the magnitude of this tragedy, they should remember that Joan's voices continued to speak to her throughout the trial. For their presence, their encouragement, gives proof that she, too, knew that she was winning, that she, too, understood that victory would one day be hers. Little wonder, then, that she should have gone to the fire confident that "God helping me, today I shall be with Him in Paradise."[75] However differently the modern world may read Joan's story, that knowledge was no small consolation for a poor, rather simple woman who scarcely knew her Pater Noster and Ave Maria.

8

The Deposition of
Edward V

Edward IV died on April 9, 1483. The death was not unexpected, nor the factional disputes to which it gave rise. As early as 1481–82, the municipal records of Canterbury note that when passing through the town, Edward's lord chamberlain, William, Lord Hastings, had stopped long enough to warn the mayor that "the king's health was not good, and another revolution, with its consequent suppression of the city charter, was not impossible."[1] Closer to the event, fears of the impending royal demise and of its likely impact became so widespread that on March 8, Anthony, Lord Rivers—the heir's uncle and his guardian-tutor at Ludlow—found it desirable to apply for a royal patent granting him authority to raise troops.[2] Premature news of the king's death reached York on April 6, and, unquestioningly, the town fathers had appropriate dirges sung on the 7th while scheduling a solemn requiem mass for the 8th.[3]

Broadly speaking, the events of the next two months, through early June, are not in dispute, only their interpretation.[4] The accession of Edward V was proclaimed in London on April 11, with his coronation scheduled for May 4. He himself received word of his father's death on the 14th, and two days later he wrote the borough of King's Lynn, announcing his imminent departure from Ludlow so that he could "be at our city of London in all convenient haste by God's grace to be crowned at Westminster."[5] He actually left on the 24th, accompanied by Rivers, Sir Thomas Vaughan, and two thousand troops.

The size of the royal entourage provoked no little debate in London. Elizabeth Woodville, the queen mother, supported by what may loosely be termed the Woodville faction, had pressed for the largest array possible, whereas others, especially Hastings, had sought an escort of more modest proportions. Two thousand had been the figure reluctantly agreed upon. It was, as Hastings reported to the duke of Gloucester, the best he could do.

At this point, Richard, that duke of Gloucester, was to be found in the north, in the vicinity of York, where he had been serving since 1478 as his brother's lord lieutenant. It was from Hastings (and never through official notification) that he received word of Edward's death, although he must earlier have known of its imminence, if only from the false solemnities at York. Finding out in this way that the late king had, among his final acts, named him, Richard, as protector of the royal heir, the duke nonetheless tarried for over ten days, probably to gather troops. Then, at some time between April 20 and 23, he left for the south, taking with him a retinue of three hundred men, all of whom had, like their leader, sworn an oath of fealty to the new king.

Before and during this journey Richard seems to have been in constant communication with Hastings, the duke of Buckingham, possibly the king, and certainly with Elizabeth Woodville, to whom he sent assurances of loyalty and obedience to the elder of her two royal sons.[6] Expected at Nottingham on the 26th, Richard arrived at Northampton on the 29th. There he joined forces with Buckingham and met with Rivers, who had ridden back from the king's party, then at Stony Stratford, to greet them.

On the morning of the 30th, the two dukes seized Rivers, proceeded to Stony Stratford, and tendered their homage to Edward V on bended knee. The royal escort was disbanded and sent back to Wales, while Rivers, Vaughan, Lord Richard Grey,[7] and Sir Richard Haute were dispatched as prisoners to the north. With the king now safely in hand, Gloucester and Buckingham returned to Northampton where, on May 2, Edward V wrote the archbishop of Canterbury, asking him to safeguard the great seal, the Tower, "and the treasure being in the same."[8] They then resumed their progress toward London, arriving on May 4 heavily encumbered with what were proclaimed to be "Woodville" arms. It was not to be a day of coronation.

If April had been a busy month for Gloucester and Buckingham, it was equally so for those in London. Not only was there a new king to be fetched and crowned, there yet remained the old one to bury, which meant that the queen and her party were largely occupied with funereal pomp at least until the 20th, when Edward was finally laid to rest at Windsor. Moreover, if those in power found themselves in sharp disagreement over such matters as the size of Edward V's escort from Ludlow, they were equally divided over the composition of the new government, the source of its authority, and especially over the role that Richard of Gloucester, the supposed protector, was to play in it. Was he to be no more than the first among equals in a broadly based council, or was he to be a true regent, with well-nigh sovereign powers? Indeed, insofar as coronations normally ended protectorates,[9] the crowning planned for May 4 demonstrates that the Woodville faction preferred a world in which Richard, denied a protector's powers, would play no part at all.

To these cares was added a growing concern over French activities in the Channel. At the time of his death, Edward IV had been moving toward renewed hostilities with the traditional foe, and it seemed increasingly likely that French corsairs led by Lord Cordes would be tempted to profit from the confusions of the interregnum by attacking first. This was a challenge that had to be met, and by late April, when Edward IV's mourners were at last free to act, the nature of their response shows the extent to which Elizabeth Woodville and her supporters had succeeded in overcoming the opposition to their dominance. Greatly though this distressed men like Hastings, they now ruled supreme, if only in London.

In military affairs the Woodvilles had certain advantages, notably the fact that the queen's son Thomas Grey, marquis of Dorset, was already constable of the Tower and, as such, custodian of the considerable treasure and armaments amassed for the expected French war. Furthermore, the queen's brother Sir Edward Woodville enjoyed a martial reputation based on years of military and naval command. Selected to head the fleet then being assembled to counter the French, he quickly made final arrangements and put out to sea on April 30.[10] Finally, to ensure that the coffers of government continued to be filled, on April 27 commissioners were appointed to collect the tax on aliens voted by Edward IV's final parliament. Most prominent among them were Rivers and Dorset, and to prevent possible questions about the source of their authority they were carefully titled, respectively, "uterine uncle" and "uterine brother" to the young king.[11]

By the end of April, then, the Woodvilles seemed to have the situation well in hand. Their opponents in London were effectively isolated; Dorset held the Tower; Sir Edward Woodville commanded the seas; and Rivers was momentarily expected with an additional two thousand men. The capstone of these efforts would be laid on May 4 when, after Edward V's coronation, all differences about Richard of Gloucester's role would come to an end. If precedent suggested that protectors were needed only so long as the king remained uncrowned, who were the Woodvilles to defy precedent?

These dreams were shattered on the night of April 30–May 1 when word reached the capital of the previous day's events in Northampton and Stony Stratford. Confusion reigned, and while each chronicle presents a different version, most of the details are fundamentally unimportant. Only two points really matter, above all the simple fact that by the evening of May 1 the queen, her daughters, and, most importantly, her younger son, the ten-year-old duke of York, had entered sanctuary at Westminster. The second point, a bit more problematic, is best conveyed in Polydore Vergil's account of what happened after Elizabeth Woodville's sudden flight:

> But the Lord Hastings who bore privy hatred to the marquis and others of the queen's side, who for that cause had exhorted Richard to take upon him the government of the prince, when he saw all in uproar and that matters fell out otherwise than he had wanted, repenting therefore that which he had done, called together unto Paul's church such friends as he knew to be right careful for the life, dignity, and estate of Prince Edward, and conferred with them what best was to be done. Here divers of them who were most offended with this late fact of Richard, duke of Gloucester, adjudged it meet with all speed to procure the liberty of Prince Edward, whom they accounted as utterly oppressed and wronged by force and violence, that so the fear, which was kindling, might be put out before it should spread further abroad; affirming that from thenceforth no device would be void of danger except the wicked enterprise, which gave good testimony that Duke Richard had inwardly no good meaning, were with present force avoided. All the residue thought that there was no need to use war or weapon at all, as men who little suspected that the matter would have any horrible and cruel end. Wherefore they concluded to tarry while Duke Richard should come and declare what the matter was, why he

had cast them who had the prince in government into prison. And this resolution finally liked them all, because in appearance it stood with the profit of the commonwealth that every[one] of the nobility, as much as might be, should avoid variance and contention.[12]

Vergil would thus have his readers believe that Hastings began to hesitate about his previous actions from the moment that Richard's forceful assertion of his rights had placed Edward V's future in doubt. Moreover, it is also true that his version of these deliberations, if accepted, would provide a more-than-satisfactory explanation for all the tensions that were going to mar the relations between protector and council during May and early June. Yet whatever the case, with Elizabeth Woodville in sanctuary, Hastings and his followers took control in London and continued to dominate it until Edward V, Gloucester, and Buckingham arrived on May 4.

For the next month, Richard's principal challenge lay in trying to consolidate and regularize his position. Upon entering London, his first act was to summon the lord mayor and all other notables of the city to receive their oaths of fealty to Edward V. Having thus attempted to reassure the doubtful that the young king would in fact reign, the duke then moved to gain recognition of the protectorship that Edward IV had conferred on him. The council agreed to it on May 10, and the earliest surviving documents in which the title appears are dated the 14th. Thereafter, most of Edward V's official actions would be taken ''by the advice of our dearest uncle the duke of Gloucester, protector and defender of this our realm during our young age.''[13]

Since, in these actions, Richard based his powers on the rightful authority that he enjoyed over his nephew, necessarily he had to proceed with plans for the reign. On May 13, writs began to be issued for a parliament that would open on June 25;[14] three days later, the archbishop of Canterbury was instructed by signet letter to assemble his province in convocation at St. Paul's, London.[15] John Russell, bishop of Lincoln and Edward's new chancellor, began drafting the sermon with which he would open parliament,[16] and at some later date, probably in early June, coronation robes were ordered.[17]

On May 20, sheriffs were told to order all unknighted persons holding £40 of land or rent to come to London on June 18 for knighting, and about June 3, the towns of Rye and Romney received invitations to the coronation.[18] Then, on June 5, some forty individuals of high rank were sent letters "charging you to prepare and furnish yourself to receive the noble order of knighthood at our coronation, which by God's grace we intend shall be solemnized the twenty-second day of this present month at our palace of Westminster, commanding you to be here at our Tower of London four days afore our said coronation to have communication with our commissioners concerning that matter."[19]

During this same period, early May through early June, the duke of Gloucester was also taking more practical steps to shore up his position, not always with complete success. Russell's appointment to the chancellorship on May 10 removed a man, the archbishop of York, whose loyalties to the queen seemed greater than his allegiance to the protectorship. On the other hand, the new chancellor was no partisan of Richard's; rather, the council appears to have picked him precisely because his previous career had made him the clear follower of neither party.[20] In addition, though, and with greater luck, Richard moved to strengthen his ties with proven or likely supporters among the old nobility. Thus, on May 14 John Howard, the future duke of Norfolk, received for life the stewardship of Lancaster south of the Trent;[21] the next day, the duke of Buckingham was similarly endowed with vast grants of authority, largely in Wales and the adjoining marches.[22] In this way power and income were rapidly bestowed on those whose new authority could extend the protector's influence far beyond the confines of London.

To reduce the danger of serious hostilities with France, letters were dispatched on May 11 "to the Lord Dunham and Sir Richard Tunstall at Calais . . . for the restitution of ships of both parties."[23] But by far the greatest threat remained that posed by the Woodvilles, for even though the queen herself had fled to sanctuary while her brother Rivers had been sent a prisoner to the north, Sir Edward Woodville and the marquis of Dorset had eluded capture and had at their disposal both a powerful fleet and, apparently, treasure from the Tower with which troops could be raised.[24]

To counter this threat, as early as May 10 Sir Thomas Fulford and John Halwell had been ordered "to rig them to the sea in all haste and to go to the Downs among Sir Edward [Woodville] and his company."[25] Similar orders were given to others on the 14th and 21st. Pardon was offered to "all that will come, except the marquis, Sir Edward Woodville, and Robert Ratcliffe."[26] And these tactics bore fruit, for the fleet was successfully dispersed, although Sir Edward himself managed to escape with two ships to Brittany, where he remained a potential source of danger.

From Richard's point of view, the whereabouts of the marquis of Dorset remained a mystery. If Tudor chronicles report that he entered sanctuary with the queen and escaped at a later date,[27] those in power at the time drew a different conclusion. For example, because the just-mentioned letters of May 14 exclude him from all offers of pardon, they demonstrate that the government, presumably after finding no signs of his presence at Westminster, must have assumed that he had sailed with Sir Edward's fleet. This was not the case, as will presently appear, but the search for him continued and, as Simon Stallworth put it on June 9, "Wheresoever can be found any goods of my lord marquis it is taken."[28] Though gone, he was not forgotten.

Since Rivers, Vaughan, Haute and Grey were already prisoners, while the queen, her brother the bishop of Salisbury, and her daughters and younger son still clung to sanctuary, they posed no immediate threat. The ultimate fate of Elizabeth Woodville and her companions remained in doubt, but on May 10, the day on which the council had recognized the new protector and agreed to change chancellors, Richard tried to move decisively against those taken as Stony Stratford. Again, though, his efforts met with ill-success. In Mancini's words:

> Accordingly he attempted to bring about the condemnation of those whom he had put into prison, by obtaining a decision of the council convicting them of preparing ambushes and of being guilty of treason itself. But this he was quite unable to achieve, because there appeared no certain case as regards the ambushes, and even had the crime been manifest, it would not have been treason, for at the time of the alleged ambushes he was neither regent nor did he hold any other public office.[29]

Those in sanctuary presented difficulties of a different order. Given the queen's scheme to exclude Richard from power by crowning her son immediately, her decision to seek refuge at Westminster is entirely understandable. After all, she had lived there throughout the readeption of Henry VI, even giving birth to the future Edward V during her stay, and that experience must have convinced her not only of the safety inherent in sanctuary, but also of her ability to endure its inherent deprivations, and this for a significant period of time. Still, whatever her fears—and whatever the protector's true motives—it was exceedingly awkward from his point of view to have his purity of purpose so blatantly doubted by the immediate family of the youth in whose name he ruled.

The practical problems created by Elizabeth Woodville's defiance had begun to become clear as early as May 7 when the executors of Edward IV's will, meeting at Baynard's Castle, had found it impossible to carry out his testamentary bequests while so many of the legatees remained in sanctuary.[30] As a result, Richard and the council were forced to devote much of their time in the ensuing weeks to negotiations aimed at ending the impasse. To illustrate, on May 23 the city council of London made it a part of its records that it had read to it the oath that the archbishops of Canterbury and York, the dukes of Gloucester and Buckingham, and all the lords of the king's council were prepared to swear to the queen regarding her safety "if the same lady wished to relinquish the privilege" of sanctuary.[31] Yet all was in vain: Stallworth's letter of June 9 reports that although "My lord protector, my lord of Buckingham with all other lords, as well temporal as spiritual, were at Westminster in the council chamber from ten to two, . . . there was none that spake with the queen."[32] By June 9, then, negotiations had foundered; once more the protector had found his powers of political persuasion inadequate to the challenge he faced.

If we pause now to consider the significance of the events in the two months following Edward IV's death, the period about which there is no serious factual disagreement, certain conclusions seem possible. First and foremost, if these events are disentangled from the interpretive biases that knowledge of later events inevitably produces, there is little evidence with which to sustain, let alone prove, the traditional charge that from the beginning Richard had aimed at the crown. On the contrary, his every move suggests more limited goals. If not, it is difficult to see why, on hearing of his brother's death, he should have immediately sought oaths of fealty to Edward V; why he should have delayed so long and gathered so few troops before starting south; or why, after establishing himself in London, he should finally have agreed to his nephew's coronation.

In modern terms, the evidence shows that at most the duke of Gloucester was trying to keep his options open. If one looks at the situation from Richard's perspective, it is quickly apparent that from the moment Edward IV died, his own position became far from easy. The limited information that had reached Yorkshire seemed to indicate that the queen and her adherents were moving rapidly to exclude him from power, and he was undoubtedly enough of a student of history to know the unhappy fate that frequently awaited royal uncles—most recently Humphrey, also of Gloucester—who had lost their voice in the councils of government. Indeed, memories of his own slain brother Rutland and of the paper-crowned head of his father could only have led him to a similar conclusion, that in times without a viable king, the lives of those with royal blood stood in considerable peril.

Little wonder, then, that Richard should have so boldly seized Rivers and the rest at Stony Stratford, or that he should have made such a point of displaying captured "Woodville" arms on his entry to London. No matter what the true situation might prove to be (and here the queen's reactions to his own moves were far from reassuring), retaining some Woodville hostages provided an obvious form of self-protection against an unknown future, while casting a few aspersions on the military preparedness of his likely opponents could surely do him no harm. Possibly he was irrational in his fear of the Woodvilles, but that proves no evil intent toward the king.

Significantly, too, Richard's difficulties hardly came to an end with his arrival in London or the recognition of his protectorship. In the most limited sense, his own security depended on the power he could exercise, and yet the prevailing situation tended to militate against his chances of retaining control. The Woodvilles were only partially subdued; the composition of the council was neither of his choosing nor entirely to his liking;[33] and even though he may not yet have known of the incident, Hastings' meeting at St. Paul's demonstrates the extent to which those in London feared his intentions in the aftermath of Northampton and Stony Stratford. If Gloucester doubted the good faith of others, so did those others doubt his own. Moreover, they possessed the ability to restrict his freedom of action, as he found to his regret when the council refused to countenance the execution of Rivers, Grey, Haute, and Vaughan after hearing the charges of ambush and treason against them.

Nowhere, one suspects, are the difficulties of Richard's position more manifest than in the train of events that culminated in his decision to crown Edward V. If power had become the tiger from which the uncle could never dismount, the nephew's coronation was likely to increase the hazards of the ride. As the Woodvilles had seen in April, formal installation of even a minor king could be used as an excuse to end a protectorship, and if Richard were to be stripped of that office, he had little guarantee that Edward V would continue to rely on his advice or grant him new titles that would continue to protect him. On the contrary, given the composition of the council and, further, given the nature of the family relationships involved, it seemed much more likely that the young king would turn once again to his mother and her upstart Woodville kin.

To avoid that contingency, the obvious solution was to postpone Edward's coronation, and it was a strategy that Richard tried, at least initially. His *coup de main* at Stony Stratford followed by his delay in entering London had ipso facto cancelled the Woodvilles' original plans, and there is nothing in the surviving record of the following month to suggest that he was in any way dissatisfied with an uncrowned king. Although oaths to Edward V were freely given from the very beginning, and writs summoning parliament began to be issued as early as May 13, it is a striking fact that no official documents mention the coronation or its date before the start of June when the government dispatched invitations to Rye and Romney and, on the 5th, to those who were to appear for knighting specifically at the time of these solemnities.[34] Similarly, even though the draft of the sermon with which John Russell expected to open parliament stresses his expectation "that the lords and commons of this land will as agreeably purvey for the sure maintenance of [Edward's] high estate as any of their predecessors have done to any other of the kings of England afore"[35]—in short, the kind of expectation usually expressed in the first parliament following a king's investiture—nowhere in the draft is there specific mention of, or even vague allusion to, the coronation that the evidence of early June says should have taken place only three days previously. Instead, Russell's emphasis falls not on the king, but on his uncle:

> And whatsoever is shaped by God for any speciality of grace expropriated to this our young king and sovereign lord by his ancestors, let it be taken to advantage. . . . In the meantime, till ripeness of years and personal rule be, as by God's grace they must once be, concurrent together, the power and authority of my lord protector is so beneficial and of reason to be assented and established by the authority of this high court, that amongst all the causes of the assembling of the parliament in this time of year, this is the greatest and most necessary first to be affirmed. God grant that this matter and such other as of necessity ought to be first moved for the well[being] of the king and

the defence of this land, may have such good and brief expedition in this high court of parliament as the ease of the people and the condition and the time requireth. So that . . . the king our sovereign lord may have cause largely to rejoice himself and congruently say with the prophet, to my said lord protector, his uncle here present: "In thee I am confirmed out of the womb of the belly of my mother, thou art my protector." Uncle, I am glad to have you . . . confirmed in this place you to be my protector in all my . . . businesses. So be it, amen.[36]

It does not take an unusually suspicious cast of mind to see in these silences of May the possibility of a consciously thought-out plan of action. Edward would be king; he would be honored; but he would not be crowned. On the contrary, Richard would continue to serve as protector until his sovereign's majority, at which time the coronation would finally take place. In the meantime, parliament would be summoned immediately—indeed, in a summer month, the awkwardness of which makes Russell apologetic, an attitude that would be incomprehensible if the government had always intended to call this meeting of parliament in conjunction with the king's coronation. As a result, everything suggests that no such ceremonies were planned and that the true purpose of the summons was to gain parliamentary approval of Richard's status. With the continuing "power and authority of my lord protector . . . assented and established by the authority of this high court," he would find his position greatly strengthened, for no longer would he have to fear that an unpredictable young king, his grasping maternal relatives, or even an independent council might thrust him from office. After all, what parliament had conferred, only parliament could take away.[37]

If these were the duke of Gloucester's initial hopes, they were shortsighted. He did not fully control the council, and if some of its members, like Hastings, appeared for the moment to be moving to his side, that did not mean that they now accepted the purity of his intentions. Rather, it was more the case that he was the one alternative for men who hated the Woodvilles and feared what they might do if allowed unrestrained power during the king's minority. Such allies were not apt to take kindly to any attempt on his part to solidify his position since that for them would have been no more than to supplant one unpleasant prospect with another. Furthermore, if the protector lacked the support needed to dominate the council, he had little hope of controlling the composition and political sympathies of any parliament it might call. To strengthen his hold, he needed an assembly of predictable malleability, and the precariousness of his position in May should have suggested to him the unlikelihood of that eventuality. This was, however, a difficulty he appears not to have appreciated until the second week of June, and his efforts then to address the problem were to make matters considerably worse.[38]

Throughout this period, Elizabeth Woodville remained Richard's greatest stumbling block. As long as she and her children stayed in sanctuary, they provided a natural rallying point for potential opposition, thereby increasing the hazards of his position while at the same time reducing his room for maneuver. For example, if he hoped initially to defer Edward's coronation, that was to threaten the queen. Her response, equally logical, was to refuse all negotiations, her refuge in Westminster providing her safety while it testified silently to her continuing opposition to the new regime. On the other hand, he could not simply strike out against Edward V and usurp the throne himself, for young Richard of York, the king's brother, had also sought sanctuary, and no action against the one could hope to succeed for long unless accompanied by action against the other.

In early June, then, those in sanctuary held the key to all future developments. Unless they could be persuaded to emerge—and here the duke of York was especially important, far more so than his mother— the protector was assured of nothing but grief in his endless search for security. It is in this context, moreover, that the decision to crown Edward V doubtless took place, an action Richard preferred not to take, and yet one made necessary by Elizabeth Woodville's stubborn defiance: Coronation alone was the one step that might induce her to give way. In the event, though, it proved insufficient, at least just the promise of it did, for to repeat Stallworth's report of the outcome on the 9th, "there was none that spake with the queen."[39]

These developments help to explain the letter that Richard dispatched to the city of York on June 10, a letter that ushered in a new and more critical stage in the ongoing crisis:

> Right trusty and well-beloved, we greet you well. And as you love the weal of us and the weal and surety of your own self, we heartily pray you to come unto us in London in all the diligence ye can possible, after the sight hereof, with as many as ye can make defensibly arrayed, there to aid and assist us against the queen, her blood, adherents and affinity, which have intended and daily doth intend to

murder and utterly destroy us and our cousin the duke of Buckingham and the old royal blood of this realm. . . . And as ever we may do for you in time coming, fail not, but haste you to us hither.[40]

This letter and its companion, a similar appeal sent to Lord Neville on the following day,[41] have generally received one of two quite different readings. Either they represent Richard's desperate response to his discovery that Hastings was conspiring against him or, more speculatively, they offer the first signs that he had just heard the allegation that his nephew was illegitimate and hence was beginning to take precautionary measures.[42] Yet neither view can survive close scrutiny. For example, since Hastings' arrest and execution took place on the 13th, it would have made little sense to summon troops from the north on the 10th and the 11th to meet such an emergency. If immediate action had to be taken, the help sought was clearly too far away to arrive in time. In fact, York received Gloucester's appeal only on the 15th, and even though he instructed its forces to reach Pontefract by the 18th, on the 21st they still had not left the city: all in all, not a very convincing timetable for a pressing crisis.[43]

Similarly, no contemporary evidence supports the view that these letters resulted from the discovery that Edward IV's children were illegitimate. Most forcefully advanced by Sir Clements Markham, this hypothesis would have Richard hearing the story from the bishop of Bath and Wells on June 8; discussing its import with the council on the 9th; and then writing for help on the 10th and 11th.[44] As many others have pointed out, however, Markham's evidence is both unreliable and late.[45] Moreover, if his reconstruction were accurate, it would be hard to understand why Mancini, our one genuinely contemporary observer, should have so blithely assumed that in the days following these letters the council was happily completing arrangements for the impending coronation.[46] Most telling of all, though proof should be deferred until discussion of the deposition itself, there is every reason to believe that the so-called revelations of Bishop Stillington came to light only long after Richard had ascended the throne.[47]

Since both of the traditional interpretations are demonstrably weak, it seems much more likely that the protector's appeals resulted not from some sudden and unexpected emergency, but from his growing realization that something had to be done to quiet the opposition that everywhere threatened his survival. Furthermore, because the decision to crown Edward V came relatively late and went against Richard's better judgment, he had every reason to summon troops. With Edward crowned, his own security would in large measure depend on the willingness of parliament to continue his protectorship, but its willingness to do so must have appeared at best uncertain, especially since Elizabeth Woodville had refused to abandon sanctuary. For it was not to be expected that this body would lightly or willingly take an action so opposed to the apparent wishes of the queen mother.

These conclusions are supported by the schedule that those coming from the north were told to follow. In planning his moves, Richard had to allow time for his letters to reach their intended recipients, and the process of gathering men would entail further delays. To assume, as Richard did on the 10th and 11th, that these troops could assemble at Pontefract by the 18th was perhaps overly optimistic, but plans for a rendezvous at that time and place make untenable their usual explanation, that on the 10th the protector was already contemplating the use of force to prevent his nephew's coronation. His existing strength was patently inadequate for such an action,[48] and this new northern army could never reach London by the 22nd. The opening of parliament three days later thus becomes the first known event in which he could have reasonably expected it to participate, for with Pontefract gained by the 18th, the 25th was a deadline it could easily meet. Like his father before him in 1460, Gloucester appears to have assumed that armed might would increase parliament's cooperativeness, especially on the matter of his continuing protectorship.

The week following Richard's appeals proved a decisive turning point. On the 13th, Hastings was accused of conspiracy and summarily executed; on the 16th, Elizabeth Woodville surrendered her son Richard of York to the protector's safekeeping; and on the 17th (or possibly late in the afternoon of the 16th), writs of *supersedeas* began to be issued, cancelling both parliament and the coronation.[49] Still, while this sequence of events is itself clear, causal relationships are less so, largely because the known facts are few and often undated. Perhaps the best approach is to look at developments as Hastings would have viewed them.

From the beginning, the lord chamberlain had been a man very much caught in the middle. Hostile to the Woodvilles and fearful of their ambitions, nonetheless he had shown himself to be equally anxious about the meaning of Northampton and Stony Stratford. On the other hand, nothing in May should have disturbed him. He had kept his offices; the protector appeared to be taking all the appropriate steps to insure Edward V's peaceful accession; and even in those instances where Richard had overreached himself, the council had brought him to heel. Hastings would have continued to be wary, doubtless, but the decision to proceed with the coronation would have allayed the worst of his immediate suspicions.

If so, the moment was brief, for doubts intensified in the aftermath of Elizabeth Woodville's refusal to abandon sanctuary even in exchange for the formal investiture of her son. Because everything suggests that Richard's appeals for troops were secret,[50] there is no proof that Hastings learned of them at the time. Yet if he had, the uncertain purposes to which these forces might be put would have been more than enough to lead to counterplotting. Moreover, since the obduracy of the queen mother left the government with only two choices, either to continue with the coronation or to have it cancelled, it is important to understand the likely consequences of the way in which Richard pursued these alternatives.

Since it would have been extraordinarily awkward to have crowned Edward V without his immediate family present—and especially Richard of York, his brother and presumptive heir—the obvious solution to a person of the protector's experience was to use force, if necessary, to insure attendance. And Mancini reports that this was, in fact, an option that Gloucester explored:

> [A]s the day [of the coronation] drew near, he submitted to the council how improper it seemed that the king should be crowned in the absence of his brother, who on account of his nearness of kin and his station ought to play an important part in the ceremony. Wherefore, he said that, since this boy was held by his mother against his will in sanctuary, he should be liberated, because the sanctuary had been founded by their ancestors as a place of refuge, not of detention, and this boy wanted to be with his brother. Therefore with the consent of the council he surrounded the sanctuary with troops.[51]

Mancini supplies no date for this incident, but insofar as his account proceeds without interruption from the arguments presented in council to the actual investment of Westminster, an event that took place on the 16th, the implication would appear to be that Richard had pursued this approach only after the fall of Hastings.

On the other hand, even though the council may well have given its final approval subsequent to the 13th, the inherent logic of the situation suggests that Richard must have first broached the subject at a much earlier date. Elizabeth Woodville enjoyed a position of strength so long as she remained in Westminster: Precisely because her defiance impeded the coronation of her son, it also undermined Richard. As long as Edward remained uncrowned, those who doubted the protector's good intentions could only continue to doubt—and to block his every move. It was his realization of this reality, one suspects, that lay behind his decision to agree to a ceremony that, under different circumstances a month earlier, he had risked his life to prevent. Unfortunately, however, this new policy failed to persuade the queen that she should abandon an opposition that had, thus far, served her so well. In turn, because Richard had just accepted the idea of his nephew's coronation, it would have been exceedingly risky for him to abandon the plan immediately, as a way of responding to the intransigence of his sister-in-law. It seems likely, therefore, that from the moment Elizabeth's attitude became clear, he would have quickly attempted to assure the doubtful that the coronation would proceed.

At the same time, though, in no way would such reassurances have changed the basic problem, that the residence of Edward's immediate family in Westminster prevented their participation in the solemnities. This was an issue that had to be addressed, and Richard appears to have done so in two ways. First, there was the threat of force so stressed by Mancini, and there is no good reason to believe that Gloucester did not employ it from the start. Second, there was the course of action suggested by the background of the writs of *supersedeas* that began to be issued only after Richard of York had been compelled to leave sanctuary and to join his brother in the Tower from which neither would emerge alive.

Although these writs were dispatched only on June 17, everything suggests that a provisional decision to issue them must have taken place sooner, before the confrontation at Westminster. Most important, because their clear intent was to cancel not just parliament, but the coronation as well, it is difficult to believe that their issuance would have occurred to anyone as late as the 17th unless the idea had already arisen earlier. By that point it was much too late to inform people in distant parts of the realm that they no longer needed to come to an event planned for the 22nd, and that many members of parliament did in fact arrive for its expected opening three days later shows just how late the writs were sent. The *supersedeas* appears to have varied in form to meet these difficulties,[52] and yet, given shortness of time, the whole approach makes sense only if it had been considered and tentatively approved at a significantly earlier date.

James Gairdner, author of the classic Victorian study of Richard's reign, knew of the *supersedeas* only from mention of it in the York House Books. Because they speak just of the cancellation of parliament, not of the coronation, he concluded that the writs must have been a device of Gloucester's all-too-numerous enemies, men who hoped that parliament's failure to meet would "prevent Richard being confirmed in the office of the protector and so . . . terminate his power."[53] Still, since evidence unknown to Gairdner demonstrates that both events were being cancelled, his interpretation becomes highly unlikely. After all, to bring the protectorship issue to a decisive end, it would have been preferable to call off the meeting of parliament while still proceeding with Edward's formal investiture as king. It follows, then, that the writs did not originate with Richard's opposition.

On the other hand, it seems equally improbable that the idea began with Richard alone, as a conscious step on the road to usurpation. If, as appears likely, the potential desirability of these writs arose some days before June 17, it also arose before the fate of Richard of York had been determined. Thus, with him still in sanctuary, the protector would have had no guarantee that the putting aside of Edward V would redound to his own benefit. In this regard, a second letter of Simon Stallworth dated June 21 may shed new light on the circumstances under which the writs were authorized.[54]

Stallworth was a prebendary of Lincoln Cathedral, so the chancellor's man, whereas his correspondent Sir William Stonor seems to have been no friend of the protector insofar as he was later to be attainted as a participant in Buckingham's rebellion.[55] On June 9, Stallworth had written Stonor that the coronation would take place "this day fortnight as we say," adding, "[w]hen I trust ye will be at London, and then shall ye know all the world."[56] Twelve days later, however, he made no mention of the coronation, and he assumed that Sir William was no longer coming to the capital. Moreover, this second letter reports that he, Stallworth, had been desperately sick for some days and even then could scarcely hold his pen to write.

Given these facts and the apparent political sympathies of the correspondents, two conclusions seem to follow: first, that Stallworth knew that a decision had been authorized to postpone or cancel the coronation and parliament; and, second, that he saw nothing exceptional or threatening in that authorization. On the contrary, if he had any concerns (and he did), they were much more immediate and specific: the execution of Hastings on the 13th; the seizure of the duke of York on the 16th; and the rumored arrival of "twenty thousand of my lord protector and my lord of Buckingham['s] men in London this week." Strikingly, the letter makes no connection between these unexpected developments and its knowledge of the postponements. It follows, then, that Stallworth believed that there was none to be made. Further, since his illness makes it likely that he knew not of the actual *supersedeas* but only of its earlier authorization, his lack of concern strongly implies that he viewed the decision to postpone as an innocent one, not a devious scheme of Richard of Gloucester. For him, the protector's evil intentions were made manifest only in the events to which he referred.

If the *supersedeas* owed its origins to something other than the plots and counterplots of Richard and his doubters, of necessity the council itself must have sanctioned it. Nor would its motivation be difficult to fathom. Although the date of the coronation had been set by June 5, the queen's implacable hostility continued, and it must soon have proved an acute embarrassment to everyone involved in the creation of policy. The protector had promised that Edward would be crowned, but to insure the participation of Richard of York he was ultimately to threaten the use of force, and he may have done so early in the proceedings. If so, the prospect of sanctuary so brutally violated would surely have horrified the council, especially its clerical members, and that in itself would have stimulated the search for other alternatives. In theory at least, the easiest solution was to try yet again to convince Elizabeth Woodville of the error of her ways, but how to do it?

Here contingent authorization for the issuance of writs of *supersedeas* begins to make sense, for the council could well have hoped that the vision of Edward's cancelled coronation would be enough to persuade the queen that she should at last yield. Her long-term ambitions, indeed her security, depended on a crowned Edward V, so it was not unreasonable to suppose that she might surrender the duke of York when, and only when, she came to see that the formal installation of one son would never take place without the presence of the other. Moreover, if this strategy succeeded, it would obviate the need to violate sanctuary. In short, the idea of cancellation began in the council as a contingency plan, little more than a negotiating ploy, and if, by the 17th, it had become a good deal more than that, nothing suggests that a bedridden Stallworth had learned of it.

Before June 13 or shortly thereafter, even all this maneuvering provides little support for the view that Gloucester had already firmly decided to depose his nephew. As Richard's supporters have again and again emphasized, his career previous to Edward IV's death suggests a man of no small family loyalty and of some military abilities.[57] On the other hand, despite the tactical skill he displayed in gaining custody over Edward V at Stony Stratford, nothing in the record of the next month and a half suggests a man of much political finesse or sagacity. Far from dominating the situation, Richard appears much more frequently to have been trapped by it, uncertain what his next move should be. In a sense, even his willingness to explore a variety of possibilities—coronation versus no coronation, negotiations versus violation of sanctuary—displays this same blundering quality, for each option appears to have been grasped on the spur of the moment, with inadequate regard for its effectiveness or likely political consequences. These were the actions more of a foolish man than a calculating one, and when taken together, they were to lead to Hastings' conspiracy.

Given the paucity of the evidence, no one will ever know for certain just what caused Hastings to turn against the protector, but that he had adequate grounds from which to choose is indisputable. If he had learned of Richard's appeals for troops, that knowledge would have been sufficient. Similarly, if Richard had already begun to urge violation of sanctuary and supported even the contingent cancellation of the coronation, either or both of those positions could easily be taken as signs of the protector's likely perfidy, especially by one whose own earlier concerns after Stony Stratford had led to the precautionary meeting of uncertain outcome at St. Paul's.

What is certain, though, is that the conspiracy was real and not just a *coup de main* on Richard's part against those whom he assumed might oppose his seizure of the crown. The speed with which the protector moved to end the plot, once discovered, not to mention the savage punishment immediately visited upon Hastings himself, suggest a genuinely frightened man since, if there had been nothing to fear, it would have been clearly safer to wait until the arrival of new troops, already summoned and imminently expected, had placed him in a stronger position. As it was, Richard appears to have concluded that his only hope lay in swift and decisive action combined with wide dissemination of the fact that northern forces would soon be available to quell all further opposition.[58] This was, one senses, yet another of Gloucester's desperate gambles, but it had to be taken—and it worked.

To understand the circumstances that would have created such desperation, one needs first to understand the nature of the conspiracy he faced. As Stallworth reported the facts as he knew them on June 21:

> As on Friday last was the lord chamberlain headed soon upon noon. . . . The lord archbishop of York, the bishop of Ely are yet in the Tower with Master Oliver King. . . . As for Foster he is in hold and men fear for his life. Mistress Shore is in prison; what shall happen here I know not.[59]

With the exception of Foster, those mentioned are familiar figures: Hastings himself; Thomas Rotherham, archbishop of York and a man whose close ties to the queen were commonly known; John Morton, bishop of Ely and Henry VII's future cardinal archbishop of Canterbury; King, a former secretary of Edward IV; and, finally, Elizabeth ("Jane") Shore, a former mistress of the late king.[60] Moreover, Foster poses no real difficulties either. He was John Forster, a lawyer and co-steward with Hastings of the Abbey of St. Albans, the records of which report that he was committed to the Tower immediately after the lord chamberlain's execution.[61]

It is easy to agree with the judgment of the Croyland Chronicle that in removing Hastings, Rotherham, and Morton, Richard was striking out at "the three strongest supporters of the new king."[62] Similarly, it is not difficult to explain Forster and King as men on the periphery of this inner circle. But what of Jane Shore? How did she come to be involved in high politics? The traditional view is best conveyed in Thomas More's familiar story of how Richard, after requesting his mess of strawberries, had returned to the council chamber in the Tower filled with accusations:

> Then said the protector: "Ye shall all see in what wise that sorceress [i.e., the queen] and that other witch of her counsel, Shore's wife, with their affinity, have by their sorcery and witchcraft wasted my body." And therewith he plucked up his doublet sleeve to his elbow

upon his left arm, where he showed a werish [i.e., shrivelled], withered arm and small (as it was never other). And thereupon every
man's mind sore misgave them, well perceiving that this matter was
but a quarrel, for well they wist that the queen was too wise to go
about such folly. And also, if she would, yet would she, of all folk,
least make Shore's wife of counsel, whom of all women she most
hated, as that concubine whom the king, her husband, had most
loved. And also no man was there present but well knew that his arm
was ever such since his birth.

Nevertheless the lord chamberlain (which fro the death of King
Edward kept Shore's wife, on whom he somewhat doted in the king's
life, saving, as it is said, he that while forbare her of reverence toward
his king, or else of a certain kind of fidelity to his friend) answered
and said: "Certainly, my lord, if they have so heinously done, they be
worthy of heinous punishment."[63]

In sum, More alleges that Jane Shore had become Hastings' mistress,
that Richard accused her of complicity in witchcraft with Elizabeth
Woodville, but that this charge is not really credible, both because the
protector's arm had always been withered and because the queen understandably hated this rival for the late king's affections. This is not, to
put it mildly, a terribly convincing story, and readers are easily to be
forgiven if they find their own doubts exceeding those of More.

There is, however, another explanation. Four months after these
events, on October 23, Richard issued a proclamation from Leicester
offering a reward to anyone capturing persons associated with the rebellion of Buckingham and the bishops of Ely and Salisbury. Among
the rebels specifically named is Thomas, marquis of Dorset, described
as "holding the unshameful and mischievous woman called Shore's
wife, in adultery."[64] Since Jane was in custody after June 13 and
primarily the king's mistress before April 9, this charge, if true, would
have applied principally to the period preceding the lord chamberlain's
conspiracy. It appears, then, that in Richard's mind Jane Shore, far
from being Hastings' mistress, was Dorset's—though it is possible, of
course, that her favors had been shared by both.

If this was the case (and one would be hard put to see why else
Richard should have mentioned the matter in October), certain aspects
of Mancini's account take on added significance. In dealing with the
events of June 13, he tells first of Richard's actions in the Tower,
moving on to a discussion of how Londoners' initial acceptance of the

protector's explanations turned rapidly to disbelief. Then, without break, he adds:

> At this same time the duke learned from his spies that the marquess had left sanctuary, and, supposing that he was hiding in the adjacent neighborhood, he surrounded with troops and dogs the already grown crops and the cultivated and woody places, and sought for him, after the manner of huntsmen, by a very close encirclement: but he was never found.[65]

Mancini does not suggest that he saw any relationship between the activities of Hastings and Dorset, but if Jane Shore was arrested for her connections with the one while in fact (or at least in Richard's mind) she was the mistress of the other, one can legitimately ask whether she may not have been a link between the lord chamberlain's plot and the marquis' decision to leave his place of hiding, wherever it may have been.[66] It is difficult to conceive of an intermediary better suited to this purpose—or less likely to arouse suspicion—than Mistress Shore. Unimportant herself, seemingly little more than the strumpet whose services Hastings had acquired after the death of his master, she was the one person involved in the conspiracy whose comings and goings would not have been the subject of undue scrutiny. And, surely, it makes much better sense psychologically for her to have been the connection between Hastings and Dorset rather than Hastings and the queen.[67]

The obvious objection to this interpretation is that most historians have viewed these two as deadly rivals. Nevertheless, politics *do* make strange bedfellows, and it is in no way improbable that the crisis precipitated by Gloucester's seizure of Edward V had brought them together. Though for contrary reasons, each desired the boy's coronation, and to achieve that end, they may well have agreed to bury their mutual antagonisms for the moment, and this as early as the short period between Stony Stratford and Richard's arrival in London. Given circumstances as these two would have seen them, apparent necessity would quickly have suggested an alliance, and if not at that point, then surely later, when both council and protector seemed on the brink of making decisions potentially prejudicial to that coronation. The enemy of my enemy is my friend, as the Arabs say, and so it was with Hastings and Dorset. Resolution of their larger differences would simply have to wait.[68]

From Richard's point of view, though, the discovery of Hastings' conspiracy—and of what he took to be its magnitude—must have been as earth-shattering as his own moves had been for Hastings. From the beginning his authority had been tenuous: Sir Edward Woodville and Dorset had escaped his grasp; the queen defied him from sanctuary; and his support from the council was at best hesitant and wavering. Now, just as his appeal for troops and apparent agreement on contingent plans for handling the queen seemed to offer the prospect of greater security, he found instead that the fragmented forces of opposition were combining against him.

The precise moment when Gloucester decided to usurp will never be known, but if he had not made that choice earlier, he did so now, only nine days before his nephew's coronation. Although the conspiracy had been nipped in the bud, Dorset had again evaded capture, and the whole nature of the plot raised the specter of continuing crisis and conflict unless and until he could effectively eliminate the one common bond among his enemies, loyalty to Edward V. As a result, he proceeded to make the contingent real, his first move being against those in sanctuary. On June 16, he invested Westminster with what Stallworth termed "great plenty of harnessed men,"[69] and when they were in place, negotiations began. Faced with this show of force, Elizabeth Woodville finally gave up the last of her sons, "trusting in the word of the cardinal of Canterbury" who "had persuaded the queen to do this, seeking as much to prevent a violation of the sanctuary as to mitigate by his good services the fierce resolve of the duke."[70]

Then, even as Richard of York departed for the Tower, Richard of Gloucester turned to what a man of his military outlook would have regarded as little more than the mopping up. By the 17th, the long-deferred writs of *supersedeas* were being prepared and dispatched. But not content with that, the protector (as he still was) returned to a problem that, on May 10, the council had refused to address. For the messenger who brought the *supersedeas* to York found himself conveying other letters too, orders for the execution of Rivers, Grey, Haute, and Vaughan, the leaders of those surprised at Stony Stratford.[71] Their journey from Ludlow had started it all, and with their death warrants, Richard would end it. The nephew would be deposed; the uncle would be king.

9

Richard III

Deposition is a risky business at best, but for Richard of Gloucester it was uniquely so. As Hastings' conspiracy had shown, fears about his intentions were already causing widespread opposition, and the situation as it existed on June 16 should have given him further cause for worry. Although he now controlled both of his nephews, the most powerful men in England had long been summoned to London, and he had little reason to suppose that, once there, they would support his cancellation of Edward's coronation and of the following parliament. The only grounds for hope lay in his knowledge that Buckingham and others of the old nobility continued to support him and that the appearance of northern troops would give him military superiority. Yet even so, he could not know just when this help would arrive, and in what numbers.

Most troubling of all, the actual deposition would raise difficulties of great magnitude. It was one thing for Isabella and Mortimer to overthrow Edward II—or Bolingbroke, Richard II, or even Edward IV, Henry VI—since in those instances the king himself could be viewed as personally responsible for a regime against which charges of unacceptable irregularity could plausibly be brought.[1] It was quite another matter for the duke of Gloucester so to depose his nephew. Edward V was a mere youth, not yet into his teens, and his age, not to mention the brevity of his reign, made it impossible to argue that he bore direct responsibility for acts demonstrating unfitness for office. Hence Richard's dilemma; if no politically viable grounds could be invented or appropriate procedures developed, the deposition was apt to be judged an outright usurpation. This was a danger to be avoided at all costs.

The principal features of Richard's solution become clear in a letter dispatched to Calais on June 28, two days after protector had been formally transformed into king. Its main purpose was to inform Lord Mountjoy, the governor, that his oath and that of his soldiers to Edward V were no longer valid:

> [S]uch oath of ligeance was made soon upon the death of the said King Edward IV to his son, not only at Calais but also in diverse places in England, by many great estates and personages being then ignorant of the very sure and true title which our sovereign lord that now is, King Richard III, hath and had the same time to the crown of England. That oath notwithstanding, now every good true Englishman is bound, upon knowledge had of the said very true title, to depart from the first oath so ignorantly given to whom it appertained not, and thereupon to make his oath anew, and owe his service and fidelity to him that good law, reason, and the concord assent of the lords and commons of the realm have ordained to reign upon the people, which is our said sovereign lord King Richard III brother to the said King Edward IV, late deceased, whom God pardon: whose sure and true title is evidently showed and declared in a bill of petition which the lords spiritual and temporal and the commons of this land solemnly presented unto the king's highness at London the 26th day of June. Whereupon the king's said highness, notably assisted by well near all the lords spiritual and temporal of this realm, went the same day unto his palace of Westminster, and there in such royal honorable [robes] appareled within the great hall there took possession, and declared his mind that the same day he would begin to reign upon his people, and from thence rode solemnly to the cathedral church of London, and was received there with procession, with great congratulations, and acclamation of all the people in every place, and by the way that the king was in, that day. The copy of the which bill the king will[s] to be sent unto Calais, and there to be read and understood together with these present.[2]

The most arresting feature of this document is the wondrously evasive way in which it conveys Richard's all-embracing claims. For reasons not stated, Edward V has never, *de jure,* been king. On the contrary, from the moment of Edward IV's death Richard III has had a "very sure and true title," although one not openly enjoyed until June 26, when he agreed "to reign upon his people." Then, to this basic claim, clearly one of inheritance, is added "good law, reason, and the concord assent of the lords and commons of the realm," a vague, sweeping phrase that is apparently designed to suggest some kind of election combined with a simple recognition of Richard's rights independent of, and prior to, this concord assent. Moreover, Mountjoy is delicately given to understand that this recognition or election had an especially solemn character insofar as it had been embodied in a bill of petition presented by all three estates. Lastly, even though the hereditary basis for the new king's title remains wholly unexplained, that it is "very sure and true" was confirmed by the presence of "well near all the lords spiritual and temporal"; by the "great congratulations and acclamation of all the people"; and by the simple fact that Richard, suitably dressed, had properly observed all the ceremonial functions and visitations incumbent upon a new ruler. Since he was dressing and acting like a king, it followed that he was to be accepted as one.

If this letter contains an impressive amount of nonsense, that is scarcely surprising. Because the decision to usurp had come only with the discovery of Hastings' conspiracy, the imminence of Edward V's expected coronation meant that Richard was faced by a multitude of immediate problems, all of which had to be addressed successfully in order to smooth the way for his own accession. The result was a period of frenetic activity that gave few opportunities for thought, and that, in turn, helps to explain why, even as late as June 28, the protector's specific justifications for claiming the crown remained as unclear in London as they were unknown in Calais.

On the 16th, once both nephews were safely in the Tower, Gloucester's most urgent task was to cancel the coronation and parliament, but he had to do so in such a way as not to provoke riot and rebellion. Throughout, caution appears to have been his watchword, but nowhere more clearly than in the case of the writs of *supersedeas* through which the cancellations were legally achieved. *The* problem was that time was short, and people were coming from great distances for these twin events. Those realities suggested that a variegated strategy had to be pursued. In London itself, the mayor and aldermen were told merely that the coronation had been postponed, not cancelled, and that the ceremony would now take place on November 9.[3] Such an assurance was unlikely to eliminate all doubt, of course, but the government could hope that it would reduce the temptation to resist at least until the time when fresh troops from the north had arrived, thus making resistance futile.

For those outside the capital, however, differences in travel time made other approaches necessary. On June 16–17, it would have appeared that those relatively nearby would not yet have left for the coronation, so towns like Romney were sent writs cancelling both the coronation and parliament.[4] Nevertheless, as distances from London increased, it became more and more likely that those intending to arrive in time for Edward's crowning on the 22nd would have already departed before their writs could reach them. As a result, the *supersedeas* sent to places like York took a different form, one in which only the meeting of parliament was countermanded.[5] In short, Richard's aim was to keep London calm while at the same time trying insofar as possible to reduce the number of those whose arrival would increase the inevitable hazards of his plans.

In the case of those whose coming could not be prevented, Richard was forced to devise a different strategy equally on the spur of the moment. Using the need to preserve order as his pretext, he persuaded newcomers to dismiss the bulk of their armed retainers as they arrived, thereby depriving them of their power to resist whenever they found out what was actually afoot.[6] The resulting confusion must have been enormous, for some had been told that the coronation had been postponed; others, that it had been cancelled; and still others, that both the coronation and the following parliament were no longer to take place. From Richard's point of view, though, these contradictions had their advantages since, with so many stories in circulation, it became difficult to form an opposition united by certain knowledge of his intentions. Indeed, he himself contributed to the general confusion when, at roughly this point, he abandoned the clothes of mourning and, to what end no man knew for sure, began to appear in public surrounded by attendants and dressed in suspiciously royal purple.[7]

All doubt came to an end on the 22nd, the day on which, only three weeks earlier, it had been agreed that Edward V's coronation would occur. To the crowds assembling just to see what would happen, everything was suddenly revealed when,

> at Paul's Cross, in the presence of the . . . lord protector and the duke of Buckingham, with a huge audience of lords spiritual and temporal,

it was declared by Dr. Ralph Shaw brother to [the] mayor and proved by such reasons as he made there and then, that the children of King Edward [IV] were not rightful inheritors of the crown, and that King Edward was not the legitimate son of the duke of York as the lord protector was.[8]

Startling though Shaw's story may seem, its revelations were hardly new. As far back as 1469 the earl of Warwick had had it bruited about that Edward IV was nothing more than the unfortunate product of an adulterous liaison of his mother Cecily of York, and, writing in 1483, Mancini added a further detail, that Cecily herself had admitted to this indiscretion as early as 1464.[9] Her husband's death in 1460 having denied her the possibility of queenship, twenty-three years later she found herself for the second time becoming a quean instead, and all so that her last surviving son could become king by displacing her grandson.

The objections to this story must have made themselves immediately apparent, not least among them the likely reactions of the dowager duchess of York at whose town house the protector had stayed during much of May and June. It seems indeed doubtful that Cecily would have accepted this charge with maternal equanimity, and it may well be that her resulting anger explains why the duke of Gloucester should have suddenly decided to give up his residence at Baynard's Castle. That he could come up with no better excuse for displacing his nephew speaks volumes both about the pressures under which he was operating and about the lack of immagination and foresight he brought to the task. Surely he should have known better, for, as Polydore Vergil reported his mother's reaction to a later generation, she, "being falsely accused of adultery, complained afterward in sundry places to right many noble men, whereof some yet live, of that great injury which her son Richard had done her."[10] If that is how she felt in later years, it is hard to believe that she would have responded any differently in 1483.

Even more troubling, perhaps—at least when Richard found time to think about it—must have been his growing realization of the extent to which an illegitimate Edward IV was apt to create more problems than he could solve. The House of York had always based its claims on legitimate hereditary succession, and in the person of its first king it had encouraged parliament to finds its Lancastrian predecessors and rivals to have been no more than *de facto* rulers of England.[11] Suddenly to proclaim that Edward had had even less right to the crown than the saintly madman he had defeated and deposed was dangerously to threaten the foundations of the whole dynasty.

Then, too, anyone in Richard's position would have had to face the practical difficulty that if Warwick had failed to carry the day in 1469 with these adultery charges—or, rather, had failed to carry it for very long—it was unlikely that they would prove any more persuasive fourteen years later. If not, and if no better case could be developed, any attempt to depose Edward V would inevitably be seen as illegal. In other words, since the challenge to Edward IV's legitimacy would receive a skeptical hearing at best, and since even acceptance of his bastardy would in no way bring into question the paternity of his son, Shaw's approach to the problem was unlikely to prove effective as a means of gaining long-term acceptance for Richard's lawful kingship.

These considerations doubtless explain why the government should have decided to change its story almost immediately. Just two days later, on June 24,

> the duke of Buckingham came unto the Guildhall, where in readiness for his coming the mayor with his brethren and a fair multitude of citizens were assembled in their liveries. To this assembly the said duke then made an oration, rehearsing the great excellency of the lord protector and the manifold virtues which God had endowed him with, and the rightful title which he had to the crown.[12]

As for the still-vague rightness of that title, Buckingham then explained that it was only the children of Edward IV who were bastards, and this because their father "on marrying Elizabeth [Woodville] was legally contracted to another wife to whom the [earl] of Warwick had joined him . . . by proxy—as it is called—on the continent."[13] Therefore, since the progeny of bigamous unions lacked rights of succession, it followed that Richard of Gloucester was his brother's rightful heir.

Like Shaw's charges, Buckingham's were far from original. In 1463–64, Louis XI had tried to arrange a marriage between his sister-in-law Bona of Savoy and Edward IV. Moreover, although Warwick's part in the negotiations is not entirely clear, what is known is that Edward's hitherto secret marriage became public in September 1464 only because the king found himself forced to reveal it as a way of ending the earl's intense pressure for a French alliance.[14] It took but little imagination to enhance the incident with tales of a proxy marriage, and with Warwick dead and Louis dying,[15] this new story ran much less risk of being denied than did that of Cecily's adultery.

This fresh approach had immediate and obvious advantages. By questioning Edward IV's marital status, not his legitimacy, Richard could hope to divert attention from the shortcomings of his first argument while at the same time continuing to concentrate on alleged defects in his nephew's title that would be sufficient to assure the latter's deposition within a politically viable framework. In other words, to bring the boy's own birth into question was no more than to redefine the grounds on which uncle sought to displace nephew, but this new impediment seemed much less likely to provoke disbelief and, with it, outright opposition.

At the same time, though, it must be said that the events of June reveal less of Richard's strengths than of his weaknesses. On the positive side, he was at all times courageous, and in responding to immediate crises he often displayed a tactical ingenuity worthy of the ablest military commander. For example, he used limited resources with notable skill when crushing Hastings' conspiracy, and in his forced removal of Richard of York from sanctuary he showed himself to be equally direct, equally effective. Similarly, the supple way in which he varied his writs of *supersedeas* suggests a man who well understood the realities of time and space—and a man who knew how to change his means to gain his ends.

Nevertheless, the negative side comes through with even greater clarity. For all Richard's forcefulness, he was not, surely, a skilled politician, a man adept at rallying others to his cause. On the contrary, in the months following the death of Edward IV, he demonstrated both a lack of political foresight and a total inability to gain the confidence either of his sister-in-law, Hastings, Stanley, Rotherham, Morton, or of more than a handful of those other people of consequence whose unswerving allegiance he needed to rule. A brave man, given to risking his all on a single toss of the dice, he appears ever to have moved from one unexpected crisis to the next, each time attempting to extricate himself from his immediate difficulties with a bold and decisive stroke.

Yet what distinguishes these strokes in the end is not so much the bold impetuosity with which Richard sought to address unexpected developments. Rather, it is the concreteness and tangibility of the specific things to which he responded. These alone appear to have been the characteristics to which he was sensitive, and crises that embodied them appear to have been the only kind that he recognized and thought he knew how to solve. Moreover, if only definite and definable problems tended to catch his attention, usually (though not always) he tried to handle them through the use of brute force, typically applied both pure and simple. Strikingly, too, in this tendency he showed himself to be one of those people who see trees rather than forests, a person never quite able to grasp the fact that events are interconnected and that actions taken in response to one event are likely to have consequences in others, often those where they are least expected. In short, he was a person who viewed the world in an incoherently fragmented way, and because he acted to contain the forces opposing him individually, without regard for potential relationships, he was to find, in the course of his reign, that matters went steadily from bad to worse. One wonders, really, whether he ever knew why.[16]

As for more amorphous, that is, more purely political problems— what to do about Elizabeth Woodville in sanctuary, for example, or how to respond to, and convert, the council's opposition during his protectorate—Richard appears to have been at a complete loss, and nowhere do his failings appear more clearly than in the blundering path he pursued to his own coronation. Even he himself was quick to see that the story of Edward IV's illegitimacy was a travesty, but if he thought that the alleged bastardy of Edward's children would improve matters, he was badly mistaken. The reality was that, whether popular or not, Elizabeth Woodville had been accepted as queen for nearly twenty years, and as the king's presumed consort she had borne no less than two sons and five daughters who had not only survived him but also had long been recognized as his.

In the world of everyday affairs, the one populated by most of Richard's intended subjects, neither the supposed adultery of Cecily of York nor the impediment posed by claims of an earlier proxy marriage was apt to be viewed as much more than technical hairsplitting or, more likely, outright lies. If, as one of Edward II's justices had put it so long before, "the only proof of filiation is the presumptive proof,"[17] Edward V remained his father's son; and if, further, Richard was soon to argue that he should be accepted as king at least in part because he dressed and acted like one, he should have seen that the same kind of reasoning supported the lawfulness of the marriage into which Edward IV and Elizabeth Woodville thought they had entered. Not to have grasped such points was totally to misconstrue the whole nature of English political culture as it had evolved by the end of the fifteenth century.

Still, to give Richard his due, he was not unmindful of precedent or of the extent to which its dictates should govern his actions. On the other hand, the precedents he chose to follow were drawn largely from the reign of his brother, from the steps that Edward had taken when seizing the crown,[18] and in practice they were to prove as narrow as his political perceptions. Such slavish imitation may well have had its commendable qualities—Richard, always the family man—but his attempts to repeat history had their dangers as well. As Marx once put them: "Hegel remarks somewhere that all great, world-historical facts and personages occur, as it were, twice. He has forgotten to add: the first time as tragedy, the second as farce."[19] In Richard's case, however, the farce was not to be without its tragedy, that of little St. Kenelm all over again.

With Buckingham's speech in the Guildhall the die was cast. Whatever the shortcomings of his story, it would have to do since, patently, a third version would have been rather too much of a good thing. On the next day, then, June 25, the day once scheduled for the opening of parliament, a few noblemen, knights, and gentlemen plus the mayor and aldermen of London accompanied Buckingham to Baynard's Castle where, with all due humility, they petitioned Richard to assume the crown.[20] Further north at Pontefract, it was also the day on which Rivers and Grey, respectively the brother and son of Elizabeth Woodville, went to the block as "conspirators of Richard's death," the treason charge to which the council had refused its assent as recently as May 10.[21]

On Thursday, June 26, duke finally became king when, in the words of The Great Chronicle of London,

> the said lord protector took possession at Westminster, in the great hall, where he was set in the king's throne or place where all kings take first possession. . . .
> And he called before him the judges, commanding them straightly, justly and duly to administer his law without delay or favor. After he had thus commanded, and performed other ceremonies, he then proceeded into the Abbey. At the church door, he was met by a procession, and the abbot or his deputy delivered to him the scepter of St. Edward. He then proceeded into the Shrine and there made offering. He was next led into the choir and sat there whilst a *Te Deum* was beautifully sung by the monks. When these ceremonies were finished, he returned into the king's palace and was there lodged.[22]

Moreover, if Duke Richard of Gloucester had now become King Richard III, it soon followed in royal logic and records that his nephew had become nothing more than "Edward bastard, late called King Edward V."[23]

Once on the throne, however, the new king still found much to do: rewarding the faithful for their support; informing the ignorant of the happy news; and making preparations both for the delayed arrival of northern troops and for his own coronation, the date of which was set for July 6. On June 27, the Wardrobe placed orders for all the finery needed for the ceremony and its attendant festivities, while John Russell was reappointed in the chancellor's office and William Catesby found himself elevated to the chancellorship of the Exchequer.[24] A day later, the pace increased. John Howard became duke of Norfolk; Buckingham was made great chamberlain "for the term of his life"; a torrent of grants—money, titles, offices, and lands—began to pour forth to followers both great and small; and Lord Mountjoy at Calais was presumably just one of the many to whom letters were dispatched, telling of, and requiring oaths to, the new king.[25] It is uncertain just when fresh troops from the west and north actually reached London, but by early July, Richard was mustering thousands of them in Moor Field, all under the command of the earl of Northumberland.[26]

Richard's coronation was to prove a notable one, lavish and probably among the best attended in the entire Middle Ages.[27] Still, for all the success it seemed to portend, appearances were deceiving. At least they should have been. Since Edward IV's death in April, Richard had managed to execute an alarming number of those who opposed him and, no matter how justified their deaths may have been in his own mind, they were scarcely calculated to increase his personal popularity. Similarly, if some like Hastings and Rivers now slept in Abraham's bosom, others like Sir Edward Woodville and the marquis of Dorset had fled into exile, while still others like King and Forster (not to mention the little princes in the Tower) were "mewed up" in prison. Elizabeth Woodville, her daughters, and others of her family remained in sanctuary, and if it had been Ralph Shaw who had preached the sermon on bastard slips not taking deep root—that is, a mere friar instead of the bishop so characteristic of earlier depositions[28]—the fact of the matter was that there were precious few of the bishops on whom Richard could have relied: Rotherham of York had showed himself opposed from the very beginning; Woodville of Salisbury was in sanctuary: and Morton of Ely had been placed in Buckingham's protective custody for participating in Hastings' conspiracy.[29] Even Russell of Lincoln, Richard's own chancellor, had, in the delicate phrase of Simon Stallworth, his prebendary, "much business and more than he is content withal."[30] As for Bourchier of Canterbury, although he proved willing in the end to crown the new king, he refused to participate in the coronation banquet, sending Dudley of Durham instead.[31] If this was "concord assent," Richard was surely making the most of it.

Similar doubts apply to the acceptance seemingly implied by the nobility's willingness to attend Richard's coronation. After all, most of them had come to London expecting another's installation, but, once there, they found their options distinctly limited: Richard had had their retainers disarmed; his northerners now provided him with overwhelming military superiority; and the violence of his recent actions suggested a man whose invitations were not lightly to be refused. One cannot say, therefore, that many attended willingly. Rather, it seems much more the case that their appearance in the capital was initially designed to show support during the potentially difficult period of Edward V's minority, but that they had then stayed on and participated was, in truth, because they had no other choice. Such choices were something that only an unknown future would bring.

Whether Richard III fully appreciated these realities seems doubtful. What he knew concretely was of a wholly different order: that he had weathered every crisis and that, contrary to all reasonable expectation and in the presence of a reassuringly large audience of his lords temporal, he had received both unction and crown from the hands of the cardinal-archbishop of Canterbury. He must have known that not all doubts had been dispelled—his sister-in-law's nearby residence in sanctuary would have been enough to remind him of that—but insofar as silence gives consent and actions speak louder than words, he had every outward justification for believing that the worst of his difficulties were over.

Thus it was that, two weeks after the coronation, Richard began his first progress through his new realm, the level of his confidence betokened by the smallness of the armed retinue accompanying him as well as by the lack of guards he had left behind to watch over the sanctuary at Westminster.[32] There seemed no one of stature left to oppose him, no one with whom Elizabeth Woodville could continue to scheme, at least not to any avail. Reading was reached by July 23, and the next two days saw the royal party stopping at Oxford for intellectual refreshment. Then it was on to Gloucester via Woodstock and Minster

Lovell, at which point Buckingham took leave of the king in order to return to Wales, Brecon Castle, and his continuing supervision of John Morton, the bishop of Ely. By August 4, Richard was at Tewkesbury, visiting the site of Edward IV's greatest victory and, in the abbey, paying his respects at the tomb of his brother Clarence. Worcester came next, and it was at Warwick Castle, on August 8, that reports first reached the royal party that rebellions were likely, rebellions aimed at freeing Edward V.[33]

Later chroniclers' tales to the contrary notwithstanding, Richard appears not to have taken this danger seriously.[34] The progress was going well, and everything suggested that the king's new subjects were receiving him warmly. At Oxford, for example, Bishop Waynflete of Winchester, the founder of Magdalen College, had the visit recorded in its registers with the words, "Long live the king unto eternity,"[35] and in August the bishop of St. David's, Thomas Langton, found it possible to report that Richard "contents the people wherever he goes better than ever did any prince; for many a poor man that has suffered wrong many days had been relieved and helped by him and his commands in his progress."[36] Therefore the tour continued from Warwick Castle to Coventry, Leicester to Nottingham, and Doncaster to Pontefract. By the end of the month, Richard had returned to York, the city from which he had departed with so much anxiety in April, but a city to which his secretary John Kendall could now exclaim: "Thanked be Jesus, the king's grace is in good health, and in like wise the queen's grace, and in all their progress have been worshipfully received with pageants, and others; and his lords and judges sitting in every place, judging the complaints of poor folk with due punishment of offenders against his laws."[37]

York was to be the pinnacle of these wanderings, for it was there, on September 8, that Richard had the satisfaction of seeing his only legitimate son, Edward of Middleham, formally invested as Prince of Wales, a title that he had initially received on the third day of his father's reign, June 28.[38] And for the proper celebration of this event, no detail was overlooked, from banners of the Virgin, the Trinity, and Saints George, Edward, and Cuthbert, to coats of arms beaten with gold and thirteen thousand badges stamped with the king's personal white boar emblem.[39] It was perhaps unfortunate that the apparent contumacy of York's archbishop impelled those in charge to replace him with the more pliant bishop of Durham for the religious parts of the ceremony,[40] but if Richard himself ever grasped the extent to which this substitution offered further proof of the fundamental weakness of his position, he gave no sign. Quite to the contrary, that he still continued to live in a fool's paradise is suggested by the fact that, within two weeks of Edward's installation, he judged the political situation apparently settled and calm enough to begin issuing writs for a new parliament that was to open on November 6 at Westminster.[41] In his mind this was doubtless to be the occasion on which the three estates could at last declare the full legitimacy of his title with proper legal solemnity.

Like the parliament summoned for June 25, though, this one never met. Instead, Richard was forced to spend much of October and early November engaged in putting down rebellion and preparing to meet the threat of possible invasion.[42] It was here, then, that he finally began to pay the price for so consistently violating the norms of his age, norms that, despite their brutality, could in no way justify his conduct. The summary executions of opponents like Rivers and Hastings had been bad enough, but at least they were mature men, presumably ones who knew the risks of the game they were playing. Justification became more difficult, however, with violation of sanctuary and the imprisonment of bishops, and for the deposition of Edward V, a twelve-year-old boy whose very youth cloaked him in the mantle of innocence, there could be no justification whatsoever: Blindly and all unknowingly, Richard III was well on his way to creating the factual basis for Shakespeare's myth of the monster. Nevertheless, for the full realization of that myth, one last deed was needed, the murder of Edward IV's sons, the little princes in the Tower.[43] Before his reign was out, there were to be other incidents that would contribute substantially to the legend, notably the incestuous court paid to his niece, but above all else it was this massacre of the innocents that was to give him his enduring reputation for pure, unadulterated evil.[44]

There is, of course, an understandable dearth of hard evidence on the subject, but if its absence makes it impossible to say with certainty precisely how—or when—Edward V and his brother met their fate, the political and human consequences of the act are much more easy to date and to document. Deposed kings have never enjoyed a long life expectancy, heaven knows, though in the case of Edward II it is worth noting that the presumption of death came only eight months after his formal deposition, when revolts aimed at his restoration began to break out.[45] The experience of Henry VI is even more instructive since, after his fall and capture, madness appears to have protected him, at least as long as it was generally believed that his lack of competence would prevent any thought of returning him to the throne. Still, when Warwick the King-maker made him the symbolic figurehead for the readeption and revolt that drove Edward IV into exile in 1470–71, the situation changed: Henry was to die in the Tower on the very night of Edward's triumphant return to London, and even though the Yorkists claimed that his death had resulted from nothing more sinister than "pure displeasure and melancholy," modern analysis of his skull suggests a weightier cause.[46]

It seems unlikely that many people expected Edward V's death to follow immediately upon his deposition.[47] For most of his former subjects, regicide remained an unthinkable act, and it was therefore to be anticipated that, just as Henry VI's madness had long preserved his life, so, too, would Edward's youth preserve his. Advancing maturity was apt to increase the hazards of his existence, not to mention that of his brother, but for the moment, most people appear to have had only contingent fears for their safety. Rather, initial concerns focused much more sharply on the injustice of their imprisonment and on the ways in which it could be most speedily ended. During the festivities associated with Richard's northern progress, for example, the Croyland Chronicle reports merely that

> while these things were going on, the two sons of King Edward before-named remained in the Tower of London, in the custody of certain persons appointed for that purpose. In order to deliver them from this captivity, the people of the southern and western parts of the kingdom began to murmur greatly, and to form meetings and con-federacies. It soon became known that many things were going on in secret, and some in the face of all the world, for the purpose of promoting this object, especially on the part of those who, through fear, had availed themselves of the privileges of sanctuary and fran-chise. There was also a report that it had been recommended by those men who had taken refuge in the sanctuaries, that some of the king's daughters should leave Westminster, and go in disguise to the parts beyond the sea; in order that, if any fatal mishap should befall the male children of the late king in the Tower, the kingdom might still, in consequence of the safety of the daughters, some day fall again into the hands of the rightful heirs.[48]

It was reports of these developments, presumably, that reached Richard at Warwick Castle on August 8, and if his response was immediate, strikingly it appears to have had as its sole purpose the ending of relative freedom of action for those in sanctuary. Again in the words of the Croyland Chronicle, probably written by Richard's own chancellor:[49]

> On this being discovered, the noble church of the monks at Westminster, and all the neighboring parts, assumed the appearance of a castle and fortress, while men of the greatest austerity were appointed by King Richard to act as the keepers thereof. The captain and head of these was one John Nesfeld, Esquire, who set a watch upon all the inlets and outlets of the monastery so that not one of the persons there shut up could go forth, and no one could enter, without his permission.[50]

Nevertheless, if both sides started the summer with cautious objectives, every month brought increasing change, especially in the camp of Richard's potential opponents. As long as most of them believed that Edward V and Richard of York remained alive and well, that belief tended to fragment the opposition and to prevent it from developing a unified strategy. It was not to be expected, after all, that Henry Tudor, the exiled Lancastrian claimant, would willingly join forces with Elizabeth Woodville, a woman whose hopes rested on the restoration of her son and of the Yorkist claims he embodied. Such an alliance would become feasible only when Yorkists and Lancastrians alike began to agree that, in all probability, both Edward V and his brother had been permanently removed from the picture. That agreement came by the end of the summer.

Precisely when the princes were killed will never be known, at least not for a certainty. On the other hand, the surviving evidence *is* suggestive. To cite but three bits of it, just one warrant is known to exist that authorizes wages for Edward V's keepers, and it is dated July 18.[51] Second, if The Great Chronicle of London reports that "at sundry times" during the term of Sir Edmund Shaw as mayor, a term that ended only on October 28, "the children of King Edward were seen shooting and playing in the garden of the Tower,"[52] the vagueness of that time reference is given greater specificity by a third piece of evidence, Mancini's chronicle. For Mancini left England in July, at which point his knowledge ended, and his account adds a crucial detail, that "after Hastings was removed, . . . the king and his brother were withdrawn into the inner apartments of the Tower proper, and day by day began to be seen more rarely behind the bars and windows, till at length they ceased to appear altogether."[53] In short, the two boys departed the

scene in advance of Mancini, and even though their absence does not
prove their murder, the longer they remained lost from view, the more
likely it became that most sensible people would draw that conclusion.
By summer's end, moreover, it was surely one that had been drawn not
just by Elizabeth Woodville, Henry Tudor, and their supporters, but
also by many churchmen, large numbers of Edward IV's former household servants, and even by the earliest of Richard III's adherents, Henry
Stafford, the duke of Buckingham.

The result was a new and much more dangerous coalition, one that
involved much of the south, center, and west of England.[54] No longer
was the objective freedom for the princes; rather, as seen through the
Chancery eyes of the Croyland chronicler, it was to be vengeance and
the installation of a new and unexpected king:

> At last, . . . public proclamation was made that Henry, duke of
> Buckingham, who at this time was living at Brecon in Wales, had
> repented of his former conduct, and would be the chief mover in this
> attempt, while a rumor was spread that the sons of King Edward
> before-named had died a violent death, but it was uncertain how.
> Accordingly, all those who had set foot on this insurrection, seeing
> that if they could find no one to take the lead in their designs, the ruin
> of all would speedily ensue, turned their thoughts to Henry [Tudor],
> earl of Richmond, who had been for many years living in exile in
> Brittany. To him a message was accordingly sent by the duke of
> Buckingham, by the advice of the lord bishop of Ely, who was then
> his prisoner at Brecon, requesting him to hasten over to England as
> soon as he possibly could, for the purpose of marrying Elizabeth, the
> eldest daughter of the late king, and, at the same time, together with
> her, taking possession of the throne.[55]

These uprisings—and their extent—appear to have caught Richard
III wholly by surprise. After investing his son as Prince of Wales, he
had resumed his progress, so confident in the strength of his position
that he saw nothing to prevent his summoning of parliament for
November. Only at Lincoln on October 11 did he hear that Buckingham
was about to rebel, and while he took immediate steps to counter the
threat, something of his shock and anger comes through in the comment
added in his own hand to a letter he dispatched on the following day to
his chancellor, John Russell:

> Here, praised be God, all is well and truly determined and ready to
> resist the malice of him that had the best cause to be true, the duke of

Buckingham, the most untrue creature living; and with God's grace we shall not be long until we shall be in that region and subdue his malice.[56]

Little wonder, too, that ever after, in Richard's documents, Buckingham would be simply and curtly dismissed as "our great Rebel" or, at times, as "our great Rebel and traitor."[57]

Still, for all Richard's surprise, these uprisings confronted him with a challenge both immediate and concrete, and it was the concrete with which he knew how to deal. In this instance, though, a good deal of luck was involved too. The rebellion was not supposed to begin until October 18, but in Kent it broke out ten days early and at a time when John Howard, the new duke of Norfolk, was in the area, inspecting his equally new Mowbray estates in Surrey and Sussex. As a result, he was able to block the rebel advance on London and quickly to suppress the insurrection itself. In the west, severe storms led to flooding that prevented Buckingham from crossing the Severn, and when he himself fled into Shropshire, he was quickly apprehended and captured. His execution followed immediately thereafter, on November 2 at Salisbury. These same storms delayed and scattered the small invasion fleet of Henry Tudor, and if a few of his Breton mercenaries made it to land, there to be captured, Henry himself beat a hasty retreat back to France and exile. Only in the southeast did fighting long continue, but when Bodiam Castle fell to the assaults of Lord Cobham and the earl of Surrey, even there resistance ended. As the Croyland Chronicle sums things up:

> The disturbances last described were prolonged from the middle of October till nearly the end of November, at which time the king . . . returned to London, . . . having triumphed over his enemies without fighting a battle.[58]

Although this triumph put Richard firmly back in control, the uprisings had inevitably disrupted his parliamentary plans. Indeed, canceling writs of *supersedeas* went out on November 2,[59] the very day on which Buckingham had gone to the block. With order restored, however, the situation began to change, and the high value that Richard placed on meeting with parliament is nowhere better demonstrated than in the speed with which he moved to call one. On December 9, only fourteen days after his return to London, new writs were dispatched, this time summoning the estates to a parliament scheduled to open on January 23,

1484 at Westminster.[60] This one would actually meet, and Richard was not to be disappointed in his expectations of it.

In terms of composition and form, the parliament of 1484 proved little different from its immediate predecessors: twenty-one principal ministers; forty-four lords spiritual; thirty-eight lords temporal; ten men of law; four receivers each of English and Gascon petitions; and two hundred ninety-six members of the commons.[61] Some lords may have seemed conspicuous in their absence—the bishops of Exeter, Ely, and Salisbury, for example, or the marquis of Dorset and the earls of Oxford and Richmond—but such were the normal realities of fifteenth-century politics. After all, every one of these men, not to mention ninety-two other members of the laity, was about to be attainted for his activities in the fall or earlier, activities that had shown each to be an enemy of Richard III.[62] Still, impressive as that total may initially appear, it was not sufficient to prevent those present from acting, and having their actions accepted, as though their decisions had been "agreed and established . . . by our lord the king, by the said prelates, earls, and barons, and by the whole community of the realm assembled in this parliament."[63]

In the month of parliament's sitting (dissolution came on February 22), most of its business fell well within the range of medieval normality. Petitions resulted in eight acts; public bills, in fifteen statutes. Other acts then provided for such things as the attainders mentioned above and Richard's right "to make grants of the lands of the persons attainted."[64] When "An Act for the Contents of a Butt of Malmesey" complains that "a butt . . . at this day scantly holdeth in measure one hundred eight gallons," thirty-two less than under Henry VI,[65] traditionalists may wonder just how this discrepancy had come to the king's attention, but the explanation is easy. Whether in responding to merchant grievances or in promising to abolish benevolences and to reform the processes of justice, Richard was using every available means to increase his own popularity.[66]

Yet it was not enough just to curry favor. For lasting success, something more was needed, a recognition of his right to rule that would settle the matter not only in law, but in the world of practical politics as well. Unsurprisingly, this was an issue on which parliament itself had no doubts whatsoever since, as it explained in Richard's act of succession:

Albeit that the right, title, and estate, which our sovereign lord the king Richard III hath to and in the crown and royal dignity of this realm of England, with all things thereunto within the same realm, and without it, united, annexed, and appertaining, be just and lawful, as grounded upon the laws of God and nature, and also upon the ancient laws and laudable customs of this said realm, and so taken and reputed by all such persons as be learned in the abovesaid laws and customs. Yet, nevertheless, forasmuch as it is considered that the most part of the people of this land is not sufficiently learned in the abovesaid laws and customs, whereby the truth and right in this behalf of likelihood may be hid, and not clearly known to all the people, and thereupon put in doubt and question. And over this, how that the court of parliament is of such authority, and the people of this land of such nature and disposition, as experience teacheth, that manifestation and declaration of any truth or right, made by the three estates of this realm assembled in parliament, and by authority of the same, maketh, before all other things, most faith and certainty; and, quieting men's minds, removeth the occasion of all doubts and seditious language. Therefore, at the request, and by the assent of the three estates of this realm, that is to say, the lords spiritual and temporal, and commons of this land, assembled in this present parliament, by authority of the same, be it pronounced, decreed, and declared, that our said sovereign lord the king was, and is, very and undoubted king of this realm of England, with all things thereunto within the same realm, and without it, united, annexed, and appertaining, as well by right of consanguinity and inheritance, as by lawful election, consecration and coronation.[67]

Insofar as Richard III's consecration and coronation appear to have been genuinely error-free, they were doubtless "lawful" within the technical meaning of that term. On the other hand, the experience of the last sixth months had graphically showed that his claims of proper election and rightful inheritance had failed to quiet men's minds or to remove the occasion for doubts and seditious language. To these points, then, his act of succession turned. It admitted honestly that those who had elected him in June had not been "assembled in form of parliament," so to rectify that deficiency it declared that what they had done "in the name and on the behalf of the said three estates out of parliament," was "now by the same three estates assembled in this present parliament, and by authority of the same, [to] be ratified, enrolled, recorded, approved, and authorized.'' Not content with that, the act even went on to declare that everything done by the estates in June was to ''be of like effect, virtue, and force, as if all the same things had been so said . . . in a full parliament and by authority of the same accepted and approved.'' Through the magic of legal fiction, the motley assemblages of June (and especially the one addressed by Buckingham in the Guildhall) were thus retrospectively found to have acted ''as if'' possessed of parliament's full power. So much for lawful election, retroactively achieved.[68]

Rather more strikingly, when it came to Richard's rights of inheritance, the act's drafters proved that in England, if not in France, it wasn't only God who could make an heir.[69] No longer did Cecily of York find herself proclaimed an adulteress or Edward IV the unfortunate victim of proxy marriage. Rather, even though the act admits to a ''more certain knowledge'' of Richard III's own ''birth and filiation'' (consanguinity was vital, after all), its own story depends on a whole host of new allegations. For example, the so-called marriage of Edward IV to Elizabeth Woodville lacked validity because it ''was made of great presumption, without the knowing and assent of the lords of this land, and also by sorcery and witchcraft.'' Worse yet, it had been celebrated ''privily and secretly, without edition of banns, in a private chamber, a prophane place, and not openly in the face of the Church, after the law of God's Church, but contrary thereunto, and the laudable custom of the Church of England.'' But worst of all, ''at the time of the contract of the same pretensed marriage, and before and long time after, the said King Edward was and stood married and trothplight to one Dame Eleanor Butler, daughter of the old earl of Shrewsbury, with whom the same King Edward had made a precontract of matrimony.'' In turn, the truth of these premises meant that Edward and Elizabeth had ''lived together sinfully and damnably in adultery, against the law of God and of His Church,'' and that all of their children were bastards, ''unable to inherit or to claim anything by inheritance, by the law and custom of England.''[70]

These charges seem scarcely more credible than those advanced in June, and few appear to have taken them seriously at the time. Secrecy, sorcery, and the lack of lordly consent lacked the weight needed to gain acceptance for the invalidation of a marriage, and when it came to the alleged precontract of matrimony—what in modern terms would be most analogous to a solemn and formal engagement—even the best canon lawyers remained uncertain whether such a commitment had the effect of delegitimating any subsequent marriage or its issue.[71] Indeed, just to mention that fact is to raise the most troubling issue of all, that in this act Richard was asking parliament to render a judgment not only on a temporal matter but on a spiritual one, the validity of a sacrament. And the Croyland chronicler, himself a churchman, makes plain the extent to which contemporaries were entirely mindful of the disquieting implications of Richard's case and of the precedent that would be set if parliament were to judge it:

> At this sitting, parliament confirmed the title by which the king had, in the preceding summer, ascended the throne; and although that lay court found itself unable to give a definition of his rights when the question of the marriage was discussed, still, in consequence of the fears entertained of the most perservering, it presumed to do so, and did do so: while at the same time attainders were made of many lords and men of high rank, besides peers and commoners, as well as three bishops, that we do not read of the like being issued by the Triumvirate even of Octavianus, Antony, and Lepidus.[72]

In short, if parliament passed Richard III's act of succession, it did so reluctantly. As a lay court, it could only doubt the propriety of its actions, and the chronicle above was probably not far wrong in believing that its primary motivation was fear: fear of a man who had defeated and executed Hastings, Rivers, and Buckingham; who was moving even then to attaint the rest of his foes; and, most ominous of all, who had had the temerity to kill his nephews, thereby transgressing possibly the most deeply felt limit of his age. It was to be expected, therefore, that this act of succession would have little practical effect, and yet this proved far from the case.

A month before parliament assembled, Henry Tudor had met with his fellow exiles, notably Dorset, the leading male member of the Woodville faction, to consider what was best to be done following the disaster of his failed invasion. The result, at Christmas, was a series of solemn vows in Rennes Cathedral, ones in which the others pledged their loyalty to Henry as king and he, in turn, swore to marry Elizabeth of York once the crown was actually his.[73] It looked, then, as though the Woodville-Tudor alliance would long continue, biding its time until opportunity arose again. Nevertheless, after parliament accepted Richard's act of succession, the alliance proceeded to come unglued rapidly. The king's factual claims may have been entirely specious, and the members of parliament may have declared them legally true only with the greatest reluctance, but once the act was law, Elizabeth Woodville abandoned her bitter resistance and began to negotiate. If the dissolution of parliament came on February 22, by March 1 all was agreed: Those still in sanctuary would leave it; Dorset would be summoned home; and all would be honored, pensioned off, or, in the case of Edward IV's daughters, married to "gentlemen born," with suitable dowries.[74] Ever mindful of the fate of her sons, though, Elizabeth attempted to drive a hard bargain, forcing Richard in the presence of witnesses to put his signature to a humiliating personal oath in which he promised on the Holy Gospels that if those daughters would

> come unto me out of the sanctuary of Westminster and be guided, ruled, and demeaned after me, then I shall see that they shall be in surety of their lives and also not suffer any manner [of] hurt by any manner [of] person or persons to them or any of them in their bodies and persons to be done by way of ravishment or defouling contrary [to] their wills, nor them or any of them imprison within the Tower of London or other prison, but that I shall put them in honest places of good name and fame, and them honestly and courteously shall see to . . . have all things requisite and necessary . . . as my kinswomen . . . . And moreover I promise them that if any surmise or evil report be made to me of them or any of them by any person or persons that I then shall not give thereunto faith or credence nor therefore put them to any manner [of] punishment before that they or any of them so accused may be at their lawful defense and answer.[75]

Although Henry Tudor was able forcibly to prevent Dorset from acting on his mother's request that he return to England,[76] Dorset in Henry's hands had nothing like the value of Elizabeth of York and her sisters in Richard's. For the aspiring Tudor, it was vital to marry one of Edward's IV's daughters, preferably the eldest, since such a marriage offered the surest means of broadening his potential base of support by enhancing a dynastic claim that was, at best, shaky. Relatively indifferent to rules of strict inheritance England may well have been,[77] but under normal circumstances it was not to be expected that its political leaders would unstintingly support claims to the crown based on nothing more substantial than illegitimate descent through the female line from the fourth son of Edward III—and direct royal descent only from Catherine of France, Henry V's widow, whose subsequent marriage to Owen Tudor, his grandfather, had been rather more tacitly assumed than publicly acknowledged.[78] Thus his best hope lay in strengthening his Lancastrian rights through union with Yorkist ones, thereby bringing both lines together so that his son, if God chose so to bless him, would ascend the throne as the heir of both houses. It was this dream, then, that Elizabeth Woodville's submission appeared so irrevocably to shatter.

To explain this change in heart, it seems insufficient to argue that the austere conditions of sanctuary life had finally broken her resolve. After all, she had stubbornly endured these same conditions at similar length during the period of Edward IV's temporary exile in 1470–71.[79] Because, in fact, she had given birth to Edward V during that first sojourn in Westminster, her stay there could even be said to have given new meaning to the whole idea of confinement. Similarly, discouraging as the defeat of 1483's rebellions must have been for her, defeat alone cannot explain why she should now have decided to end her resistance. As Edward IV's triumphant return in 1471 had shown, conditions could change with startling rapidity; there were always grounds for optimism; and, even though hopes could no longer rest on the liberation of her sons, the fact remains that a victorious Henry Tudor would soon mean an eager son-in-law. That was not quite the same as a son, perhaps, and yet it was surely worth waiting for, at least a bit longer.

Given the timing of Elizabeth's decision and the insufficiency of alternative explanations, Richard III's act of succession emerges as the crucial element in her changed outlook. Doubtless the factors just cited also played a part in her thinking, but what seems most striking in the end is the simple fact that defiance turned into submission only after the three estates had "pronounced, decreed, and declared, that our said sovereign lord the king was, and is, very and undoubted king of this realm of England . . . as well by right of consanguinity and inheritance, as by lawful election, consecration and coronation." Far from undoubted though these claims may have remained in Elizabeth's mind, the very process of their declaration in parliament appears to have tipped the balance, thereby creating a new situation.

Historians have often assumed that the parliament of the later Middle Ages had little practical authority and that its chief purpose in the king-making process was merely to lend an air of specious legality to accessions that were, in truth, no more than the brutal results of conquest.[80] If so, though, the parliamentary legitimation of a usurper should have had no effect on the conduct of those opposed to him, whereas the present case shows just the opposite. Once parliament had declared Richard to be England's legal king, Elizabeth concluded that the game was lost, dubious though everyone knew his title to be. She would take what she could get, and in so doing, she demonstrated that she, too, believed that "the court of parliament is of such authority, and the people of this land of such nature and disposition, as experience teacheth, that manifestation and declaration of any truth or right, made by the three estates of this realm assembled in parliament, and by authority of the same, maketh before all other things, most faith and certainty." Small wonder, then, that Richard should have so doggedly sought a meeting of parliament, for even a man of his limited political perceptions had to recognize that in its approval lay his best hopes for long-term success.

More important, this approach underscored Richard's continuing faith in the practical effectiveness of parliamentary authority. He had earlier demonstrated the same faith, during the previous June when he had seen the approval of parliament as the one way to extend the life of his protectorate even after the coronation of Edward V, but his views probably arose less out of personal commitment than out of a more-or-less unconsidered adherence to Yorkist precedent.[81] As far back as 1459, for example, his future father-in-law the earl of Warwick had refused to surrender the captaincy of Calais in response to Henry VI's personal orders, arguing that "forasmuch as he was made [captain] by authority of parliament, he would not obey the privy seal."[82] In Warwick's mind, apparently, what one parliament had done, only another could undo. Similarly, when Richard of York sought the crown itself in 1460, Henry VI's judges and lawyers responded, when pressed, that they lacked the authority needed to determine which man was king, but that "since this matter . . . is above the law and passed their learning, . . . it pertained to the lords of the king's blood, and the peerage of this land, to . . . meddle in such matters." Strikingly, too, the lords of the October parliament had accepted this advice and, with specific appeals to the authority of parliament, they had then proceeded to make Richard Henry's heir, thereby disinheriting young Edward of Lancaster in the process.[83] Lastly, even though York's dreams came to an end in the battle of Wakefield, his son Edward IV was to make 1460's act of accord one of the legal principles undergirding the parliamentary declaration of his title.[84] Indeed, when Edward returned from exile in 1471, initially he disavowed all intention of deposing Henry VI again. Instead, he emphasized his proper status under the still-unrepealed accord by rather ostentatiously having his men wear the ostrich feathers of the Prince of Wales, a title that only this same act had given him, as heir to his father.[85] In other words, Richard III's high view of parliament had far more behind it than his own political instincts, and if he went well beyond Yorkist precedent in claiming that parliament had spiritual as well as temporal jurisdiction, he found for the moment, at least, that others were prepared to accept his claim.

Nevertheless, that moment proved brief, and for reasons that shed considerable light on the complex nature of English political culture at the end of the fifteenth century. As demonstrated by Elizabeth Woodville's initial response, Richard had legitimate grounds for believing that his act of succession would end opposition to his rule even to the point of calming a mother's vengeful fury over the murder of her sons. What no one could have anticipated, though. was that less than a month later, the Prince of Wales, Edward of Middleham, would take sick and, in early April, die.[86] At the immediate level of practicality, his death meant that Richard III no longer had an heir, and his means for remedying this defect were soon to be destroyed by the illness of Anne Neville, his queen, an illness so grave that "the king entirely shunned her bed, declaring that it was by the advice of his physicians that he did so."[87] In short, if there were ever to be further heirs, they would have to be born of a different mother.

Yet there was a deeper level at which the death of Edward of Middleham proved even more disastrous in its consequences. If, by 1484, many Englishmen had come to believe that parliament was a mystical body through which the Holy Spirit spoke inerrantly,[88] God's support as declared in Richard's act of succession now seemed voided by the loss of this son. For the tragedy of his passing was also a judgment of God. Just as He had finally intervened to punish Cynefrith for her role in the martyrdom of little St. Kenelm,[89] so, too, did He visit His wrath on Richard III for *his* massacre of the innocents. By thus taking away Richard's own nine-year-old son, God had no more than justly applied His own law of an eye for an eye or, as the Croyland chronicler put it, in this judgment "was fully seen how vain are the thoughts of a man who desires to establish his interests without the aid of God."[90]

By midsummer, the resulting moral bankruptcy of the regime was becoming ever more apparent, but nowhere more vividly than in the mocking couplet that was affixed to a door of St. Paul's on July 18:

> The Cat, the Rat, and Lovell our dog
> Rule all England under a hog.

Thus did Richard's principal advisers, William Catesby, Sir Richard Ratcliffe, and Francis, viscount Lovell, find themselves harshly lampooned, though not as harshly, perhaps, as the king they served, a man sardonically transformed into a brutish caricature of his own white boar emblem. William Collingbourne was the supposed author of the lines— at least he was accused of it—but if he soon paid with his life, far more serious from Richard's point of view were the court's additional findings, ones that found the poet guilty of having "plotted the death of the king by provoking war, disturbances and dissension within the realm of England," and also of having conspired to invite "the so-called earl of Richmond to arrive in the land of England at Poole in the county of Dorset."[91] The opposition was again forming, and this time it would be strengthened not just by its sense of God's support, but also—and more practically—by growing southern resentment of the northerners on whom Richard had freely bestowed the lands confiscated from the southern rebels of 1483.[92]

As early as June, the government had begun to prepare ships to counter possible attacks from Brittany, but although a truce with its duke soon ended that threat, in August Richard still found it necessary to warn mariners and port authorities that while they should allow a Breton truce ship free passage, this safe-conduct did not extend to any "persons therein . . . being our enemies or rebels."[93] By September, all mayors, sheriffs, and other officials were being warned of "certain persons in sundry places in the west parts of this our realm which be detected of certain things that they . . . do and attempt against their natural duty and ligeance."[94] And December was to see yet another flurry of activity. The inhabitants of Harwich were told "to resist rebels if they arrive there," while commissioners in Surrey, Middlesex, and Hertfordshire were reminded of the steps they should take "against the malice of our rebels and traitors if the case [should so] require."[95]

Such orders gave new meaning to Advent, surely, and even Christmas brought no relief:

> The feast of the Nativity was kept with due solemnity at the palace at
> Westminster, and the king appeared with his crown on the day of the

Epiphany. While he was keeping this festival with remarkable splendor in the great hall, just as at his first coronation, news was brought to him on that very day, from his spies beyond the sea, that, notwithstanding the potency and splendor of his royal state, his adversaries would, without question, invade the kingdom during the following summer, or make an attempt to invade it.[96]

Other men might have quailed at this news, but Richard III welcomed it. This was the kind of specific challenge with which he knew how to deal and, as the Croyland Chronicle continues, "he imagined that it would put an end to all his doubts and troubles."

Nevertheless, if 1485 was to be the year of decision, the crushing finality of that decision, and the ways in which it has resounded in literature ever since, cannot fully be grasped without reference to one last bit of Ricardian folly that began at these same Yuletide festivities. There was, for the moment, much gaiety and dancing—far too much, in fact, for the tastes of our chronicler—during the course of which both Queen Anne and Elizabeth of York appeared in gowns

> of similar color and shape, a thing that caused the people to murmur and the nobles and prelates greatly to wonder thereat; while it was said by many that the king was bent, either on the anticipated death of the queen taking place, or else, by means of divorce, . . . on contracting a marriage with the said Elizabeth. For it appeared that in no other way could his kingly power be established, or the hopes of his rival be put to an end.[97]

Only a mind as brilliantly limited as Richard III's could have devised such a scheme. On the one hand, he was shrewd enough to see that marriage to Elizabeth would deprive Henry Tudor of Yorkist dynastic claims, and if increasing numbers of rebels and traitors were coming to doubt the legitimacy with which he himself ruled, those same claims could also be used to strengthen his own. On the other hand—and here his true blindness shows through—he failed totally to grasp the difficulties inherent in a match not just with a niece, but with one that parliament had declared an illegitimate bastard only the year before. Rather, as a conventionally pious man, he knew his Leviticus, and his reading in that source of all sources for incest taboos appears to have convinced him that while aunts were prohibited from marrying nephews, there was nothing to prevent the union of uncles and nieces, a subject not specifically covered in its text.[98] As events were to show, he could not have been more mistaken.

On March 16, 1485, Anne Neville died. Richard's marital plans could now be launched, or so he thought, but when Catesby and Ratcliffe got wind of them, their opposition was intense. Unlike their sovereign, they seem instantly to have understood that this further violation of God's law was likely to sound the death knell for Richard and all those associated with him. To add incest to the slaughter of children was more than subjects could be expected to bear, though persuading the king of this truth proved far from easy:

> [T]he king was told to his face that if he did not abandon his intended purpose, and that, too, before the mayor and commons of the city of London, opposition would be offered to him not merely by the warnings of the voice; for all the people of the north, in whom he placed the greatest reliance, would rise in rebellion against him, and impute to him the death of the queen, the daughter and one of the heirs of the earl of Warwick, . . . in order that he might, to the extreme abhorrence of the Almighty, gratify an incestuous passion for his said niece. Besides this, they brought to him more than twelve Doctors of Divinity, who asserted that the pope could grant no dispensation in the case of such a degree of consanguinity.[99]

Still not entirely convinced, but worn down by the arguments of his advisers, Richard III finally went to the Hospital of St. John shortly before Easter. There, in the presence of "the mayor and aldermen of our city of London, together with the most sad and discreet persons of the same city in great number, being present many of the lords spiritual and temporal of our land, and the substance of all our household,"[100] he denied "in a loud and distinct voice" that he had ever had any intention of wedding his niece. But the damage had already been done. The rumor was out and, on April 5, he was forced to write his city of York that if its citizens should hear any "false and abominable language and lies," any "noise and slander against our person," they were to believe none of it: Such tales were entirely the invention of "divers evil disposed persons both in our city of London and elsewhere within this our realm."[101] Seldom has any ruler undergone a greater self-inflicted public humiliation, though the Richard Nixon of "I am not a crook" may have come close.

The disaster of Richard's marital plans proved the final straw. Across the Channel, Henry Tudor prepared his invasion, while those at home were equally caught up in plans either to oppose or to assist him. In early June, the king moved his headquarters to Nottingham for the summer. Ever the good tactician, he had grasped the fact that its location made it the ideal spot for the rapid assembly of those northern forces on which success would so heavily depend, just as that same geography enhanced the possibility of swift response to invasion from almost any quarter. On June 22, a proclamation went out, warning "all . . . subjects to be ready in their most defensible array to do his highness service of war, . . . for the resistance of the king's . . . rebels, traitors and enemies." Nevertheless, the list of those so identified was to prove woefully incomplete, but even so, its names provide impressive testimony on the extent to which Richard's two years of blundering had thoroughly alienated Yorkists and Lancastrians alike: Jasper Tudor, "calling himself the earl of Pembroke," finds himself linked to Sir Edward Woodville, the bishop of Exeter to the earl of Oxford, and if all are dismissed as "disabled and attainted by the authority of the high court of parliament, . . . many be known for open murderers, adulterers, and extortioners contrary to the pleasure of God, and against all truth, honor, and nature."

Understandably, though, the proclamation reserves its greatest wrath for the darkest renegade of them all:

> The said . . . rebels and traitors have chosen to be their captain one Henry Tudor, son of Edmund Tudor, son of Owen Tudor, which of his ambitiousness and insatiable covetousness encroacheth and usurpeth upon him the name and title of royal estate of this realm of England, whereunto he hath no manner, interest, right, or color, as every man well knoweth, for he is descended of bastard blood, both of his father's side and of his mother's side. . . . [I]f he should achieve his false intent and purpose, every man's livelihood and goods shall be in his hands, liberty and disposition, whereby should ensue the disheriting and destruction of all the noble and worshipful blood of this realm, for ever. . . . And in more proof and showing of his said purpose of conquest, the said Henry Tudor . . . and others, the king's rebels and traitors aforesaid, have extended at their coming, if they may be of power, to do the most cruel murders, slaughters, and robberies, and disherisons, that ever were seen in any Christian realm.[102]

Perhaps some Englishmen found themselves persuaded by this apocalyptic rhetoric, but for most, Richard's own record must have made it appear that these dire predictions were little more than a case of the pot calling the kettle black. If so, to have been as unknown as Henry Tudor was not without its advantages. Just as later generations were to assume that Richard III's disastrous moves stood as proof of his satanic malignity, so, too, were they and contemporaries prepared to view Henry as their angelic deliverer, a man whose feats in battle would end "these bloody days" and whose heirs would, with God's blessing,

> Enrich the time to come with smooth-faced peace,
> With smiling plenty and fair prosperous days![103]

Still, when Henry set sail on August 1, he had with him no more than three to four thousand men, of whom possibly a tenth were fellow exiles and the rest, mostly French and Breton mercenaries. All knew that this force alone would prove grossly insufficient, but before departure, and like Richard before him, Henry had made an appeal to those in England whose help he would need:

> Right trusty, worshipful, and honorable good friends, and our allies, I greet you well. Being given to understand your good devoir and intent to advance me to the furtherance of my rightful claim [and] due and lineal inheritance of the crown, and for the just depriving of that homicide and unnatrual tyrant which now unjustly bears dominion over you, I give you to understand that no Christian heart can be more full of joy and gladness than the heart of me your poor exiled friend, who will, upon the instance of your sure [report of] what powers ye will make ready and what captains and leaders you get to conduct, be prepared to pass over the sea with such forces as my friends here are preparing for me. And if I have such good speed and success as I wish, according to your desire, I shall ever be most forward to re-member and wholly requite this your great and most loving kindness in my just quarrel.[104]

The fleet reached Milford Haven late in the afternoon of August 7.[105] Henry disembarked immediately, knelt, and, after making the sign of the cross, invoked divine aid through the words of Psalm 43: "Judge me, O God, and plead my cause." By the next morning he was off for North Wales. The pace was leisurely—just 92 miles in the first week—but Henry saw no need to hurry since, of course, it was better to allow time for reinforcements to reach him than to rush pell-mell into battle outmanned and unprepared. And in this tactic he proved successful: The first Welsh contingents joined him on August 8, but the real turning point came a week later when, as the invaders approached Shewsbury, the leading lord of Carmarthenshire Rhys ap Thomas also threw in his lot with them. Tradition holds that by this one stroke alone Henry added almost two thousand men to his growing army.

Confused word of Henry's landing reached Nottingham on August 11, and Richard, too, began his final preparations. Fresh orders went out to all sheriffs and commissioners of array; individuals like Henry Vernon of Haddon, Derbyshire, were told to bring their quotas of men "upon pain of forfeiture unto us of all that ye may forfeit and lose."[106] In response, the magnates of England turned to their own preparations. For example, the duke of Norfolk instructed his levies to rendezvous at Bury St. Edmunds on August 16, not untypically telling John Paston to appear with "such a company of tall men as you can easily make up at my expense, as well as what you have promised the king."[107] There were, however, few signs of enthusiasm. The earl of Northumberland proceeded toward Nottingham at a pace that was leisurely at best, and if the Stanleys were quick to mobilize, neither Lord Thomas nor Sir William was to join Richard at all. For theirs was to be the waiting game.

On August 15, Henry crossed over into England, reaching Shrews-, bury two days later. From there he continued eastward, attracting more and more men as he went. Shrewsbury itself contributed its militia; two days later, it was Sir Gilbert Talbot with five hundred Shropshiremen; and almost simultaneously Sir Richard Corbet added eight hundred more. By the time Henry reached Stafford, his new adherents were reaching flood proportions: old followers of Edward IV, servants of the long-dead Clarence, even men from the estates of the more recently departed duke of Buckingham. And it was at Stafford, too, on August 19, that Henry had his first meeting with Sir William Stanley, whose own forces numbered some three thousand.

Although it will never be known just what each man said to the other, it seems likely that Sir William passed on two important bits of information: first, that Richard's headquarters at Nottingham meant that he intended to block any advance on London; and, second, that insofar as Lord Strange, Sir William's nephew, found himself a royal hostage, neither Stanley could give Henry open support. Instead, the waiting game would continue, the Stanleys shadowing every Tudor move, thereby seeming to assist Richard while actually giving comfort to neither side. This aloofness must have frustrated both parties in nearly equal measure, but, whatever the motives involved, Lord Strange survived.

The time of testing now drew near. In the early hours of August 20, Henry entered Lichfield. By the next day, he was marching down Watling Street, toward Atherstone. There he encountered the two Stanleys; parleyed again; and then spent the night. At the same time, though, because Watling Street runs in a southerly direction, ultimately to London, this new line of march stirred the royal forces to action. They left Nottingham on the morning of the 20th (though possibly late the preceding day), and by evening they were camped at Leicester. On Sunday the 21st, crown on head and troops in battle formation, Richard III proceeded on to the Cistercian abbey of Merevale, about a mile west of Atherstone. With dusk approaching, he pitched his tents on the plain of Redmoor, better known to posterity as Bosworth Field.

At dawn on the 22nd, Richard III prepared for battle, but

> there were no chaplains present to perform divine services . . . nor any breakfast prepared to refresh the flagging spirits of the king; besides which, . . . in the morning he declared that during the night he had seen dreadful visions, and had imagined himself surrounded by a multitude of demons. He consequently presented a countenance which . . . was on this occasion more livid and ghastly than usual. . . . He also declared that it was his intention, if he should prove the conqueror, to crush all the supporters of the opposite faction.[108]

It was not to be. By midmorning, Richard III lay vanquished, having died very much as he had lived: blindly unrepentant, fittingly unshriven, and in a characteristically dramatic charge. It was but the last of his bold and impetuous gambles, a desperate attempt to win back a kingdom that he knew was on the verge of being lost, though not for the lack of a horse.

To the end, however, there were those who supported him. Some, mainly northerners, remembered that he had once been Warwick's son-in-law and that, as Edward IV's lord lieutenant, he had governed them firmly but well. In those memories, they recognized one of their own. As the city of York recorded its grief on the following day:

> Were assembled in the council chamber, where and when it was showed by divers persons, especially by John Spooner sent unto the field of Redmoor to bring tidings from the same to the city, that King Richard, late mercifully reigning over us, was through the great treason of [those] that turned against him, with many other lords and nobility of these northern parts piteously slain and murdered, to the great heaviness of this city.[109]

Others, advisers like Catesby and new peers like Norfolk, had gained much through Richard—and hence had much to lose if another were to take his place. As did the northerners, such men fought on to the last.

Still, and in spite of this last full measure of devotion, the loyalties of the fallen were soon forgotten. What endured instead were the views of the living, those fiercely divided antagonists on whose newly united allegiance would depend Henry VII's ability to enrich the time to come with fair prosperous days. And, surely, of all the captured Yorkists, none better expressed those views, or more clearly defined the meaning of Bosworth, than did Thomas Howard, the earl of Surrey whose feats of arms in 1483 had done so much to crush the last vestiges of Buckingham's rebellion. Every inch the soldier, the earl appears not to have been an overly reflective man, but when forced to confront the victorious Tudor, even in captivity he found it possible to defend his support of Richard with an outlook much more promising for that time to come than the acquisitive selfishness of Norfolk his father or the narrow regionalism of those northerners at whose side he had so recently stood. "He was my crowned king," Surrey explained, "and if the parliamentary authority of England set the crown upon a stock, I will fight for that stock. And as I fought for him, I will fight for you, when you are established by the said authority."[110] Strikingly, too, when Henry was, Surrey did, and in that conjunction the parliamentary character of English government was both confirmed and founded.

Notes

PART I. INTRODUCTION

1. Personal communication of Helen Maud Cam to the author dated October 18, 1954. The examples cited in the first paragraph were observed by the author while living in Paris in 1958–59.

2. Joseph R. Strayer, "Taxation under Philip the Fair," Joseph R. Strayer and Charles H. Taylor, *Studies in Early French Taxation* (Cambridge, Mass., 1939), p. 94.

3. Anglo-Saxon Chronicle, E ("Laud") Version, as translated in David C. Douglas and G. W. Greenaway, eds., *English Historical Documents 1042–1189* (New York, 1953), II, 161.

4. Cited in Charles Holt Taylor, "Assemblies of French Towns in 1316," *Speculum*, 14 (1939), p. 289 and n. 3.

5. Quoted in Edgard Boutaric, *Saint Louis et Alfonse de Poitiers* (Paris, 1870), p. 51.

6. Walter of Hemingburgh, *Hemingburgh's Chronicle* (London. 1848–49), II, 6, as translated in William Stubbs, *Constitutional History of England* (Oxford, 1880), II, 120. For doubts on the historicity of Hemingburgh's story, though not entirely relevant here, see Sir Maurice Powicke, *The Thirteenth Century 1216–1307* (Oxford, 1953), p. 521.

CHAPTER 1

1. Ernest Lavisse, *Histoire de France* (Paris, 1901–2), III², 212–216.

2. May McKisack, *The Fourteenth Century 1307–1399* (Oxford, 1959), pp. 83–92.

3. J. Strachey et al., eds., *Rotuli Parliamentorum* (London, 1767–77), II, 53. Hereafter *RP*.

4. McKisack, p. 102.

5. E.g., Martin Bouquet et al., eds., *Recueil des historiens des Gaules et de la France* (Paris, 1738–1904), XX, 609–610, 691; XXI, 40–41, 151, 197, 658–659, 663, 806. Hereafter *HF*, The only reticence I have found comes in an interpolation added to the Anonymous Chronicle of Saint Martial of Limoges (XII, 806, n. 7) that says that the d'Aunays "transgressed against the king in ways that ought not to be disclosed."

6. Stubbs, II, 388, n. 1.

7. Charles T. Wood, *The French Apanages and the Capetian Monarchy 1224–1328* (Cambridge, Mass., 1966), pp. 48–65.

8. *HF*, XXI, 197.

9. Wood, pp. 57–63; Gabrielle M. Spiegel, "The *Reditus Regni ad Stirpem Karoli Magni:* A New Look," *French Historical Studies*, 7 (1971), 156, 163.

10. Paul Viollet, "Comment les femmes ont été exclues de la succession à la couronne de France," *Mémoires de l'Institut de France*, 34² (1895), 131–148.

11. *HF*, XXI, 663. The chronicles are much more explicit about the problem of illegitimacy than are official documents, which never mention it. Until the succession question was resolved, Jeanne's paternity was officially no more than "hidden agenda" about which no records were kept.

12. Stubbs, II, 388.

13. Charles T. Wood, "Personality, Politics, and Constitutional Progress: The Lessons of Edward II," *Studia Gratiana [Post Scripta]*, 15 (1972), pp. 524–525.

14. Jehan Froissart, *Chronicles of England, France, Spain, and the Adjoining Countries* (London, 1839), I, 13.

15. Galfridus le Baker de Swinbroke, ed. J. A. Giles, *Chronicon Angliae Temporibus Edwardi II et Edwardi III* (London, 1847), p. 95; Wood, "Personality," pp. 524–525.

16. Chalfont Robinson, "Was King Edward the Second a Degenerate?" *American Journal of Insanity*, 66 (1909–10), p. 455, n. 27.

17. On sodomy as a standard charge in depositional proceedings, see below, Chapter 6, pp. 103–104. In essence, sodomy was viewed as a form of heresy.

18. I am indebted to Elizabeth A. R. Brown, who kindly did the appropriate chronological calculations and checked the itineraries of both king and queen. In addition, it is probably worth noting that Edward II appears to have fathered an illegitimate son named Adam; at least the Great Wardrobe accounts for 1322 record payments to "Ade filio domini Regis bastardo," as reported in F. D. Blackley, "Adam, The Bastard Son of Edward II," *Bulletin of the Institute for Historical Research*, 37 (1964), p. 76.

19. Lavisse, III², 214.

20. McKisack, p. 93.

21. The standard account of Edward II's death remains Thomas F. Tout, "The Captivity and Death of Edward of Carnarvon," *The Collected Papers of Thomas Frederick Tout* (Manchester, 1934), III, 145–190, but the claim has recently been revived that Edward may in fact have escaped the new government's attempts to slay him: G. P. Cuttino and Thomas W. Lyman, "Where Is Edward II?" *Speculum*, 53 (1978), pp. 522–544. On the other hand, the Cuttino-Lyman tale of possible escape to Italy so resembles those told in the cases of Edward V and of France's John the Posthumous that one assumes in the absence of concrete evidence to the contrary that it reflects not the true facts, but only the dreams of those who were unwilling to accept the possibility that even kings might die tragically young or unnaturally.

22. McKisack, pp. 80–81, 83, 85, 93.

23. Frederick Pollock and Frederick W. Maitland, *The History of English Law*, 2nd ed. (Cambridge, 1968), II, 396–397; André Esmein, *Cours élémentaire d'histoire du droit français* (Paris, 1925), p. 236.

24. F. W. Maitland, ed., *Year Books of Edward II* (London, 1903), I, 186.

25. Ibid., I, 187.

26. Pollock and Maitland, II, 398.

27. W. C. Bolland, *The Year Books* (Cambridge, 1921), p. 76. I am indebted to the late William Huse Dunham, Jr. for this citation and, more generally, for having drawn the interest of the common law to my attention.

28. McKisack, pp. 90–91.

29. Carl Stephenson and Frederick G. Marcham, *Sources of English Constitutional History*, rev. ed. (New York, 1972), I, 192.

30. Fritz Kern, *Kingship and Law in the Middle Ages* (Oxford, 1956), pp. 12–13; Henry G. Richardson, "The Coronation in Medieval England," *Traditio*, 16 (1960), p. 116.

31. Robert Fawtier, tr. Lionel Butler and R. J. Adam, *The Capetian Kings of France* (London, 1960), pp. 48–49; in the case of England, I am thinking primarily of William I's selection of Rufus; Henry I's initially of his son William Adelin and then of his daughter Matilda; Stephen's attempts to designate his son Eustace and then his agreement in 1153 to accept the future Henry II as heir, thereby disinheriting his second son William; and, finally, Henry II's crowning of his own son Henry in 1170. For a more general discussion of the restructuring of families that occurred in the twelfth century, see David Herlihy, *Medieval Households* (Cambridge, Mass., 1985), pp. 79–111.

32. Kern, pp. 54–55.

33. Ernst Kantorowicz, *The King's Two Bodies* (Princeton, 1957), pp. 328–330; Marc Bloch, *The Royal Touch* (Montreal, 1973), p. 127. In weighing the significance of this change, though, it is important to remember the unusual circumstances under which both new kings ascended the throne. Philip III

succeeded while his father was on crusade, and the difficulties with which the expedition was faced undoubtedly encouraged immediate succession. In much the same way, because Edward I was himself returning from crusade when Henry III's death occurred, doubtless the government found it desirable to recognize his reign immediately in order to preserve continuity, it being uncertain just when Edward would return.

34. Ralph Giesey, "The Juristic Basis of Dynastic Right to the French Throne," *Transactions of the American Philosophical Society,* new series, Part 5, LI (1961), p. 5.

35. Bloch, pp. 1–4.

36. Achille Luchaire, *Histoire des institutions monarchiques de la France sous les premiers Capétiens (987–1180),* 1st ed. (Paris, 1883), I, 66. The statement carries more than the usual weight since Arnoul was no friend of the Capetians and hence unlikely to accord them hereditary right unless he truly believed that they had achieved it.

37. Spiegel, pp. 145–146, 152, 160–162.

38. The whole of Spiegel's article is relevant here, though I should add that my own interpretation of the sources differs from hers insofar as I take most seriously the likelihood that they were written to legitimate dynastic thinking whereas she stresses their importance to later territorial ambitions. In citing her article here and in the notes that follow, my references are therefore more to her sources than to her interpretation of them. In this regard, my own thinking has been heavily influenced by Andrew W. Lewis, *Royal Succession in Capetian France: Studies on Familial Order and the State* (Cambridge, Mass., 1981), and especially by its fourth chapter, "The Growth of Capetian Dynasticism," pp. 104–154.

39. Spiegel, p. 151; John Baldwin, *The Government of Philip Augustus* (Berkeley and Los Angeles, 1986), pp. 362–393.

40. Georgia Sommers [Wright], "Royal Tombs at St. Denis in the Reign of Saint Louis" (1966 Columbia University doctoral dissertation, copyright 1967), pp. 94–100.

41. Spiegel, pp. 145–146.

42. Bloch, pp. 127–128.

43. Spiegel, pp. 160–162. Unfortunately, though, Charlemagne's canonization came only at the hands of an antipope.

44. Spiegel, pp. 155, 172.

45. Spiegel, pp. 170–173.

46. Kantorowicz, pp. 252–253; Joseph R. Strayer, *Medieval Statecraft and the Perspectives of History* (Princeton, 1971), pp. 302–303, 305–308, 312–313.

47. Robert Branner, "The Montjoies of Saint Louis," *Essays in the History of Architecture Presented to Rudolf Wittkower,* ed. D. Fraser et al. (London, 1967), I, 15–16.

48. Henri F. Delaborde, ed., *Oeuvres de Rigord et de Guillaume le Breton* (Paris, 1882), I, 164. The Latin original of the phrase is: *regis Philippi unigenitus.*

49. Philippe de Beaumanoir, ed. A. Salmon, *Coutumes de Beauvaisis* (Paris, 1889–1900), I, 146, no. 294.

50. Kern, p. 20, n. 4.

51. As translated in Charles T. Wood, ed., *Philip the Fair and Boniface VIII*, 2nd ed. (New York, 1971), p. 65.

52. Strayer, *Medieval Statecraft*, pp. 300–314, an article titled "France: The Holy Land, the Chosen People, and the Most Christian King."

53. Kantorowicz, p. 333.

54. Douglas and Greenaway, II, 142–144, 146, 214, 215–216, 217, 221, 224, 230–231, 285.

55. In June 1119 William Adelin attested a royal charter as "Dei gratia rex designatus"; *Regesta Regum Anglo-Normannorum, II, Regesta Henrici Primi, 1100–1135*, ed. Charles Johnson and H. A. Cronne (Oxford, 1956), no. 1204. I am indebted to C. Warren Hollister for this citation.

56. Rufus, Henry I, and Richard had no legitimate sons that survived them; deaths are almost too numerous to mention.

57. I am thinking primarily of the struggles of Henry I, Robert Curthose, and William Clito; of Stephen and the Angevins; and of Henry II and his sons. Without developing the point, it seems apparent that these cross-Channel conflicts confused the succession and undermined royal legitimacy.

58. Spiegel, p. 152.

59. Charles T. Wood, "England: 1216–1485," *Dictionary of the Middle Ages,* ed. Joseph R. Strayer et al. (New York, 1981–), IV, 485a; W. L. Warren, *Henry II* (Berkeley and Los Angeles, 1973), pp. 222–223.

60. W. L. Warren, *King John* (Berkeley and Los Angeles, 1961), pp. 2–3.

61. Geoffrey of Monmouth, tr. Lewis Thorpe, *The History of the Kings of Britain* (Harmondsworth, 1966), pp. 171ff. Geoffrey's would appear to be one of the earliest examples extant of this kind of dynastic myth-making, something that proved much more successful when tried at a later date in France.

62. Valéry had supposedly told Hugh Capet that he would become king but that his line would fail after the seventh generation: see Spiegel, p. 147.

63. Arthur was born on March 29, 1187, whereas his father had died on August 19, 1186. His mother Constance of Brittany appears to have suggested the name (Warren, *King John,* pp. 81–82), but in accepting this choice Henry II took dynastic responsibility for it. Upon accession, Richard recognized Arthur almost immediately as his own heir, in a letter of November 11, 1190, to the pope.

64. Bloch, p. 346, n. 73.

65. Bertie Wilkinson, *Constitutional History of Medieval England 1216–1399* (London, 1948–52), I, 68–98; see also below, Chapter 2, pp. 39–40.

66. Kern, p. 55, n. 33.

67. A hard point to prove, given the relatively scant attention paid to the subject in France. But cf. Richardson, pp. 161–174, and Robert S. Hoyt, "The Coronation Oath of 1308: The Background of 'Les Leys et les Custumes,' " *Traditio,* 11 (1955), 235–257. That the French had an entirely different approach to charters of liberties, and totally different reasons for granting them, was brilliantly suggested in a paper, "Charters, Leagues, and Liberties in Thirteenth- and Fourteenth-Century England and France," given by Elizabeth A. R. Brown at the Eighth Conference on Medieval Studies sponsored by the Medieval Institute of Western Michigan University, Kalamazoo, May 1, 1973.

68. Kantorowicz, p. 380.

69. Bloch, p. 133.

70. Bloch, pp. 137–139; T. A. Sandquist, "The Holy Oil of St. Thomas of Canterbury," *Essays in Medieval History Presented to Bertie Wilkinson,* ed. T. A. Sandquist and M. R. Powicke (Toronto, 1969), pp. 331–332, 335–336.

71. Viollet, pp. 139–141.

72. *HF,* XX, 645.

73. Bloch, pp. 275–282; Kantorowicz, pp. 218–223.

74. Fawtier, p. 57; Kantorowicz, pp. 221–223.

75. Richardson, pp. 145–146, 150.

76. S. B. Chrimes, *English Constitutional Ideas in the Fifteenth Century* (Cambridge, 1936), p. 24, n. 1.

77. Chrimes, p. 7, n. 2.

78. Sandquist, pp. 336–339; Chrimes, p. 7; Bloch, p. 139; Bertie Wilkinson, *Constitutional History of England in the Fifteenth Century* (New York, 1964), p. 196. Sandquist believes (p. 340) that "the evidence which links the new dynasty with the oil of St. Thomas will not support the notion that in 1399 the Lancastrians sought to bolster their claim to the English throne by emphasizing the special character of Henry IV's unction." He is clearly right insofar as Henry's propaganda stressed other factors, especially his recognition/election by the estates and the people (on which see below, Chapter 6, pp. 112–114), but Henry's very decision to use this oil surely suggests that he saw in it some potential value.

79. Quoted in Chrimes, p. 32, from a 1399 case heard by the commons. Chrimes (pp. 22–32) takes the Yorkists' claims of dynastic legitimacy with the utmost seriousness as the major prop of their authority; Wilkinson, on the other hand (*Fifteenth Century,* pp. 138–142, 162–163), properly points out that all of them in practice had to rely on parliamentary support to such an extent that it undercut their purely hereditary claims. Moreover, as is pointed out below, Chapter 6, pp. 113–115, Yorkist claims of dynastic legitimacy and hereditary right were of no value unless and until they were legally recognized by an authority high enough to do so, and in practice that authority turned out to be parliament's.

80. Mary was illegitimate because, in the Protestant view, Henry VIII had never been married to her mother; in the case of Elizabeth, shortly before her mother Anne Boleyn's execution Archbishop Cranmer determined that she, too, had never been married to Henry, thanks to a precontract of marriage into which she was alleged to have entered. Thus their right to succeed depended entirely on Henry's various acts of succession as declared in parliament.

81. Obviously, much more is involved in the deposition of kings, or the lack thereof, than simple differences in theories of kingship. In particular, of no little significance are the differing political organizations of England and France and the contrary geographic ways in which power was organized. Such differences may therefore help to explain why the idea of deposition never took root in France, but the fact remains that, as stressed in this chapter, the French failure to develop depositional theory—or to put it into practice—seems more fundamentally related to the success of French royalty in producing heirs—and then in developing mythic theories to explain why no one other than the proper man had the right to rule.

82. P. S. Lewis, *Later Medieval France: The Polity* (London, 1968), p. 114.

83. Ibid., p. 61. But for proof that not all agreed with Charles and Joan, see Bloch, p. 144. I would argue, however. that the evidence Bloch cites comes late, after the death of Isabeau, and that by that point the nature of the argument against Charles' right to the crown had changed significantly; see below, Chapter 7, pp. 147–149.

CHAPTER 2

1. Thomas Rymer, ed., *Foedera* . . . (London, 1704–35), VII, 151; *Calendar of Close Rolls 1377–1381* (London, 1914), I, 74.

2. H. T. Riley, ed., *Munimenta Gildhallae Londoniensis* (London, 1860), II², 456. Insofar as Gaunt was anxious to stress the youthful innocence of the boy he was crowning (below, pp. 30,84), it seems likely that he avoided a Sunday coronation because, in 1376, Holy Innocents' Day had fallen on a Sunday. Popular belief held that the day of the week on which it fell remained a red letter one throughout the following year, a day on which all travel and important activities should be avoided: Johan Huizinga, *The Waning of the Middle Ages* (Garden City, N. Y., 1954), p. 154. Why he should have picked a Thursday instead is, however, something that remains obscure.

3. The one chronicle that uses the St. Swithun dating is *The Anonimalle Chronicle 1333 to 1381*, ed. V. H. Galbraith (Manchester, 1927), p. 107. "St. Kenelm the king" is used by: Thomas Walsingham, ed. H. T. Riley, *Historia Anglicana* (London, 1863), I¹, 332, and A Monk of St. Albans [Thomas Walsingham], ed. E. M. Thompson, *Chronicon Angliae ab anno Domini 1328 usque ad annum 1388* (London, 1874), pp. 156, 162–163. For "St. Kenelm the king and martyr": Ranulph Higden, ed. Joseph R. Lumby, *Polychronicon* (London, 1882), VIII, 393, and Adam of Murimuth, ed. Thomas Hog, *Adami*

Murimuthensis Chronica . . . cum eorundem continuatione (London, 1846), p. 228.

4. *Oxford Dictionary of Saints,* ed. David Farmer (Oxford, 1978), article "Swithun"; *The Book of Saints,* 5th ed. (New York, 1966), article "Swithun."

5. Riley, *Munimenta,* II², 476.

6. A Monk of St. Albans, *Chronicon,* p. 150, as translated in McKisack, p. 398. It could be, of course, that the double Winchester linkage is what suggested the inappropriateness of a Swithun dating to Walsingham, which would explain why he failed to use it in any of his chronicles.

7. The fullest account of the whole legend, its development and sources, is to be found in E. Sidney Hartland, "The Legend of St. Kenelm," *Transactions of the Bristol and Gloucestershire Archaeological Society,* 39 (1916), pp. 13–65. For a modern view, more scholarly than Hartland's, see Wilhelm Levison, *England and the Continent in the Eighth Century* (Oxford, 1946), pp. 32, 249–251, 253, 258. Brief articles on Kenelm will also be found in the reference works cited in n. 4 above.

8. William Caxton as quoted in modernized spelling in Hartland, p. 37.

9. White Kennett et al., *A Complete History of England . . .* (London, 1706), I, 51. In terms of Milton's poetic failings here, it should be explained that he was merely rendering a late-thirteenth-century poem into the English of his day: cf. Carl Horstmann, ed., *The Early South-English Legendary of Lives of the Saints . . .* (London, 1887), pp. 347ff and, for the passage in question, p. 352.

10. Ibid.

11. James Orchard Halliwell-Phillips, ed., *Letters of the Kings of England* (London, 1848), I, 136–144; Elizabeth Jenkins, *The Princes in the Tower* (New York, 1978), pp. 96–97. For the best study of the real love people bore toward children during this period, see Lorraine C. Attreed, "From *Pearl* maiden to Tower princes: towards a new history of medieval childhood," *Journal of Medieval History,* 9 (1983), pp. 43–58. See also Nicholas Ormes, "The Education of Edward V," *Bulletin of the Institute of Historical Research,* 57 (1984), pp. 119–130.

12. Huizinga, p. 154; Attreed, passim; John F. Benton, "Les entrées dans la vie: Étapes d'une croissance ou rites d'initiation?" *Annales de l'Est,* 5ᵉ série, no. 1–2 (1982), pp. 9–14.

13. *Vermont Statutes Annotated,* Title 33, Chapter 12, §635a.

14. François André Isambert et al., eds., *Recueil général des anciennes lois françaises* (Paris, 1822–33), II, 541–542, 450, 452.

15. Sir William Holdsworth, *A History of English Law,* 5th ed. reprint (London, 1966), III, 510–511; Pollock and Maitland, II, 438–441.

16. If (and this is a problematic "if") previous commentators are correct in assuming that the otherwise unqualified term "legal age" means 21 in both

English and French documents, then French kings who attained their majority at that age (or who were earlier expected to, even though, in practice, they did not) include: Louis IX (in Louis VIII's deathbed intent, though not in practice), the sons of Philip IV (according to their father's regency plans), and Charles VI (in practice, though not in his father's intent, as is explained below, pp. 35–37). English kings who came of age at 21 include: Henry III, Edward I, and Richard II. See Isambert, II, 694 and 726, and VI, 640; Pierre Dupuy, *Traité de la Maiorité de nos Rois* . . . (Paris, 1655), p. 135; and John Nicholas, ed., *A Collection of All the Wills Now Known to be Extant of the Kings and Queens of England* . . . (London, 1780), pp. 15–16 (Henry III, 1253), 18–20 (Edward I, 1271). On Richard II, see J. S. Roskell, "The Office and Dignity of Protector of England with special reference to its origins," *English Historical Review*, 68 (1953), p. 193.

17. Isambert, I, 181, 182.

18. On Confirmation, see the article of that name in *The New Catholic Encyclopedia* (New York, 1967) and also A. Vacant et al., *Dictionnaire de Théologie Catholique* (Paris, 1909–50), III¹, "Confirmation," cols. 1075–1076. On the ages of reason and discretion, see the relevant articles in the same works or, more briefly, the articles "Age (Canon Law)," "Age of Discretion," and "Age of Reason" in the *Maryknoll Catholic Dictionary* (New York, 1965).

19. William C. Jordan, *Louis IX and the Challenge of the Crusade* (Princeton, 1979), pp. 3–13.

20. Dupuy, pp. 60–61. For the re-emergence of 30 as a possibly significant age in 1563, see below, p. 40.

21. *Maryknoll Catholic Dictionary*, "Age (Canon Law)."

22. Siméon Luce, ed., *Chronique des quatre premiers Valois (1327–1393)* (Paris, 1862), p. 244.

23. Isambert, V, 415–423; E.-J. de Laurière et al., eds., *Ordonnances des Rois de France* . . . (Paris, 1723–1849), VII, 517. Hereafter *Ordon*. Fourteen as here specified means the beginning of the fourteenth year of life, not the fourteenth birthday, and two precedents are worth noting: In 1270, Philip III specified fourteen years completed as the age of majority for his sons (Isambert, II, 644–645). Then, in 1344, Philip VI specified that his son Philip would be of age for oaths and *partages* also at fourteen (Dupuy, p. 6). Philip VI's provisions seem based on those of canon law and parallel the similar provisions of English common law discussed above, pp. 33–34. Lastly, twenty-five for majority comes from Roman Law: cf. Theodore Mommsen, ed., *Corpus Juris Civilis* (Berlin, 1886), I, "Iustiniani Digesta," IIII:4, "De Minoribus Viginti Quinque Annis," pp. 56–62.

24. Isambert, V, 419.

25. Dupuy, pp. 224–227.

26. Sir Frank Stenton, *Anglo-Saxon England*, 3rd ed. (Oxford, 1971), pp. 367–368.

27. *RP*, III, 16 (Clause 50). Thirty did, however, reappear as an unusually significant age for Richard II, on which see below, Chapter 5, pp. 88–90.

28. Sir Harris Nicolas, ed., *Proceedings and Ordinances of the Privy Council of England* (London, 1834–37), III, 232 (with variant on p. 233). Fourteen was also stressed in one other English instance, the arrangements governing the duke of York's first protectorship over Henry VI. The duke was to be protector, but Henry's son Edward of Lancaster had the right to take over, assuming a protectorship was still needed and that Edward wanted the job, when he reached the age of 14: Roskell, pp. 226–227; Ralph A. Griffiths, *Henry VI* (Berkeley and Los Angeles, 1981), p. 726.

29. Griffiths, p. 234. For further examples of ambiguity, see pp. 231ff, the first part of Chapter XI, "The Ending of the King's Minority."

30. Lavisse, VI², 192–193.

31. Wilkinson, *1216–1399*, I, 68–98; G. J. Turner, "The minority of Henry III, Part I," *Transactions of the Royal Historiocal Society*, n. s. 18 (1904), 245–295; M. T. Clanchy, *England and Its Rulers 1066–1272* (London, 1985), pp. 201–207; Anthony Steel, *Richard II* (Cambridge, 1962), pp. 176–177; Anthony Tuck, *The Crown & Nobility 1272–1461* (London, 1986), p. 197.

32. Lavisse, IV¹, 296–297.

33. Sarah Hanley [Madden], "L'idéologie constitutionnelle en France: le lit de justice," *Annales*, 37 (1982), pp. 30–63, especially 40–42; Dupuy, pp. 356–397, especially 376.

34. Wilkinson, *1216–1399*, I, 68–98; Clanchy, pp. 201–206. The list as given in the text is misleading since, as in other instances, ambiguity clouds potential significance. For example, Philip Augustus was crowned while still a minor in 1179, but the ceremony also took place during the lifetime of his father and hence was not inconsistent with procedure followed earlier with regard to those who were being recognized purely as *reges designati*. That was not entirely the situation in Philip's case, but neither would it be fair to say that his age, 14 in 1179, proves the normality of coronation for minors, even though 14 was later to become France's theoretical age of majority.

35. *RP*, IV, 337; Roskell, p. 221; Charles T. Wood, "The Deposition of Edward V," *Traditio*, 31 (1975), p. 251.

36. See below, Chapter 7, pp. 140–141.

37. Dupuy, pp. 28–29.

38. *RP*, IV, 326. Although the codicil, only recently discovered, confirms Gloucester's long-doubted claim that he had received tutelage, from the beginning the council also refused to accept it. For will, codicil, analysis, and the statement quoted in the text, see Patrick and Felicity Strong, "The last will and codicils of Henry V," *English Historical Review*, 96 (1981), pp. 78–102; see also Griffiths, pp. 17–19.

39. Nicolas, III, 233.

40. The best and most recent discussion of this point came in Elizabeth A. R. Brown, "Queens, Regencies, and Royal Power in Thirteenth- and Fourteenth-Century France," a paper given at the annual meetings of the American Historical Association, December 29, 1982, Washington, D. C. See also F.-J.-M. Olivier-Martin, *Études sur les régences I: les régences et la majorité des rois sous les Capétiens directs et les premiers Valois (1060–1375)* (Paris, 1931) and Dupuy, pp. 35–40 and *Preuves*.

41. *Foedera*, I¹, 145, an official description of these events as sent to Ireland.

42. Wilkinson, *1216–1399*, I, 69–88; Jordon, pp. 3–13; Dupuy, pp. 35–40 and *Preuves*.

43. Matthew Paris, ed. H. R. Luard, *Chronica Majora* (London, 1882), VI, 69–70, as translated in Wilkinson, *1216–1399*, I, 97–98.

44. Roskell, pp. 212, 213, n. 1.

45. James H. Ramsay, *A History of the Revenues of the Kings of England 1066–1399* (Oxford, 1925), II, 298; McKisack, p. 402.

46. Kantorowicz, pp. 374ff, 377–381.

47. Nicolas, III, 233.

48. Dupuy, pp. 2, 297–298.

49. Ibid., pp. 12–13, 212–217; Édouard Perroy, *The Hundred Years War* (London, 1951), pp. 219–227.

50. *Foedera*, I¹, 152; T. D. Hardy, ed., *Rotuli Litterarum Patentium* (London, 1835), I, 177.

51. Jordan, pp. 53–58, 63–64. Jordan stresses that Louis accepted responsibility for the misdeeds uncovered, and that is clearly the case insofar as he took it upon himself to correct all wrongs and believed that doing so was his personal obligation. My point in the text is rather different in that he also believed during his minority he had lacked the power needed to stop abuses and hence was not to blame in terms of intentionality.

52. Tuck, p. 197; Steel, pp. 176–177.

53. Nicolas, IV, 95; J. G. Dickinson, *The Congress of Arras* (Oxford, 1955), p. 215.

54. Nicolas, IV, 296–298.

55. Ibid., IV, 132–137.

55. Christopher St. German, *Doctor and Student* (London, 1751), Dialogue I, Chapter XXI, 65.

PART II. INTRODUCTION

1. Letter of 796 to Pope Leo III as translated in Heinrich Fichtenau, *The Carolingian Empire* (Oxford, 1957), p. 61.

2. For more detail on the discussion that follows, see Charles T. Wood,

"*Regnum Francie:* A Problem in Capetian Administrative Usage," *Traditio,* 22 (1967), pp. 117–147, and Introduction to Part III below, pp. 94–97.

3. Felix Liebermann, *Gesetze der Angelsachsen* (Halle, 1903–16), I, 214f, as translated in Stephenson and Marcham, I, 18.

CHAPTER 3

1. Stubbs, II, 95.

2. Reginald F. Treharne, "The Mise of Amiens, 23 January 1264," *Studies in Medieval History Presented to Frederick Maurice Powicke,* ed. Richard W. Hunt et al. (Oxford, 1948), p. 235; Reginald F. Treharne, *The Baronial Plan of Reform, 1258–1263* (Manchester, 1932), p. 337.

3. Charles-Victor Langlois, *Saint Louis-Philippe le Bel: Les derniers Capétiens directs,* Lavisse, III², 50, 82.

4. Fawtier, pp. 29–33.

5. Jordan, p. 217.

6. William Stubbs, ed. H. W. C. Davis, *Select Charters,* 9th ed. (Oxford, 1929), pp. 378–387.

7. For Henry's complaints in 1260 see Charles Bémont, *Simon de Montfort comte de Leicester* (Paris, 1884), pp. 343–353 (pièce justificative no. XXXVII); for those of 1261, Ernest F. Jacob, "The Complaints of Henry III against the Baronial Council in 1261," *English Historical Review,* 41 (1926), pp. 564–571; for those presented at Amiens in 1264, Treharne, "Mise," pp. 237–239.

8. *Foedera* (1816 ed.), I¹, 405–406, 416. In these bulls neither pope made reference to their possible jurisdiction as feudal overlord of England; rather, they spoke entirely in their pontifical capacity.

9. Treharne, *Baronial Plan,* pp. 260–263, 275–277, and especially p. 289 and n. 9.

10. *Foedera* (1816 ed.), I¹, 433–434.

11. Ibid., as translated in Stephenson and Marcham, I, 148.

12. Treharne, "Mise," pp. 228–235.

13. For a fuller discussion of this point see Wood, *Apanages,* pp. 17–19.

14. Charles Petit-Dutaillis, *The Feudal Monarchy in France and England* (London, 1936), p. 269; Gerard J. Campbell, "The Protest of Saint Louis," *Traditio,* 15 (1959), pp. 405–418.

15. Jacob, pp. 565–566.

16. Wood, "*Regnum Francie,*" passim, and especially pp. 136–139 (quotation from p. 139).

17. Jordan, pp. 35–64, 135–181, 236–246.

18. Jean de Joinville as translated in Jean de Joinville and Geoffroi de Villehardouin, tr. Sir Frank Marzials, *Memoirs of the Crusades* (London, 1908), p. 308; for the treaties of Corbeil and Paris, Michel Gavrilovitch, *Étude sur le traité de Paris de 1259* (Paris, 1899), pp. 5–86.

19. Pierre Chaplais, "Le Traité de Paris de 1259 et l'inféodation de la Gascogne allodiale," *Le Moyen Âge*, 61 (1955), pp. 121–137.

20. Treharne, "Mise," pp. 228–235, especially p. 231.

21. *Foedera* (1816 ed.), I¹, 383–384; Treharne, *Baronial Plan*, p. 225; Fredric L. Cheyette, "*Suum cuique tribuere*," *French Historical Studies*, 6 (1970), pp. 287–299.

22. Gavrilovitch, p. 58.

23. Charles Bémont, *Simon de Montfort Earl of Leicester*, new ed. (Oxford, 1930), p. 187; for other aspects of Louis' aid to Henry, see also pp. 179, 192, and Treharne, *Baronial Plan*, pp. 225, 227 n. 5, 236, 252, 264, 272, 290, 300, 319, 321–322.

24. Treharne, "Mise," pp. 230–231.

25. Ibid., p. 231.

26. Treharne, *Baronial Plan*, pp. 319–322. Although not all the barons in revolt were vassals of the king of France, their leader Simon de Montfort was, thus making this scheme at least partially feasible.

27. Ibid., pp. 319–320.

28. Jordan, pp. 35–64; see also above, Introduction to Part I, pp. 8–9.

29. Joinville and Villehardouin, p. 321.

30. Beaumanoir, II, 23–24, no. 1043.

31. See above, Chapter 1, pp. 21–22; Joinville and Villehardouin, pp. 277, 326; Jordan, pp. 182–213.

CHAPTER 4

1. For bibliography, see Wilkinson, *1216–1399*, I, 187, and Richard W. Kaeuper, "Royal Finance and the Crisis of 1297," *Order and Innovation in the Middle Ages*, ed. W. C. Jordan, C. B. McNab, and T. F. Ruiz (Princeton, 1976), p. 45, nn. 1–3.

2. Stubbs, *History*, II, 157.

3. Wilkinson, *1216–1399*, I, 207–208.

4. Strayer and Taylor, pp. 44–45.

5. Ibid., p. 56 and n. 182.

6. Ibid., p. 58.

7. Elizabeth A. R. Brown, "*Cessante Causa* and the Taxes of the Last Capetians: The Political Application of a Philosophical Maxim," *Studia Gratiana [Post Scripta]*, 15 (1972), pp. 565–587. In 1314, Philip suspended the tax on November 28, the day before he died, but no restitution was ordered until the following January when Louis X, the new king, instructed collectors to return only those monies received after the date of the suspension.

8. Strayer and Taylor, pp. 56–57.

9. Ibid., p. 44, demonstrates briefly the adequacy of the purely French background, one that parallels that found in England as cited below, n. 15. Because

the French Chambre des Comptes was destroyed by fire in 1737, few financial records survive on which to judge the extent of French use of English precedent.

10. F. M. Powicke, *The Thirteenth Century* (Oxford, 1953), p. 675, n. 1. For background and the bull itself, see Wood, *Philip and Boniface*, pp. 19–32.

11. Powicke, pp. 665–666.

12. Stubbs, *History*, II, 145 and n. 1.

13. Powicke, p. 666.

14. Francis Palgrave, ed., *Parliamentary Writs* (London, 1827–34), I, 282–283, 290.

15. Powicke, pp. 541–553.

16. Ibid., p. 680. Wilkinson argues (*1216–1399*, I, 192–197) that the *Monstraunces* were drawn up at this point, probably by the so-called knights, and I agree, adding only that the emphasis on the military issue in this document demonstrates the extent to which its author did not fully understand either the nature of the situation or Edward's real plan.

17. Rose Graham, ed., *Registrum Roberti Winchelsey Cantuariensis Archiepiscopi A. D. 1294–1313* (Oxford, 1952–56), I, 179–180; Powicke, p. 676.

18. Ibid., p. 680; Stubbs, *History*, II, 147. It should be noted also that Philip the Fair used remarkably similar appeals to the emotions in 1302: Wood, *Philip and Boniface*, p. 44.

19. Graham, I, 189–190; Stubbs, *History*, II, 148; Powicke, pp. 676, 680.

20. Ibid., pp. 680–681, 680, n. 1.

21. Ibid., pp. 676–677.

22. *Foedera*, I, 872–873.

23. In general, for this passage I accept the reconstruction of Wilkinson, *1216–1399*, I, 199–204.

24. Powicke, p. 683.

25. Ibid.

26. Ibid., pp. 677, n. 2, 683.

27. Strayer and Taylor, pp. 91–94; John Bell Henneman, *Royal Taxation in Fourteenth Century France: The Development of War Financing 1322–1356* (Princeton, 1971); John Bell Henneman, *Royal Taxation in Fourteenth-Century France: The Captivity and Ransom of John II, 1356–1370* (Philadelphia, 1976). The French need and willingness to enter into individual negotiations show up clearly in secret instructions to collectors in 1302 that first specify the rate and then suggest that officials should, in effect, settle for anything they can get: *Ordon.*, I, 350–351, n. (b).

28. See above, n. 19.

29. Wilkinson, Powicke, and Kaeuper are only three of the many who have subscribed in varying degrees to this general view within the last generation.

30. Stubbs, *History*, II, 160–169. Joseph R. Strayer reports (personal communication of February 15, 1976) that in the Scheide Collection of Princeton

University there is a roll from around 1300 that illustrates Stubbs' point perfectly insofar as the *recto* lists a series of specific grievances relating to the forests while the *verso* contains the results of an actual perambulation of the forest of Wychwood. As Strayer sums up the burden of the *recto* side: "What was wanted was immediate remedy of concrete grievances, not constitutional theory."

31. A. Luders et al., *Statutes of the Realm* (London, 1818–28), I, 189. Hereafter *Statutes*.

32. *Foedera*, I, 978, as translated in Wilkinson, *1216–1399*, I, 230, 231.

33. Powicke, pp. 699–704. That the forests continued to be a bone of contention between king and barons is suggested by the frequency with which clauses relating to them appear in the Ordinances of 1311: cf. *Statutes*, I, 157, for example, articles 18, 19, 31, and 38.

34. For a fuller discussion of the points in this paragraph, see below, Introduction to Part III, pp. 97–99.

35. What was probably the last statement of these views, and only reviewed by Richardson in general terms, is to be found in G. O. Sayles, *The King's Parliament of England* (London, 1975).

CHAPTER 5

1. The quotations are drawn from the National Gallery's description as it hangs beside the Diptych. Modern discussion of the piece begins with Maude V. Clarke, "The Wilton Diptych," M. V. Clarke, ed. L. S. Sutherland and May McKisack, *Fourteenth Century Studies* (Oxford, 1937), pp. 272–292. Important recent studies include: Joan Evans, "The Wilton Diptych Reconsidered," *Archaeological Journal*, 105 (1948); Francis Wormald, "The Wilton Diptych," *Journal of the Warburg and Courtauld Institutes*, 17 (1954); and John H. Harvey, "The Wilton Diptych: A Re-evaluation," *Archaeologia*, 98 (1961). In addition, I am especially indebted to Sumner J. Ferris, who kindly shared with me his then-unpublished paper, "The Wilton Diptych and the Absolutism of Richard II," *Journal of the Rocky Mountain Medieval and Renaissance Association*, 8 (1987). Although Professor Ferris and I do not always agree on the Diptych's meaning, it was unquestionably his work that first drew its interest to my attention and suggested paths for fruitful exploration.

2. The nails and crown of thorns do not appear in most reproductions, but are clearly visible in the original. Professor James Gillespie has also suggested (personal communication of January 24, 1987) that the positioning of Richard's hands so resembles that of a priest that he may be preparing not just to kiss Christ's foot but to receive Him as the Living Eucharist. I find this parallel both intriguing and likely.

3. This point is not absolutely certain insofar as part of the difference in hue seems to result from the use of color modeling to suggest a light source. On the

other hand, Richard had clear reasons for wanting the angels' garments to be of a hue modestly different from Mary's, on which see below, pp. 89–90 and n. 48.

4. McKisack, p. 467 n. 2, p. 475.

5. T. F. T. Tout, *Chapters in the Administrative History of Medieval England* (Manchester, 1920–33), V, 204.

6. This is the view advanced by Wormald, and it appears based in part on the seeming parallels between the Diptych and Michelino da Basozzo's *Christ Crowning Giangaleazzo Visconti in Heaven*, a work painted in 1403. On the other hand, in that painting Giangaleazzo is shown already in heaven, actually in the process of kissing Christ's foot, and the crown involved is that of martyrdom, not kingship. As a result, the similarities between the two works are in fact more apparent than real.

7. McKisack, p. 393. The most substantial version of these allegations is printed in Jean Froissart, ed. Kervyn de Lettenhove, *Oeuvres* (Brussels, 1867–77), VIII, 460–462, but see also *Chronique des quatre previers Valois*, p. 259.

8. *RP,* II, 330.

9. Ibid.

10. *Foedera,* VII, 126.

11. McKisack, p. 395.

12. *RP,* II, 362. The magi are called "the three kings of Cologne" since its cathedral claimed to possess their relics.

13. *Foedera,* VII, 151.

14. Matthew 3:17.

15. Matthew 21:5, itself based on the prophecy of Zechariah 9:9.

16. *RP,* III, 3.

17. Harvey, p. 19 and n. 4, was the first to argue the present identifications, though Evans, p. 3, appears first to have suggested a linkage between saints and ancestors by demonstrating that in all probability Edward the Confessor also stood for Edward III.

18. McKisack, p. 467.

19. Anne F. Sutton and P. W. Hammond, eds., *The Coronation of Richard III: The Extant Documents* (Gloucester and New York, 1983), p. 238.

20. Harvey, pp. 10–11, 20–21, and Plate XII.

21. Evans, pp. 1–5.

22. See above, Chapter 2, pp. 41–42.

23. *Polychronicon,* IX, 111; Thomas Walsingham, ed. H. T. Riley, *Annales Ricardi Secundi* (London, 1866), pp. 260–261; *RP,* III, 418.

24. It would have been unexceptional, however, across the Channel, on which see below, Chapter 7, pp. 149–150. For Richard's royalism and its sources, see Richard H. Jones, *The Royal Policy of Richard II* (Oxford, 1968), esp. pp. 64–99, 164–175.

25. The eleventh year hypothesis has been frequently advanced, most recently by Eleanor L. Scheifele in a paper, "The Political Significance of the Wilton Diptych," presented at the 1987 International Congress of the Medieval Institute of Western Michigan University. Harvey, p. 19, argues the esoteric counterpart of the Garter. In addition, Scheifele proposes that the angels may also refer to the merciless parliament of 1388, which met in the eleventh year of Richard's reign, as well as to the eleven new titles of nobility he created in 1397. In general, I am more inclined to accept her first hypothesis than her second insofar as the latter one runs counter to views presented in n. 27 below. In brief, if the dating of the Diptych there argued is correct, the eleven new titles of 1397 would no more than echo the Diptych's reference rather than being one of its sources because, by that point, the commission to paint it would have already been given. On the other hand, I see none of these interpretations as being contradictory of my own: As this chapter demonstrates, the Diptych's symbols usually refer to many things, not just one.

26. Harvey, p. 19, understands the reference, but tends to miss its true significance (on which below, pp. 89–90) since he is more concerned with demonstrating the existence of his "esoteric counterpart of the Order of the Garter."

27. This reasoning leads to three other points, none of which seems capable of absolute proof. The first and most hypothetical is that Richard's decision to grow a beard was somehow closely related to his own increasing self-identification with Christ. We do not know, however, precisely when the beard first appeared. About all that can be said with certainty is that it came late, its first datable appearance in the surviving evidence being 1397, the year in which Richard's bearded effigy and Westminster portrait were both completed (Clarke, pp. 284–285). That is a suggestive date, of course, but it really proves very little about actual first appearance. Second, and possibly more convincingly, because the Diptych's vision is patently of vengeance anticipated but not yet achieved, it seems overwhelmingly likely that it was commissioned in the period before Richard struck out at some (though not all) of the former Appellants in 1397. A commission given at any later date would surely have emphasized the downfall of Gloucester and his supporters, not just Richard's anticipation of that event. In turn, that conclusion leads to the third point, again hypothetical. Since Richard's actions in 1397 seem never to have been directed against Mowbray and Bolingbroke; and since, further, the Diptych appears to have been commissioned before those actions and, as will be shown below (pp. 89–90), includes Bolingbroke as the particular target of royal wrath, the following becomes an attractive scenario: Gloucester, Arundel, and Warwick were probably struck down because of recent conduct, but at the same time that conduct undoubtedly triggered Richard's well-known temper and caused him to seethe with fury not just about recent offenses, but earlier ones as well, ones in

which others like Bolingbroke and Mowbray had been full participants. Only when calmed down did he decide to vent his anger solely on Gloucester, Arundel, and Warwick. If that was what actually happened, then the most likely date for the commissioning of the Diptych would be in that brief period during which Richard, at the height of his anger, would have taken no little pleasure in planning retributive vengeance on all those who had ever insulted his royal majesty.

28. Harvey, pp. 8–10, 19–20, demonstrates that the collars antedate the first negotiations for Richard's French marriage and do not resemble contemporary French ones. As a result, the Plantagenet symbolism becomes preferred, not the marriage influence preferred by Clarke, pp. 278–284, a preference that is still repeated in the National Gallery's explanatory description of the Diptych.

29. F. S. Haydon, ed., *Eulogium Historiarum* (London, 1863), III, 369–370.

30. See above, Chapter 2, p. 30.

31. Sutton and Hammond, pp. 238–239. Peter Hammond (personal communication of January 22, 1985) does not believe that the sapphire ring was that of Richard's coronation, and I agree with him. Similarly, there is nothing in the known versions of the story of St. Edward and the beggar to demonstrate that it was that ring either. My purpose in the text is not to identify any one ring as having been specifically intended, but only to suggest the range of associations *any* ring held by Edward would have called forth in Richard's mind. It should be noted, too, that when Richard gave the Abbey a new coronation ring for the use of his successors, it was described quite differently, as an *Annulum . . . aureum cum quodam lapide precioso vocato ruby* (Sutton and Hammond, p. 239 n. 61).

32. Walsingham, *Chronicon Angliae*, pp. 142–143. Although the story of Alice's theft of Edward III's rings is doubtless apocryphal, Richard II may well have known it. If so, the derogation of royal majesty therein involved would surely have made the Confessor's ring into an even richer source for Richard's meditations.

33. McKisack, p. 412.

34. Walsingham, *Chronicon Angliae*, pp. 222–223; *Anonimalle Chronicle*, p. 114.

35. *Polychronicon*, IX, 222.

36. Walsingham, *Annales*, pp. 184–185. For a general account of all these events, see McKisack, Chapters XIII–XV.

37. William Caxton, tr., *The Golden Legend or Lives of the Saints as Englished by William Caxton* (London, 1900), VI, 243–246.

38. McKisack, p. 444.

39. *Polychronicon*, IX, 114–115.

40. McKisack, p. 454.

41. S. B. Chrimes, "Richard II's Questions to the Judges, 1387," *Law*

Quarterly Review, 72 (1956), pp. 365–390. It is McKisack, p. 448, who posits that Tresilion had been the man who suggested this strategy, and I agree with her.

42. McKisack, pp. 412–414.

43. McKisack, pp. 476–477. By 1397, he was being officially called "entier Emperour" of England: *RP*, III, 343.

44. *Eulogium Historiarum*, III, 378.

45. Walsingham, *Annales*, p. 201.

46. McKisack, p. 479.

47. McKisack, pp. 479–485; *RP*, III, 347–385, and esp. p. 357 for the quashing of all acts of the merciless parliament.

48. Nicholas Harris Nicolas, *History of the Orders of Knighthood of the British Empire* . . . (London, 1842), I, 40–42; William A. Shaw, *The Knights of England* (London, 1906), I, i–ii, 1, 5. The teams for jousting are mentioned only in the first years of the Order, but that the basic concept continued is demonstrated by the fact that in St. George's Chapel the knights' stalls were arranged thirteen on each side (king and prince here being included), and the stalls were numbered on the basis of their location, either on the sovereign's side or the prince's: Nicolas, p. 40 n. 9. Since Garter robes were also blue, I assume that they, rather than the Virgin's, were meant to be recalled in the angelic robes shown in the Diptych—and that it was this intended reference that explains why their gowns are of a seemingly lighter hue than Mary's. At present, of course, Garter blue is a significantly darker shade than the one depicted, but that was not always the case. As Peter Hammond has pointed out (personal communication of February 12, 1987), George I deepened the color in 1715 to eliminate all possible Jacobite associations. Before that date it would have been lighter than Mary's, as it is in the Diptych.

49. Maurice Keen, *Chivalry* (New Haven and London, 1984), pp. 174–178, 198.

50. De Grailly's was the third stall on the sovereign's side (Nicolas, I, 40* n. 9), which means that Henry became a member of Richard II's twelve-knight team from the moment that the latter became king.

51. McKisack, pp. 487–490.

PART III. INTRODUCTION

1. For bibliography as well as excerpts from works, the interpretations of which are typical of the views summarized below, see Thomas N. Bisson, ed., *Medieval Representative Institutions: Their Origins and Nature* (Hinsdale, Ill., 1973).

2. For much of the aforegoing on the nature of customary law, see Susan Reynolds, *Kingdoms and Communities in Western Europe 900–1300* (Oxford, 1984), especially Chapters 1 and 5.

3. See above, Chapter 3, p. 53.

4. Stubbs, *Charters*, p. 400, as translated in Stephenson and Marcham, I, 151.

5. Stubbs, *Charters*, p. 403, as translated in Stephenson and Marcham, I, 151.

6. Stubbs, *Charters*, p. 379, as translated in Stephenson and Marcham, I, 144.

7. *Statutes*, I, 189, as translated in Stephenson and Marcham, I, 205.

8. The classic expression of this judicial view is to be found in Sayles' *The King's Parliament of England*. It should be noted, though, that he does not draw the analogy here made with judge and jury, nor does he concern himself with any explanation of why such a body could successfully have declared statute law.

9. For a brilliant discussion of the petitioning process and its significance, see J. R. Maddicott, "Parliament and the Constituencies, 1272–1377," *The English Parliament in the Middle Ages*, ed. R. G. Davies and J. H. Denton (Philadelphia, 1981), pp. 61–87.

10. For a discussion of this transformation in its French form, though equally applicable to the English instance here under review, see Wood, *Apanages*, pp. 85–88.

11. As translated from a Year Book case of 39 Edward III printed in Chrimes, p. 352. Insofar as G. R. Elton has argued that the phrase "the body of the whole realm" was first used under the Tudors and had great significance in terms of the transformation he sees as only then taking place in the nature of parliament, it should be noted that Thorpe's appeal to *le corps de tout le Royalme* predates Tudor usage by some 150 years and appears to carry with it very similar significance. Cf. G. R. Elton, *"The Body of the Whole Realm": Parliament and Representation in Medieval and Tudor England* (Charlottesville, Va., 1969), passim.

CHAPTER 6

1. C. Cocquelines, ed., *Bullarum . . . Romanorum . . . amplissima collectio* (Rome, 1741), III², 142.

2. Ibid.

3. For bibliography and a brief sketch of Peter's career, see Charles T. Wood, "Celestine V, Pope," *Dictionary of the Middle Ages*, III, 214.

4. Wood, *Philip and Boniface*, passim.

5. Robert Fawtier, "L'attentat d'Anagni," *Mélanges d'archéologie et d'histoire*, 60 (1948), pp. 153–179.

6. Wood, "Personality," pp. 519–536; William Huse Dunham, Jr., and Charles T. Wood, "The Right to Rule in England: Depositions and the Kingdom's Authority, 1327–1485," *American Historical Review*, 81 (1976), pp.

738–761; Natalie Fryde, *The Tyranny and Fall of Edward II, 1321–1326* (Cambridge, 1979). See also above, Chapter 1, pp. 12, 14–15.

7. This interpretation is in direct conflict with older views, ones that stressed feudal defiance to the near-exclusion of all other possibilities. See, for example, F. W. Maitland, *The Constitutional History of England* (Cambridge, 1926), p. 191, and J. E. A. Jolliffe, *The Constitutional History of Medieval England* (London, 1937), p. 488.

8. T. S. R. Boase, *Boniface VIII* (London, 1933), p. 288; Teofilo F. Ruiz, "Reaction to Anagni," *Catholic Historical Review*, 65 (1979), pp. 390–392.

9. Brian Tierney, *Foundations of the Conciliar Theory* (Cambridge, 1955), pp. 161–164.

10. Gerard E. Caspary, "The Deposition of Richard II and the Canon Law," *Proceedings of the Second International Congress of Medieval Canon Law* (Rome, 1966), I, 200.

11. Mary Mildred Curley, *The Conflict Between Boniface VIII and King Philip IV, the Fair* (Washington, D. C., 1927), p. 35. It is generally assumed that Celestine's language and the principles underlying it were suggested to him by Cardinal Benedict Gaetani, soon to become Boniface VIII. As Boniface's later editing of *The Sext* demonstrates, he was unusually well informed on the kinds of legal points that had to be made in order to validate Celestine's renunciation.

12. J. Stevenson, ed., *Chronicon de Lanercost* (Edinburgh, 1839), p. 236. Since Spiritual Franciscans played a leading role in the debates over Celestine V and Boniface VIII, it should be noted that this Austin chronicle derives from a lost Franciscan model, something that may help to account for the extent to which it stresses failings in Edward that were also important in the two papal cases.

13. Edward Peters, *The Shadow King: Rex Inutilis in Medieval Law and Literature* (New Haven, 1970), passim.

14. Pierre Dupuy, ed., *Histoire du différend d'entre le pape Boniface VIII et Philippes le bel, roy de France* (Paris, 1655), pp. 102–106; Jean Leclercq, "La renonciation de Célestin V et l'opinion théologique en France du vivant de Boniface VIII," *Revue d'histoire de l'église de France*, 25 (1939), pp. 183–192.

15. Robinson, p. 449.

16. Dupuy, p. 104 (article 15).

17. E. A. Bond, ed., *Chronica Monasterii de Melsa* (London, 1868), II, 355.

18. Vern L. Bullough and James Brundage, *Sexual Practices and the Medieval Church* (Buffalo, N. Y., 1982), p. 70. For the significance of heresy in depositional proceedings and for a further instance of how it was applied in the case of Edward II, see below, pp. 104–105 and n. 22. It should be noted,

though, that the chronicles that accuse him of sodomy and buggery come late and are not contemporaneous with his reign or deposition. It may well be, then, that the attribution of homosexual behavior to Edward was no more than an *ex post facto* application of evolving depositional theory to the "facts" of his case.

19. Curley, p. 32.

20. Dunham and Wood, pp. 740–741; William Stubbs, ed., *Chronicles of the Reigns of Edward I and Edward II* (London, 1883), II, 313–315.

21. Brian Tierney, *Origins of Papal Infallibility 1150–1350* (Leiden, 1972), pp. 141–142; Tierney, *Foundations*, p. 49.

22. S. B. Chrimes and A. L. Brown, eds., *Select Documents of English Constitutional History, 1307–1485* (London, 1961), pp. 34–36. From the reign of Edward II on, the whole idea of "fundamental law" (usually meaning, at a minimum, both the coronation oath and Magna Carta) took on increasing importance in English affairs. The legal assumptions underlying this development appear remarkably similar to those sketched out for the Church in the next-to-last sentence of the previous paragraph.

23. Cf. Dupuy, pp. 102–106.

24. Tierney, *Origins*, p. 158.

25. Tierney, *Foundations*, pp. 58–62; Tierney, *Origins*, pp. 50, 57. A modern jury, although possessing no sovereign powers, nevertheless has the capacity to determine and to declare which of many competing "facts" are legally true. That appears to be the essence of Huguccio's point and helps to explain how a court without ultimate authority can nonetheless take positions on which definitive action can be based.

26. See above, Introduction to Part III, pp. 97–99.

27. Tierney, *Origins*, p. 52.

28. Reynolds, *Kingdoms and Communities*, demonstrates the extent to which the idea of a community being superior to its single-person ruler was an absolute commonplace throughout continental Europe during this period and not just a theory of canon lawyers. In England the centrality of the community to all parliamentary proceedings found its most familiar expression in the *Modus tenendi parliamentum*, as stressed in G. P. Cuttino, "A Reconsideration of the 'Modus tenendi parliamentum,'" *The Forward Movement of the Fourteenth Century*, ed. Francis Lee Utley (Columbus, Ohio, 1961), pp. 31–60. Cuttino, p. 33, accepts Galbraith's dating of the *Modus* to the period 1316–1324, and I agree.

29. Richard Scholz, *Die Publizistik dur Zeit Philipps des Schönen und Bonifaz VIII* (Stuttgart, 1903).

30. J. P. Migne, ed., *Patrologia Latina* (Paris, 1844–65), CXXXVII, 845: "Quia Spiritus sancti testatur praesentia et congregatio sacerdotum, certum esse quod legimus, quia nec potest veritas nostra mentiri, cuius in Evangelio ista est sententia: 'Ubi duo vel tres congregati fuerint,'" etc.

31. H. R. Luard, ed., *Flores Historiarum* (London, 1890), II, 454.

32. Tierney, *Origins*, pp. 34–35; Kantorowicz, pp. 193–272.

33. Herbert Maxwell, tr., *The Chronicle of Lanercost* (Glasgow, 1913), pp. 254–255.

34. Tierney, *Foundations*, p. 135.

35. Ibid., pp. 87–153.

36. Ibid., pp. 110–115, 118–119.

37. Ibid., pp. 157–178. For a fuller discussion of this "double plenitude" theory, one that explains how papal (or, implicitly, monarchical) authority can have both divine and human origins, see M. J. Wilks, *The Problem of Sovereignty in the Later Middle Ages: The Papal Monarchy With Augustinus Triumphus and the Publicists* (Cambridge, 1963), pp. 488–523.

38. Maxwell, p. 255.

39. *Foedera*, I, 650.

40. H. G. Richardson and G. O. Sayles, eds., *Rotuli Parliamentorum Angliae Hactenus Inediti* (London, 1935), p. 101. The insistence here that Edward was losing every shred of royal dignity seems designed to counter a point in papal depositional theory, that while a pope could be removed from the particular office of bishop of Rome because it was humanly bestowed, he would after his removal still retain his character as bishop, something of divine origin. An English variant of this papal theory appeared only in 1399, when Richard II insisted that the Lancastrians could never take away from him the royal character that had been "inoiled" in him at his coronation: see above, Chapter 1, pp. 26–27.

41. Fawtier, "L'attentat," pp. 169–170.

42. Scholars used to insist on the assembly's nonparliamentary status, but there seems a growing trend to refer to the meeting as a parliament: see, for example, G. L. Harriss, "The Formation of Parliament, 1272–1377," Davies and Denton, pp. 29, 37–38.

43. Maxwell, p. 255; McKisack, p. 91.

44. This representational character, seemingly based on a vague conception of estates, appears with great frequency, notably in the composition of the body that made the future Edward III *custos* of the realm in October 1326; of the delegations that visited the imprisoned king at Kenilworth; of the Westminster assembly itself; and of those groups of men who swore allegiance to the new king at the Guildhall in late January 1327: Dunham and Wood, pp. 740–742.

45. Wood, "Personality," pp. 526–530; Wood, "Deposition," pp. 277–278.

46. The classic study on this subject remains Charles H. McIlwain, *The High Court of Parliament and Its Supremacy* (New Haven, 1910).

47. Almost no literature exists for the medieval period on the differences between political and constitutional approaches to conflict resolution, but the

issues involved were discussed in preliminary fashion in Wood, "Personality" and "Deposition." In recent experience, possibly the clearest illustration of the text's point lies in the way in which Congressman Peter Rodino, the Democratic chairman of the House Judiciary Committee, modified both his rhetoric and behavior over the course of the so-called Watergate crisis. During most of 1973, he acted very much as one would expect any politician to act, looking for practical ad hoc solutions while at the same time attempting to score political points at the expense of Richard Nixon and the Republican Party he headed. By fall, however, as it became clear that Watergate was not going to be solved in any normal political way, Rodino's conduct became increasingly statesmanlike and his rhetoric began to emphasize issues of principle, the need for impartial procedures, and other elements equally foreign to standard Congressional behavior. By July 24, 1974, he found it perfectly appropriate to open his committee's impeachment hearings with a statement stressing the antiquity of the principle that "the law must deal fairly with every man," a point he then buttressed by observing that "[s]even centuries have now passed since the English barons proclaimed [this] principle by compelling King John, at the point of a sword, to accept the great doctrine of Magna Carta." In twentieth-century British experience, a similar transformation seems to occur in the career of Winston Churchill, the limited politician of the gold standard and general strike who became the statesman of 1940.

48. On these events, see in particular Gaillard Lapsley, "The Parliamentary Title of Henry IV," *English Historical Review,* 49 (1934), pp. 423–449, 577–606.

49. Dunham and Wood, pp. 744–747.

50. Walter Ullmann, *Origins of the Great Schism* (London, 1948); E. F. Jacob, *Essays in the Conciliar Epoch,* 3rd ed. (Manchester, 1963); E. F. Jacob, *Essays in Later Medieval History* (Manchester, 1968), pp. 98–140.

51. Dunham and Wood, pp. 744–747.

52. See above, Chapter 1, pp. 26–27.

53. *RP,* III, 455–457, 523–542; *Statutes,* II, 151–156, 170, 243–244, 340–342; G. R. Elton, "The early journals in the house of lords," *English Historical Review,* 89 (1974), pp. 481–512; William Huse Dunham, Jr., " 'The Books of Parliament' and 'The Old Record,' 1396–1504," *Speculum,* 51 (1976), pp. 694–712.

54. *RP,* II, 200, 225, 236, 254, 264, 268.

55. Chrimes, pp. 165–166. Parliamentary sermons existed under Edward III, but only later did they begin to be stressed as a part of that process that validated any royal program for which parliamentary approval was needed. Such stress first appears under Richard II and becomes clear only in the fifteenth century. Chrimes' list of sermons must be correlated with the appropriate passages as printed in *RP* (for example, IV, 3, 15, 34, 62, 70, 94, 106, 123, and 150, the

sermons preached under Henry V, all of which support the point in the text). To give all the citations for the whole century would, however, strain the patience of any publisher: Chrimes is sufficient guide.

56. *RP*, III, 459, 466; Kantorowicz, pp. 227–228.

57. This interpretation appears to explain most persuasively why such emphasis was placed on continuity of membership in the records of Henry's first parliament: *RP*, III, 415ff.

58. Dunham and Wood, p. 747.

59. *RP*, III, 378; Dunham and Wood, pp. 748–751.

60. *RP*, VI, 241; Wood, "Deposition," pp. 283–285.

61. J. S. Brewer et al., eds., *Letters and Papers . . . Henry VIII* (London, 1862–1910), VI, 94.

62. As quoted in G. R. Elton, *Reform and Renewal: Thomas Cromwell and the Common Weal* (Cambridge, 1973), p. 67. Mores, the receiver of the monastery of Syon, was responding to Cromwell's query on how statute law could overcome papal positions expressed in general councils "whereunto some affirm and hold opinion that the Holy Ghost be present."

63. Raphael Holinshed, *Holinshed's Chronicles of England, Scotland, and Ireland* (London, 1807), III, 826. Elton expresses some concern in *The Tudor Constitution: Documents and Commentary* (Cambridge, 1960), pp. 230 and 257, n. 1, that Holinshed may not have recorded Henry's statement accurately, his principal objection being that "the metaphor he used usually applied to the whole nation and the realm" rather than to parliament alone. On the other hand, in canon law the concept of bishop and chapter so clearly meant a corporation of head and members that was, legally speaking, the whole church, that I do not find these doubts persuasive. Besides, a review of the medieval record would quickly show that the whole community of the realm was usually deemed not just to be represented, but actually present, as meetings of parliament: Wood, "1216–1485," p. 481. As a result, one does not have to appeal to canon law to demonstrate the absolute ordinariness of the statement.

PART IV. INTRODUCTION

1. G. D. G. Hall, ed. and trans., *The Treatise on the Laws and Customs of the Realm of England, Commonly Called Glanvill* (London, 1965), p. 71.

2. The numbers and percentages given here treat Hugh Capet and William the Conqueror as founders of a line, not as interrupters of the previous line. If the latter approach is used, between 987 and 1461, France experienced four successions that weren't father to son, or 19 percent. In England, the corresponding figures for the period 1066–1485 would be nine and 47.4 percent respectively.

3. H. G. Koenigsberger and George L. Mosse, *Europe in the Sixteenth Century* (New York, 1968), p. 249; see also n. 2. For a graphically suggestive

exploration of just how bedeviling illness and infertility could be in sixteenth-century royal families, see Mark Hansen, *The Royal Facts of Life: Biology and Politics in Sixteenth-Century Europe* (Metuchen, N. J., and London, 1980).

4. Andrew W. Lewis, "Dynastic Structures and Capetian Throne-right: The Views of Giles of Paris," *Traditio*, 33 (1977), pp. 241–242. As Lewis shows, Giles regarded both Hugh Capet and William I as usurpers, but their heirs as legitimate kings. What seems clear, though, is that the French kings overcame memories of that initial usurpation much more successfully than did their English counterparts, which is the real point of the John of Warenne quotation, whether apocryphal or not.

5. Beaumanoir, II, 264, no. 1515.

6. Wood, *Apanages*, pp. 87–88, 101–102; Wood, *"Regnum Francie,"* pp. 143–144.

7. *Ordon.*, I, 665. When facing difficult decisions, ones on which baronial opposition to royal policy could be anticipated, the king often relied solely on consultation with members of the royal family, apparently hoping that their consent would be accepted (however reluctantly) as fulfilling the requirements of general consultation: cf. Wood, *Apanages*, p. 108, n. 83.

8. Gavin I. Langmuir, "Counsel and Capetian Assemblies," *Studies Presented to the International Commission for the History of Representative and Parliamentary Institutions* (Louvain, 1958), pp. 28–34; Thomas N. Bisson, *Assemblies and Representation in Languedoc in the Thirteenth Century* (Princeton, 1964); Susan Reynolds, *Kingdoms and Communities.*

9. Gavin I. Langmuir, "Community and Legal Change in Capetian France," *French Historical Studies*, 6 (1970), pp. 275–286.

10. *Chronique Parisienne Anonyme, Mémoires de la Société de l'Histoire de Paris*, 11 (1884), pp. 60–62.

11. Paul Varin, ed., *Archives administratives de la ville de Reims, Documents inédits sur l'histoire de France* (Paris, 1839–43), II¹, 272.

12. For a brief summary of Marcel's career, see Perroy, pp. 132–136.

13. For a brief review of the medieval evidence followed by a massive presentation of early modern practice, see J. Russell Major, *Representative Government in Early Modern France* (New Haven, 1980). Major is, however, much more concerned with what estates actually did than with the kinds of authority that gave them legitimacy.

14. See, for example, Robert Fawtier, "Parlement d'Angleterre et États Généraux de France au Moyen Âge," *Comptes-rendus de l'Academie des Inscriptions et Belles-Lettres* (1953), pp. 276–284.

CHAPTER 7

1. The decree *Haec sancta synodus,* usually and wrongly titled *Sacrosancta,* as translated in Henry Bettenson, ed., *Documents of the Christian Church* (New York, 1947), pp. 192–193.

2. See above, Chapter 6, pp. 101–110, 112–113.

3. W. P. Barrettt, ed. and tr., *The Trial of Jeanne d'Arc* (New York, 1932), p. 179. The phrase in brackets appears elsewhere, in the cut parts of the letter.

4. Christine de Pisan, ed. Angus J. Kennedy and Kenneth Varty, *Ditié de Jehanne d'Arc* (Oxford, 1977), vv. 97, 101–109, 111–112. I am indebted to my colleague Kevin Brownlee for having shared with me his as yet unpublished "Structures of Authority in Christine de Pizan's *Ditié de Jehanne d'Arc*," a paper in which he uses the Kennedy and Varty translation, though with modest emendations. Here and in subsequent quotations from Christine I have accepted Brownlee's alterations whenever it seemed to me that they rendered the text more precisely.

5. Christine de Pisan, vv. 161–165, 169–173.

6. Barrett, p. 178.

7. Barrett, p. 180.

8. W. S. Scott, ed. and tr., *The Trial of Joan of Arc* (Westport, Conn., 1956), p. 84; cf. Barrett, pp. 178, 179. In general, in what follows I shall be using the Scott translation since it is based on the so-called Orleans manuscript, which is in French, whereas Barrett uses the official Latin text. Like Scott, I believe (see below, n. 14) that the French version is the one actually taken down at the trial and then only later translated into Latin. As a result, it is one step closer to what Joan herself actually said.

9. Barrett, p. 68.

10. T. Douglas Murray, *Jeanne d'Arc: Maid of Orleans, Deliverer of France . . . Set Forth in the Original Documents* (New York, 1902), p. 159.

11. *Ordon.,* XI, 86–90, especially clauses 1, 21, 22, and 29.

12. See above, Chapter 1, pp. 14–16. In fact, though, Henry's rights as French heir depended in Troyes not on succession *through* Catherine but on his having become Charles VI's true son by virtue of his consummation of the marriage. Technically, then, his rights did not depend on female succession in the normal sense, though since this is legal hair-splitting, I continue to use the traditional view in the text.

13. Scott, p. 126.

14. Scott, p. 122. Scott translates "will himself be" in the final clause, whereas Barrett, p. 126, uses the conditional "should," as I have. In oral French the two tenses sound almost the same in the third person singular, and I assume that the scribe used the wrong one when taking down Joan's testimony. Seeing his error, he then changed it when making his Latin translation. Such differences convince me that the Latin was based on the French, not vice versa, since the error here cited could have arisen only if the French came first.

15. See above, Chapter 6, pp. 111–112.

16. Scott, pp. 67, 120, 104.

17. The specifics on which this interpretation rests are treated below, pp. 132–139.

18. Scott, p. 67.

19. Scott, p. 74.

20. Scott, pp. 66–67; Marina Warner, *Joan of Arc: The Image of Female Heroism* (New York, 1981), pp. 40–43. I take Joan's denial of ever having had anything to do with the adult tending of cattle as an insistence on status. She finds nothing wrong with more "elevated" occupations, insisting, for example, that she can outsew any woman in Rouen (Scott, p. 66), but she clearly regards herding as beneath her dignity.

21. Scott, pp. 104 and note, 106.

22. Scott, p. 120.

23. Jacobus de Voragine, tr. Granger Ryan and Helmut Ripperger, *The Golden Legend* (London, 1941), II, 578–583.

24. Ibid., II, 613. For a discussion of transvestite saints and of Joan's relationship to them, see Caroline Walker Bynum, *Holy Feast and Holy Fast: The Religious Significance of Food to Medieval Women* (Berkeley, 1987), pp. 290–291 and accompanying bibliographic notes.

25. *The Golden Legend*, II, 613–614.

26. Ibid., II, 709. The rest of the story comes from pp. 709–716.

27. Ibid., II, 715. See also Robert Fawtier, "Les reliques rouennaises de Sainte Catherine d'Alexandrie," *Analecta Bollandiana*, 41 (1923), pp. 357–368.

28. Scott, p. 106.

29. Scott, pp. 104–105. I take the "king's daughter" reference here to be an unconscious echo of the Catherine story.

30. Scott, pp. 105–106. The parental forgiveness is reported on p. 104.

31. E.g., Scott, pp. 72, 77, 91, 93, 100, 107, 125. That St. Catherine's was the voice involved is explicit only in the testimony on p. 107, but it seems the logical one in the other instances as well, where no name is given. Such silences in Joan's answers—as well as their specifics—often seem governed by the questions asked of her. If a questioner refers only to "a voice," so does she, but if one specifies a particular saint such as Catherine, she will also.

32. Deborah Fraioli, "The Literary Images of Joan of Arc: Prior Influences," *Speculum*, 56 (1981), p. 828.

33. Fraioli, pp. 811–830 passim; Warner, pp. 24–27.

34. Scott, pp. 75–76. The ultimate source of this prophecy about the Bois Chenu is to be found in Geoffrey of Monmouth, ed. Acton Griscom, *The Historia regum Britanniae* (London, 1929), pp. 390–391, where Merlin predicts that a *puella* will emerge *ex urbe canuti nemoris* to bring peace through her healing arts.

35. Régine Pernoud, tr. J. M. Cohen, *The Retrial of Joan of Arc* (London, 1955), p. 67. Cf. Douglas Murray, pp. 21 n. 1 and 226.

36. Douglas Murray, p. 227; cf. Pernoud, p. 75.

37. Pernoud, p. 88; Warner, p. 24; Douglas Murray, pp. 269–270; Fraioli, p. 817 n. 36. The prophecy itself appears in Jules Quicherat, ed., *Procès de condamnation et de réhabilitation de Jeanne d'Arc* (Paris, 1841–49), III, 83–84, though it is not based on any of Marie's independently known visions.

38. Douglas Murray, p. 239.

39. Scott, p. 135.

40. All quotations here from *The New Catholic Encyclopedia* (New York, 1967), IV, article "Confirmation."

41. Description and quotation both from Jules Michelet, tr. Albert Guérard, *Joan of Arc* (Ann Arbor, 1967), p. 42. Michelet does not cite his source, but it is the "Journal du siége d'Orléans, et du voyage de Reims," Quicherat, IV, 186. Given the argument later to be developed (see below, pp. 147–150), that in the process of Joan's rehabilitation Charles himself gave new emphasis and meaning to this kind of quasi-sacramental interpretation of his coronation as a form of confirmation, it is worth noting that the physical contact here mentioned is also supported by contemporary evidence. For example, on the very day of that coronation, three Angevins wrote Charles' wife and mother-in-law from Reims about the ceremony. Among other things they reported: "Et durant ledit mystère, la Pucelle s'est toujours tenue joignant du roy, tenant son estendart en sa main": Quicherat, V, 129.

42. Barrett, pp. 175–176.

43. Christine de Pisan, vv. 229–231, 233–234, 239–245, 225–228, 257–259, 265–270, 377–378, 406–408, 272.

44. Douglas Murray, p. 285. This testimony comes from Brother Jean Pasqueral at Joan's rehabilitation trial, and even though there are reasonable grounds for doubting much of what he said (below, pp. 149–150), on this specific point I see no reason for doubt.

45. Scott, pp. 97–98, 111–112, 115–116, 119–120, and 121 for the incident at Beaurevoir; p. 104 for the parental forgiveness.

46. Christine de Pisan, vv. 417–421, 424–426, 329–334, 337–344.

47. Scott, pp. 110, 138.

48. Scott, pp. 111, 119.

49. Scott, p. 119. It is true, of course, that during her captivity her voices foretold many events that never came true, the most concrete of which was her expected meeting with Henry VI (Scott, p. 117). At that point, though, she was obviously trying to put up a brave front and had no opportunity to change her testimony in light of subsequent events. One can only wonder how she would have emended it if she had survived.

50. Scott, p. 74.

51. Fraioli, pp. 826–827; Marjorie Reeves, *The Influence of Prophecy on the Later Middle Ages: A Study in Joachimism* (Oxford, 1969), pp. 320–331; see also the comments by Kennedy and Varty in Christine de Pisan, pp. 63–65.

52. Scott, p. 122; see also above, p. 130 and n. 14. It should be noted, however, that if Joan's trial record reflects little knowledge of this prophecy, seeming allusions to it appear with some regularity in her letters. See, for example, Barrett, p. 176; Quicherat, V, 126; and esp. Antonio Morosini, ed. Léon Dorez and Germain Lefèvre-Pontalis, *La chronique d'Antonio Morosini* (Paris, 1898–1902), III, 83–85. On the other hand, one cannot be certain that Joan actually said all that her scribes attributed to her, whereas the letters reported by Morosini may not be genuine.

53. Pernoud, p. 105.

54. Scott, p. 135.

55. Above, pp. 140–142.

56. Scott, p. 135. It should be noted how the advice of Joan's voices to speak and act "boldly" is here unconsciously transferred to her own counsel. The example is not untypical.

57. On French estates and parlements conceiving of themselves as mystical bodies, see the index of Kantorowicz under *Corpus mysticum* and also Ralph E. Giesey, "The French Estates and the Corpus Mysticum Regni," *Album Maud Cam* (Louvain, 1960), I, 153–171. On English parliaments within the same framework, see above, Chapter 6, pp. 106–115. On the Council of Basel, my main point is that when it tried to claim an authority superior to the pope's, Eugenius IV simply dissolved it and then held a new one first at Ferrara, subsequently at Florence. Although the extreme conciliarists tried to keep Basel in being as the "true" council, over time they found that their position attracted little practical support. Their failure involved very human politics, of course, but a key element in Basel's downfall appears to have been the very different position that conciliarists there enjoyed as compared to the one they had possessed during the early sessions of Constance. That is, once people were generally agreed as to who the true pope was (as they were by the time of Basel), they seem also to have accepted the proposition however slowly and grudgingly that under a restored papal headship a council could be considered "lawfully assembled in the Holy Spirit" only when it had received its authority from Christ not directly, as at Constance, but by virtue of delegation from the pope. In other words, once the schism was healed, and whenever popes and councils disagreed, the latter were to find that they had no ultimate authority, independently received, to which they could appeal—and to which others would respond.

58. Jean Anouilh, adapted Lillian Hellman, *The Lark*, in Jean Anouilh, *Five Plays* (New York, 1959), II, 280.

59. Above, Chapter 1, pp. 20–22.

60. Dickinson, pp. 175–186; Urbain Plancher, *Histoire générale et particulière de Bourgogne* (Paris, 1739–81), IV, cli–clv, no. CXXII.

61. On the lack of adultery charges against Isabeau during Joan of Arc's lifetime, see R. C. Famiglietti, *Royal Intrigue: Crisis at the Court of Charles VI 1392–1420* (New York, 1986), pp. 42–45.

62. Above, p. 139; Pernoud, p. 111. The reference to "the back of archers" is derived ultimately from the prophecies of Merlin as they appear in Geoffrey of Monmouth's *Historia regum Britanniae,* Book 7, and the prediction "Ascendet uirgo dorsum sagittarii," etc. Sagittarius was transformed into archers, and ascending into riding by an author and manner unknown. For the original, see Griscom, ed., p. 397.

63. Pernoud, p. 106.

64. Pernoud, pp. 63–67.

65. Pernoud, p. 125 n. 1.

66. Douglas Murray, pp. 282–283.

67. Scott, p. 31. Obviously I add the point that the views expressed may reflect opinions other than Joan's since, of course, she was illiterate. On the other hand, at her trial (Scott, p. 69), when the letter was read to her, although she objected to some phrases as not being her own, she failed to mention the ones here cited.

68. Pernoud, pp. 117–118.

69. Douglas Murray, pp. 229–230.

70. Scott, p. 82.

71. Pernoud, p. 105.

72. Pernoud, p. 141.

73. Barrett, p. 427.

74. Pernoud, p. 209.

75. Scott, p. 171. A further sign of Joan's belief that she was doing well in the contest with her judges was her elation when proved right on the accuracy of her memory: Pernoud, p. 169.

CHAPTER 8

1. Historical Manuscripts Commission, *Reports of the Royal Commission on Historical Manuscripts* (London, 1883), IX[1], 1452. Hereafter cited as *HMC.*

2. Dominic Mancini, ed. and tr. C. A. J. Armstrong, *The Usurpation of Richard the Third,* 2nd ed. (Oxford, 1969), p. 115, n. 45.

3. Angelo Raine, ed., *York Civic Records* (York, 1938), I, 71; R. Davies, ed. *York Records: Extracts from the Municipal Records of the City of York* (London, 1843), p. 142.

4. The following standard accounts, quite different in their interpretations, agree on the chronology and basic facts: James Gairdner, *History of the Life and Reign of Richard the Third,* rev. ed. (Cambridge, 1898); Sir Clements R. Markham, *Richard III: His Life & Character* (London, 1906); Paul Murray Kendall, *Richard the Third* (New York, 1965); Giles St. Aubyn, *The Year of Three Kings 1483* (London, 1983); and Charles Ross, *Richard III* (Berkeley and Los Angeles, 1981). In what follows, I shall assume the basic chronology, also briefly set forth in Sutton and Hammond, pp. 13–46, citing only specific sources.

5. *HMC*, XI, App. III (1887), p. 170. Edward's "convenient haste" confirms what is otherwise purely a chronicler's story about the coronation being planned for May 4.

6. The evidence for this correspondence, all from chronicles, is reviewed by Kendall, pp. 172–185.

7. Grey, the younger of Elizabeth Woodville's two nonroyal sons, had been sent from London on the previous day: Kendall, p. 189.

8. Printed in Mancini, p. 119, n. 59.

9. See above, Chapter 2, p. 38.

10. Mancini, p. 118, n. 55, and p. 119, n. 59; Kendall, pp. 191–192.

11. *Calendar of Patent Rolls: Edward IV-Edward V-Richard III, 1476–85* (London, 1901), pp. 352–353.

12. Polydore Vergil, ed. Henry Ellis, *Three Books of Polydore Vergil's English History, Comprising the Reigns of Henry VI., Edward IV., and Richard III.* (London, 1840), pp. 175–176.

13. John G. Nichols, ed., *Grants, Etc. from the Crown During the Reign of Edward the Fifth* (London, 1854), pp. 46, 54, 57, etc. The title "defensour" appears to have been added only in the latter part of May; on the 21st, for example (p. 29), Richard is still only "protectour."

14. Nichols, p. xiii; *Seventh Report of the Deputy Keeper of the Public Records* (London, 1846), Appendix II, 212.

15. Nichols, p. 13.

16. Chrimes, pp. 168–178.

17. Caroline Halsted, *Richard III. as Duke of Gloucester and King of England* (Philadelphia, 1844), pp. 447–448, doc. SS. I find convincing Halsted's argument, there given, for accepting the clothes described as Edward V's coronation robes.

18. Nichols, pp. xxxii, 23; Anne F. Sutton and P. W. Hammond, eds., *The Coronation of Richard III: The Extant Documents* (Gloucester and New York, 1983), p. 19. The May 20 knighting orders mention no coronation, so the invitations to Rye and Romney are, to my knowledge, the first in which the government mentioned that event.

19. Nichols, pp. 69–71, quotation on p. 70.

20. Charles T. Wood, "Richard III, William, Lord Hastings and Friday the Thirteenth," *Kings and Nobles in the Later Middle Ages*, ed. Ralph A. Griffiths and James Sherborne (Gloucester, 1986), p. 164. The loyalties of Rotherham of York were suspect especially after he had momentarily ceded the great seal to Elizabeth Woodville in sanctuary. Such a cession violated the specific instructions that Gloucester had sent on May 2 (above, p. 153), though it is likely that the event took place before the letter arrived.

21. Nichols, p. 4.

22. Nichols, pp. 5–9, 11–14, 31, 33–36, 49.

23. Nichols, p. 2.

24. Mancini, pp. 81 and 119, n. 59.

25. Nichols, p. 2.

26. Nichols, p. 3; Mancini, pp. 121–122, n. 67.

27. See Armstrong's citations and discussion in Mancini, p. 117, n. 52. Since Dorset survived into Tudor times, he himself may be the source for the Tudor version.

28. C. L. Kingsford, ed., *The Stonor Letters and Papers 1290–1483* (London, 1919), II, 159.

29. Mancini, p. 85. It appears that the council refused to recognize treason here because it, the council, had not yet appointed Richard protector. If so, its position echoes that taken by Henry VI's council when it refused to recognize the provisions of Henry V's will that had granted tutelage over Henry VI to Humphrey of Gloucester: see above, Chapter 2, pp. 38–39.

30. F. R. H. du Boulay, ed., *Registrum Thome Bourgchier* (Oxford, 1957), pp. 52–53; Kendall, p. 199.

31. Printed in Mancini, pp. 124–125, n. 74.

32. *Stonor Letters,* II, 160. That real crisis arose at this point is further suggested by the fact that writs under the privy seal and grants recorded in Harleian ms. 433 for Edward V all come to an end on June 8–9: Sutton and Hammond, p. 20.

33. Kendall, pp. 203–213, has the best general discussion of the composition of the council and of the tensions and rivalries within it.

34. Nichols, pp. 69–71. As additional support for the hypothesis that the government agreed to the coronation only after some delay, note that Stallworth's first letter of June 9 (*Stonor Letters,* II, 159–160) reports the date of the coronation as recent news. Note also that Vergil, p. 18, asserts that Russell's part of the council was still only preparing to proclaim the date of the coronation publicly at the time that Hastings' conspiracy was discovered, on June 13. Ross, p. 74, n. 36, believed that the date of the coronation became known as early as May 20, but the documents he cites do not support his point: cf. Wood, "Friday the Thirteenth," p. 166, n. 21.

35. Chrimes, pp. 176–177.

36. Chrimes, p. 178.

37. Dunham and Wood, p. 751 and n. 26.

38. See below, pp. 163–170.

39. See above, pp. 158–159.

40. *York Civic Records,* I, 73, as modernized in Gairdner, pp. 59–60.

41. James Gairdner, ed., *The Paston Letters* (London, 1904), VI, 71–72.

42. E.g., Gairdner, *Richard the Third,* pp. 59–64 (the Hastings' conspiracy explanation) and Markham, pp. 93–98 (the Stillington interpretation, though combined with discovery of Hastings' opposition).

43. Kendall, pp. 223–224, 234–235; Mancini, pp. 132–134, n. 104.

44. Markham, pp. 93–98.

45. E.g., Mortimer Levine, "Richard III—Usurper or Lawful King?" *Speculum*, 34 (1959), pp. 391–401, especially 392–393 and n. 8.

46. Mancini, p. 89.

47. See below, pp. 178–181, 194–195.

48. Cf. Gairdner, *Richard the Third*, p. 60.

49. On the dating of the *supersedeas*, see Wood, "Deposition," pp. 259–260, and below, Chapter 9, pp. 177–178.

50. No copies survive in the official record, thus suggesting that they were written by a person or persons outside the circle of normal governmental procedures. Furthermore, the tone of both is personal, with Richard appealing on the basis of previous ties, not on that of his position as protector. This personalism is understandable, surely, but still suggestive of unofficial action.

51. Mancini, p. 89.

52. See below, Chapter 9, pp. 177–178. On the arrival of MP's in London and Richard's concern, Mancini, p. 95. These writs are mentioned only in the records of York and New Romney (*York Civic Records*, I, 75; *HMC*, V, 547a), so evidence is scanty, but for a more detailed discussion of the issues they raise, see Wood, "Deposition," pp. 259–261, and below, Chapter 9, pp. 177–178.

53. Gairdner, p. 86.

54. *Stonor Letters*, II, 160–161.

55. Gairdner, p. 58.

56. *Stonor Letters*, II, 159.

57. Probably the most impartial presentation of this point will be found in A. R. Myers, "The Character of Richard III," *History Today*, 4 (1954), pp. 511–521.

58. It seems likely that the imminent arrival of northern troops became public knowledge only at this point. For example, even though Stallworth's letter to Stonor of June 21 reports the expected arrival of "xx thousand of my lord protectour and my lord of Bukyngham men in London this weeke" as though it was still new news, it must be remembered that Stallworth had been ill for some days, unable to write, and the way in which he lumps together his account of Hastings' death, York's removal from sanctuary, and these troops suggests that he thought of all three as things about which he had heard simultaneously: *Stonor Letters*, II, 161; see above, pp. 168–169.

59. *Stonor Letters*, II, 161.

60. On Jane Shore's real name, see N. Barker and R. Birley, "Jane Shore," *Etoniana*, no. 125 (June 1972). For the sake of convenience and familiarity, though, the text will continue to use "Jane."

61. I am indebted to Alison Hanham for this identification, she having discovered a mention of Forster's arrest in H. T. Riley, ed., *Register Abbatiae*

Johannis Whethamstede (London, 1872-73), II, 265-267. For Forster's likely role in the plot, see below, pp. 172–173, and n. 66. It should be noted that neither in Stallworth nor in the two most contemporaneous chroniclers, Mancini and Croyland, is any part given to Thomas, Lord Stanley, in all of this plotting. My suspicion is that he had none—but that he found it useful to claim that he did, once Henry VII was on the throne, thus leading to his inclusion in later Tudor accounts and in Shakespeare.

62. H. T. Riley, ed. and tr., *Ingulph's Chronicle of the Abbey of Croyland* (London, 1854), p. 488.

63. St. Thomas More, ed. Richard S. Sylvester, *The History of King Richard III and Selections from the English and Latin Poems* (New Haven, 1976), pp. 48–49.

64. Halsted, p. 456, doc. HHH.

65. Mancini, p. 91.

66. Since Hastings and John Forster were the co-stewards of St. Albans, it seems likely that Dorset had sought refuge there. Such a hypothesis would explain why Forster came to be arrested after Hastings' death, something that would otherwise seem inexplicable.

67. For a fuller discussion of this point, see Wood, "Friday the Thirteenth," pp. 157–159.

68. Ibid.

69. *Stonor Letters,* II, 161. John Howard, soon to be the duke of Norfolk, alone supplied "8 botes uppe and down from Westminster": J. P. Collier, ed., *Household Books of John, Duke of Norfolk and Thomas, Earl of Surrey, 1481–1490* (Roxburghe Club, 1844), p. 402.

70. Mancini, p. 89.

71. This conclusion depends on the dates and distances involved. York received the *supersedeas* on June 21, whereas Rivers appears to have heard of the imminence of his death at least by the 23rd, the day on which he drew up his last will and testament. Since Rivers and the others were being held at Sheriff Hutton, about a day's ride north of York and since, moreover, it seems unlikely that two messengers would have been dispatched to such proximate destinations, the text's point naturally follows.

CHAPTER 9

1. For Henry IV's "record and process" as well as the specific charges that were brought against Richard II, see *RP,* III, 415–434. On the other depositions cited, see Dunham and Wood, passim, and Chapter 6 above.

2. Henry Ellis, ed., *Original Letters,* 2nd Series (London, 1827), I, 148.

3. Sutton and Hammond, p. 22 and nn. 77, 80. Given the London announcement of a postponement to November 9 and reference to that same date of postponement in The College of Arms Chronicle, a nonofficial source, Sutton

and Hammond assume that postponement to November 9 was mentioned in all the writs of *supersedeas* issued. That is a possibility, but the interpretation about to be presented seems better to account for the different ways in which the terms of the writs received were recorded at New Romney and York.

4. *HMC*, V, 547a. The term used for this cancellation is *contradicendi*, itself ambiguous enough to allow the possibility of mere postponement. In what follows, I assume the New Romney writ as a model for all those received by persons and places relatively close to London.

5. *York Civic Records*, I, 75. I assume, similarly, the York writ as a model for those received by persons and places far removed from London.

6. Mancini, p. 95.

7. Ibid.

8. A. H. Thomas and I. D. Thornley, eds., *The Great Chronicle of London* (London, 1938), p. 230, as modernized in A. R. Myers, ed., *English Historical Documents 1327–1485* (New York, 1969), pp. 334–335. The reconstruction of events presented here depends on the close analysis of highly contradictory evidence. For that analysis, see Wood, "Deposition," pp. 271–275.

9. Mancini, pp. 61–63; Kendall, pp. 241–242. That Mancini, a foreigner who resided in England for only a year, knew this story and could add a new detail to it demonstrates conclusively that it was current in 1483.

10. Vergil, pp. 183–185, for the whole Shaw incident, p. 185 for the quotation. The reader should recognize, however, that as a court historian of Henry VII Vergil would have had strong grounds for stressing Cecily's anger: the wish to undercut any possible doubts about the legitimate royal descent of Henry's queen, Elizabeth of York.

11. *Statutes*, II, 380–391.

12. *Great Chronicle* as modernized in Myers, *Documents*, pp. 334–335.

13. Mancini, pp. 95–97.

14. Kendall, pp. 43, 51–52.

15. Louis XI died on August 20, 1483, an event that had been long expected.

16. The basis for the assessment of Richard's character as presented in the last three paragraphs is more fully presented in Wood, "Friday the Thirteenth," pp. 155–168.

17. See above, Chapter 1, p. 17.

18. The parallels involved are reviewed in detail in C. A. J. Armstrong, "The Inauguration Ceremonies of the Yorkist Kings and their Title to the Throne," *Transactions of the Royal Historical Society*, 30 (1948), pp. 51–73.

19. Karl Marx, *The Eighteenth Brumaire of Louis Bonaparte* (New York, n.d.), p. 13.

20. More, pp. 77–78. It is unclear here whether Richard had not yet left Baynard's Castle; whether he had returned momentarily to meet this delegation in the same place where his brother Edward IV had met a similar group in 1461;

or whether More is simply in error about the place of meeting. It is, however, a minor point.

21. Dunham and Wood, pp. 754–755. See also above, Chapter 8, pp. 158, 174.

22. *Great Chronicle,* p. 232. Richard dated the start of his reign from these events, on the significance of which dating, see Wood, "Deposition," p. 282, n. 100.

23. Rosemary Horrox and P. W. Hammond, eds., *British Library Harleian Manuscript 433* (Upminster, 1979–83), II, 2. Hereafter *Harleian 433.*

24. Sutton and Hammond, pp. 153–173; *Foedera,* XII, 189; *Calendar of Patent Rolls,* p. 360; Kendall, p. 271.

25. *Calendar of Charter Rolls, 1427–1516* (London, 1927), VI, 258; *Harleian 433,* I, 65ff; and above, p. 176.

26. Chroniclers seem generally agreed that about 4,000–5,000 men were involved, on which see Armstrong's discussion in Mancini, pp. 132–133, n. 104. Not all of these troops were northerners, however; some were Buckingham's men, summoned from Wales.

27. For details on the range of food and finery provided, see Sutton and Hammond, passim, but most of the peers who attended are succinctly presented in Markham, p. 109. For a fuller record of attendees, see Samuel Bentley, ed., *Excerpta Historica* (London, 1831), pp. 379–384.

28. Wood, "Deposition," p. 271; Dunham and Wood, pp. 740–741, 746–747, 753.

29. Ross, p. 42; Wood, "Deposition," pp. 252, 265–266.

30. Gairdner, *Richard the Third,* p. 58; *Stonor Letters,* II, 161.

31. *Excerpta Historica,* p. 382; Mancini, pp. 100–101 and n. 111. It could also be that the elderly Bourchier was merely tired, though I doubt it.

32. St. Aubyn, p. 171; *Croyland,* pp. 490–491.

33. Richard's itinerary has to be reconstructed from the chronicles, from *Harleian 433,* and from ancillary documents, but it is most succinctly presented in St. Aubyn, pp. 171–175.

34. More claims, for example, that it was in response to this news that Richard sent Sir James Tyrell from Warwick to do in the princes: More, pp. 83–84.

35. William D. Macray, ed., *Register of Magdalen College, Oxford,* new series (London, 1894), I, 11–12.

36. Joseph B. Sheppard, ed., *Christ Church Letters,* Camden Society new series (Westminster, 1877), XVII, 45, as quoted in St. Aubyn, p. 183.

37. *York Civic Records,* I, 78.

38. St. Aubyn, pp. 165–166, 184–185.

39. *Harleian 433,* II, 42.

40. St. Aubyn, p. 185.

41. Josiah C. Wedgwood, *History of Parliament* (London, 1936–38), II, 473. Wedgwood estimates that the date of issuance for these writs must have been ca. September 25.

42. The nature of the rebellion and its participants is most fully discussed in Ross, pp. 105–124.

43. On the overwhelming likelihood of Richard's responsibility, see Ross, pp. 96–104, and Charles T. Wood, "Who killed the little princes in the Tower?" *Harvard Magazine*, 80, no. 3 (January–February 1978), pp. 34–40.

44. On the courting of Elizabeth of York see below, pp. 201–202. On the centrality of the princes' murder to Richard's villainous reputation, and on the effect that reputation had, see above, Chapter 2, pp. 32–33, and Attreed, passim. On the reasons why even the most contemporaneous and reliable of the chroniclers, notably Croyland, should have judged Richard a villainous schemer rather than as the semi-incompetent blunderer presented here, see Wood, "Friday the Thirteenth," pp. 163–165.

45. Above, Chapter 1, pp. 15–16.

46. W. H. St. John Hope, "The Discovery of the Remains of King Henry VI in St. George's Chapel, Windsor Castle," *Archaeologia*, 2nd series, 62 (1911), pp. 533–542. Ross argued, p. 99, that Edward IV also hesitated to kill Henry as long as his son and more competent heir remained at large, and hence that death came only after that son had been eliminated. I agree that this difficulty may well have been a contributing factor.

47. In so arguing, I recognize that I fly in the face of Mancini's testimony, pp. 92–93, that people generally believed Edward dead before Mancini's own departure from London, which came in July 1483, but I take his view to be largely rhetorical retrojection from an author writing in November, a time when the deaths of both princes were much more universally assumed. That these deaths were not so assumed for much of the summer, at least not by the ordinary Englishman, is demonstrated by Croyland's testimony now to be cited.

48. *Croyland*, pp. 490–491.

49. Ross, pp. xliii–xliv. Russell's authorship has been challenged by H. A. Kelly, "The Last Chroniclers of Croyland," *The Ricardian*, 7, no. 91 (December 1985), pp. 142–177. Kelly prefers "Dr. Richard Lavender, . . . Bishop Russell's second-in-command" (p. 162), but from the point of view of the present argument, the difference is relatively unimportant: Lavender was presumably in almost as good a position as Russell, his master, to report accurately on Richard's actions.

50. *Croyland*, p. 491.

51. *Harleian 433*, II, 2.

52. *Great Chronicle*, p. 234.

53. Mancini, pp. 92–93.

54. The composition of the new alliance is best analyzed in Ross, pp. 105–115.

55. *Croyland*, p. 491.

56. *Original Letters*, I, 129.

57. E.g., *Harleian 433*, II, 30ff, and passim thereafter.

58. Ross, pp. 115–117; *Harleian 433*, II, 66; *Croyland*, p. 495.

59. Wedgwood, II, 473.

60. Ibid., II, 475.

61. Ibid., II, 475, 479–493.

62. *RP*, VI, 244–249, 250–251.

63. See above, Introduction to Part III, p. 96.

64. *RP*, VI, 249–250.

65. *Statutes*, II, 496–497.

66. *Statutes*, II, 477–498.

67. *RP*, VI, 241–242.

68. J. W. McKenna expresses puzzlement about this view in "The myth of parliamentary sovereignty in late-medieval England," *English Historical Review*, 94 (1979), p. 499, but his puzzlement arises only from his lack of understanding of the legal force of "as if" when used in this kind of context. It is a legal fiction that gives retroactive parliamentary authority to earlier actions not taken lawfully. It seems overwhelmingly to have been a Yorkist innovation, as in Edward IV's 1461 statute (*Statutes*, II, 380–388) that declared Lancastrian judicial acts legally valid "as if" there had been "any king lawfully reigning" at the time such acts "were begun, sued, had, or determined."

69. See above, Chapter 1, pp. 22–27.

70. *RP*, VI, 241.

71. For the best legal analysis of the uncertainties involved, see R. H. Helmholz, "The Sons of Edward IV: A Canonical Assessment of the Claim That They Were Illegitimate," *Richard III: Loyalty Lordship & Law*, ed. P. W. Hammond and Rosemary Horrox (London, 1986), pp. 91–103.

72. *Croyland*, pp. 495–496.

73. Ralph A. Griffiths and Roger S. Thomas, *The Making of the Tudor Dynasty* (New York, 1985), pp. 103–105.

74. *Harleian 433*, III, 190; for Dorset's summons home, Ross, p. 198.

75. *Harleian 433*, III, 190.

76. Ross, p. 198.

77. See above, Chapter 1, pp. 23–27.

78. Griffiths and Thomas, pp. 1–4, 28–32.

79. Charles Ross, *Edward IV* (Berkeley and Los Angeles, 1974), pp. 152–177, for the period of Edward's exile and return. The precise dates of Elizabeth's stay in sanctuary are not certain, but she appears to have entered Westminster in early November 1470 and left in mid-April 1471.

80. The most recent expression of this view, one that incorporates and synthesizes most earlier expressions of it, is to be found in McKenna, pp. 481–506 passim.

81. Armstrong, pp. 51–73.

82. Davies' English Chronicle as quoted in Dunham and Wood, p. 751.

83. *Statutes*, II, 378–379.

84. *RP*, V, 463, 464, 466.

85. John Bruce, ed., *Historie of the Arrivall of Edward IV. in England* . . . (London, 1838), p. 4; John Warkworth, ed. James O. Halliwell, *A Chronicle of the First Thirteen Years of the Reign of King Edward the Fourth* (London, 1839), p. 14.

86. *Croyland*, p. 496; St. Aubyn, p. 201.

87. *Croyland*, p. 499.

88. See above, Chapter 6, pp. 112–115.

89. See above, Chapter 2, pp. 30–31.

90. *Croyland*, p. 496.

91. Henry Grimston, ed., *The Third Part of the Report of Sir George Croke* (London, 1683), pp. 122–123, as translated in St. Aubyn, pp. 204–205.

92. On the northerners in the south and the problems they caused, see A. J. Pollard, "The Tyranny of Richard III," *Journal of Medieval History*, 3 (1977), pp. 147–166.

93. *Harleian 433*, II, 145, 156–157.

94. Ibid., II, 164.

95. Ibid., II, 182, 183.

96. *Croyland*, p. 498.

97. *Croyland*, pp. 498–499.

98. Leviticus 20; H. A. Kelly, "Canonical Implications of Richard III's Plan to Marry His Niece," *Traditio*, 23 (1967), pp. 269–311.

99. *Croyland*, p. 499.

100. Halsted, p. 466, doc. VVV.

101. Ibid.; *Croyland*, p. 500, also reports these denials, the truth of which it then denies, and an account of Richard's statement at the Hospital of St. John from a London merchant point of view appears in Laetitia Lyell, ed., *Acts of Court of the Mercers' Company* (Cambridge, 1936), pp. 173–174.

102. Halsted, p. 469, doc. ZZZ. Only the beginning of this proclamation appears in *Harleian 433*, II, 230, but it appears in full in Gairdner, *The Paston Letters*, VI, 81–84.

103. William Shakespeare, *The Tragedy of King Richard III*, V.v.36, 33–34.

104. Halsted, p. 470, doc. AAAA, from British Library, Harleian ms. 787, fo. 2.

105. For the general narrative of Henry's invasion and Richard's responses, I rely heavily on the excellent syntheses to be found in the two most recent works treating the subject, Griffiths and Thomas, pp. 127–158, and Michael Bennett, *The Battle of Bosworth* (New York, 1985), pp. 82–97.

106. Quoted in D. T. Williams, *The Battle of Bosworth* (Leicester, 1973), p. 4.

107. British Library, Additional Ms. 43490, fo. 53, as quoted in Bennett, p. 89.

108. *Croyland,* p. 503.

109. York City Archives, House Book B 2–4, fo. 169 verso, as modernized in Jeremy Potter, *Good King Richard?* (London, 1983), p. 94.

110. William Camden, ed. R. D. Dunn, *Remains Concerning Britain* (Toronto, 1984), p. 247.

Bibliography

With very few exceptions, the bibliography that follows is based entirely on works cited in the notes and not on those myriad others that directly or indirectly inform the judgments found in the text. In the interests of economy, however, the bibliography does not list reference manuals, works of pure fiction, or historical materials that, although cited, appear to have only a distant relationship to the main themes of this book.

SOURCES

Adam of Murimuth, ed. Thomas Hog, *Adami Murimuthensis Chronica . . . cum eorundem continuatione*. London, 1846.
le Baker de Swinbroke, Galfridus, ed. J. A. Giles, *Chronicon Angliae Temporibus Edwardi II et Edwardi III*. London, 1847.
Barrett, W. P., ed. and tr., *The Trial of Jeanne d'Arc*. New York, 1932.
Beaumanoir, Philippe de, ed. Amadée Salmon. *Coutumes de Beauvaisis*. 2 vols. Paris, 1889–1900.
Bentley, Samuel, ed., *Excerpta Historica*. London, 1831.
Bettenson, Henry, ed., *Documents of the Christian Church*. New York, 1947.
Bond, E. A., ed., *Chronica Monasterii de Melsa*. 3 vols. London, 1866–68.
du Boulay, F. R. H., ed. *Registrum Thome Bourgchier Cantuariensis Archiepiscopi 1454–1486*. Oxford, 1957.
Bouquet, Martin, et al., eds., *Recueil des historiens des Gaules et de la France*. 24 vols. Paris, 1738–1904.
Brewer, J. S., et al., *Letters and Papers, Foreign and Domestic, of the Reign of Henry VIII*. 37 vols. London, 1862–1910.

Bruce, John, ed., *Historie of the Arrivall of Edward IV. in England.* . . . London, 1838.

Calendar of Charter Rolls, 1427–1516. Vol. VI. London, 1927.

Calendar of Patent Rolls: Edward IV–Richard III, 1476–85. London, 1901.

Caxton, William, tr., ed. F. S. Ellis, *The Golden Legend or Lives of the Saints as Englished by William Caxton.* 6 vols. London, 1900.

Chartier, Jean, ed. Vallet de Viriville, *Chronique de Charles VII roi de France.* 3 vols. Paris, 1858.

Chrimes, S. B., and A. L. Brown, eds., *Select Documents of English Constitutional History, 1307–1485.* London, 1961.

Chronique Parisienne Anonyme. Mémoires de la Société de l'Histoire de Paris, 11 (1884).

Cocquelines, Carlo, ed., *Bullarum privilegiorum ac diplomatum Romanorum Pontificum amplissima collectio.* 6 vols. Rome, 1739–62.

Collier, J. P., ed., *Household Books of John, Duke of Norfolk and Thomas, Earl of Surrey, 1481–1490.* London, 1844.

Davies, R., ed., *York Records: Extracts from the Municipal Records of the City of York.* London, 1843.

Delaborde, Henri F., ed., *Oeuvres de Rigord et de Guillaume le Breton.* 2 vols. Paris, 1882.

Douglas, David C., and G. W. Greenaway, eds., *English Historical Documents 1042–1189.* New York, 1953.

Douglas Murray, T., ed., *Jeanne d'Arc: Maid of Orleans, Deliverer of France . . . Set Forth in the Original Documents.* New York, 1902.

Dupuy, Pierre, ed., *Histoire du différend d'entre le pape Boniface VIII et Philippes le bel, roy de France.* Paris, 1655.

Ellis, Henry, ed., *Original Letters.* 2nd Series. 4 vols. London, 1827.

Elton, G. R., ed., *The Tudor Constitution: Documents and Commentary.* Cambridge, 1960.

Froissart, Jehan, *Chronicles of England, France, Spain, and the Adjoining Countries.* London, 1839.

Gairdner, James, ed., *The Paston Letters.* 6 vols. London, 1904.

Galbraith, V. H., ed., *The Anonimalle Chronicle 1333 to 1381.* Manchester, 1927.

Geoffrey of Monmouth, tr. Lewis Thorpe, *The History of the Kings of Britain.* Harmondsworth, 1966.

Graham, Rose, ed., *Registrum Roberti Winchelsey Cantuariensis Archiepiscopi A. D. 1294–1313.* 3 vols. Oxford, 1952–56.

Hall, G. D. C., ed. and tr., *The Treatise on the Laws and Customs of the Realm of England Commonly Called Glanvill.* London, 1965.

Halliwell-Phillipps, James Orchard, ed., *Letters of the Kings of England.* 2 vols. London, 1848.

Bibliography 253

Hardy, T. D., ed., *Rotuli Litterarum Patentium.* Vol. I¹. London, 1835.
Haydon, F. S., ed., *Eulogium Historiarum.* 3 vols. London, 1858–63.
Hemingburgh, Walter of, *Hemingburgh's Chronicle.* 2 vols. London, 1848–49.
Higden, Ranulph, ed. C. Babington and Joseph R. Lumby, *Polychronicon.* 9 vols. London, 1865–86.
Historical Manuscripts Commission, *Reports of the Royal Commission on Historical Manuscripts.* Multivolumed and continuing. London, 1840– .
Holinshed, Raphael, *Holinshed's Chronicles of England, Scotland, and Ireland.* 6 vols. London, 1807–8.
Horrox, Rosemary, and P. W. Hammond, eds., *British Library Harleian Manuscript 433.* 4 vols. Upminster, 1979–83.
Horstmann, Carl, ed., *The Early South-English Legendary of Lives of the Saints.* . . . London, 1887.
Isambert, François André, et al., eds., *Recueil général des anciennes lois françaises.* 29 vols. Paris, 1822–33.
Johnson, Charles, and H. A. Cronne, eds., *Regesta Henrici Primi, 1100–1135. Regesta Regum Anglo-Normannorum,* vol. II. Oxford, 1956.
Joinville, Jean de, and Geffroi de Villehardouin, tr. Sir Frank Marzials, *Memoirs of the Crusades.* London, 1908.
Kingsford, C. L., ed., *The Stonor Letters and Papers 1290–1483.* 2 vols. London, 1919.
de Laurière, E.-J. et al., eds., *Ordonnances des Rois de France de la Troisième Race.* . . . 23 vols. Paris, 1723–1849.
Luard, H. R., ed., *Flores Historiarum.* 3 vols. London, 1890.
Luce, Siméon, ed., *Chronique des quatres premiers Valois (1327–1393).* Paris, 1862.
Luders, A., et al., eds., *Statutes of the Realm.* 12 vols. London, 1818–28.
Lyell, Laetitia, ed., *Acts of Court of the Mercers' Company.* Cambridge, 1936.
Macray, William D., ed., *Register of Magdalen College, Oxford.* New series, 7 vols. London, 1894.
Maitland, F. W., ed., *Year Books of Edward II.* London, 1903.
Mancini, Dominic, ed. and tr. C. A. J. Armstrong, *The Usurpation of Richard the Third.* 2nd ed. Oxford, 1969.
Matthew Paris, ed. H. R. Luard, *Chronica Majora.* 7 vols. London, 1872–80.
Maxwell, Herbert, tr., *The Chronicle of Lanercost.* Glasgow, 1913.
Monk of St. Albans, A [Thomas Walsingham], ed. E. M. Thompson, *Chronicon Angliae ab anno Domini 1328 usque ad annum 1388.* London, 1874.
More, St. Thomas, ed. Richard S. Sylvester, *The History of King Richard III and Selections from the English and Latin Poems.* New Haven, 1976.

Morosini, Antonio, ed. Léon Dorez and Germain Lefèvre–Pontalis, *La chronique d'Antonio Morosini*. 4 vols. Paris, 1898–1902.

Myers, A. R., ed., *English Historical Documents 1327–1485*. New York, 1969.

Nicholas, John, ed., *A Collection of All the Wills Now Known to be Extant of the Kings and Queens of England*. . . . . London, 1780.

Nichols, John G., ed., *Grants, Etc. from the Crown During the Reign of Edward the Fifth*. London, 1854.

Nicolas, Sir Harris, ed., *Proceedings and Ordinances of the Privy Council of England*. 7 vols. London, 1834–37.

Palgrave, Francis, ed., *Parliamentary Writs*. 2 vols. London, 1827–34.

Pisan, Christine de, ed. Angus J. Kennedy and Kenneth Varty, *Ditié de Jehanne d'Arc*. Oxford, 1977.

Quicherat, Jules, ed., *Procès de condamnation et de réhabilitation de Jeanne d'Arc*. 5 vols. Paris, 1841–49.

Raine, Angelo, ed., *York Civic Records*. 2 vols. York, 1938.

Richardson, H. G., and G. O. Sayles, eds., *Rotuli Parliamentorum Angliae Hactenus Inediti*. London, 1935.

Riley, H. T., ed., *Ingulph's Chronicle of the Abbey of Croyland*. London, 1854.

———, ed., *Munimenta Gildhallae Londoniensis*. 2 vols. London, 1860.

———, ed., *Register Abbatiae Johannis Whethamstede*. 2 vols. London, 1872–73.

Rymer, Thomas, ed., *Foedera, conventiones, literae, et cujuscunque generis Acta publica*. . . . 20 vols. London, 1704–32.

Scott, W. S., ed. and tr., *The Trial of Joan of Arc*. Westport, Conn., 1956.

Stephenson, Carl, and Frederick G. Marcham, eds., *Sources of English Constitutional History*. 2 vols., rev. ed. New York, 1972.

Stevenson, J., ed., *Chronicon de Lanercost*. Edinburgh, 1839.

Strachey, J., et al., eds., *Rotuli Parliamentorum*. 6 vols. London, 1767–77.

Stubbs, William, ed., *Chronicles of the Reigns of Edward I and Edward II*. 2 vols. London, 1882–83.

———, ed. H. W. C. Davis, *Select Charters*. 9th ed. Oxford, 1929.

Sutton, Anne F., and P. W. Hammond, eds., *The Coronation of Richard III: The Extant Documents*. Gloucester and New York, 1983.

Thomas, A. H., and I. D. Thornley, eds., *The Great Chronicle of London*. London, 1938.

Tisset, Pierre, and Yvonne Lanhers, eds. *Procès de condamnation de Jeanne d'Arc*. 3 vols. Paris, 1960–71.

Varin, Paul, ed., *Archives administratives de la ville de Reims. Documents inédits sur l'histoire de France*, II[1]. Paris, 1839–43.

Vergil, Polydore, ed. Henry Ellis, *Three Books of Polydore Vergil's English*

History, Comprising the Reigns of Henry VI., Edward IV., and Richard III. London, 1840.

Voragine, Jacobus de, tr. Granger Ryan and Helmut Ripperger, *The Golden Legend.* 2 vols. London, 1941.

Walsingham, Thomas, ed. H. T. Riley, *Annales Ricardi Secundi.* London, 1866.

———, ed. H. T. Riley, *Historia Anglicana.* 2 vols. London, 1862–64.

Warkworth, John, ed. James O. Halliwell, *A Chronicle of the First Thirteen Years of the Reign of King Edward the Fourth.* London, 1839.

SECONDARY WORKS

Baldwin, John, *The Government of Philip Augustus.* Berkeley and Los Angeles, 1986.

Bémont, Charles, *Simon de Montfort comte de Leicester.* Paris, 1884.

———, *Simon de Montfort Earl of Leicester.* New ed. Oxford, 1930.

Bennett, Michael, *The Battle of Bosworth.* New York, 1985.

Bisson, Thomas N., *Assemblies and Representation in Languedoc in the Thirteenth Century.* Princeton, 1964.

———, ed., *Medieval Representative Institutions: Their Origins and Nature.* Hinsdale, Ill., 1973.

Bloch, Marc, tr. J. E. Anderson, *The Royal Touch.* Montreal, 1973.

Boase, T. S. R., *Boniface VIII.* London, 1933.

Bolland, W. C., *The Year Books.* Cambridge, 1921.

Boutaric, Edgard, *Saint Louis et Alfonse de Poitiers.* Paris, 1870.

Bullough, Vern L., and James Brundage, *Sexual Practices and the Medieval Church.* Buffalo, N. Y., 1982.

Chrimes, S. B., *English Constitutional Ideas in the Fifteenth Century.* Cambridge, 1936.

Clanchy, M. T., *England and Its Rulers 1066–1272.* London, 1985.

Clarke, M. V., ed. L. S. Sutherland and May McKisack, *Fourteenth Century Studies.* Oxford, 1937.

Curley, Mary Mildred, *The Conflict Between Boniface VIII and King Philip, the Fair.* Washington, D. C., 1927.

Davies, R. G., and J. M. Denton, eds., *The English Parliament in the Middle Ages.* Philadelphia, 1981.

Dickinson, J. G., *The Congress of Arras.* Oxford, 1955.

Dupuy, Pierre, *Traité de la Maiorité de nos Rois. . . .* Paris, 1655.

Elton, G. R., *"The Body of the Whole Realm": Parliament and Representation in Medieval and Tudor England.* Charlottesville, Va., 1969.

———, *Reform and Renewal: Thomas Cromwell and the Common Weal.* Cambridge, 1973.

Esmein, André, *Cours élémentaire d'histoire du droit français.* Paris, 1925.

Famiglietti, Richard C., *Royal Intrigue: Crisis at the Court of Charles VI, 1392–1420*. New York, 1986.

Fawtier, Robert, tr. Lionel Butler and R. J. Adam, *The Capetian Kings of France*. London, 1960.

Fichtenau, Heinrich, *The Carolingian Empire*. Oxford, 1957.

Fryde, Natalie, *The Tyranny and Fall of Edward II, 1321–1326*. Cambridge, 1979.

Gairdner, James, *History of the Life and Reign of Richard the Third*. Rev. ed. Cambridge, 1898.

Gavrilovitch, Michel, *Étude sur le traité de Paris de 1259*. Paris, 1899.

Griffiths, Ralph A., *Henry VI*. Berkeley and Los Angeles, 1981.

————, and Roger S. Thomas, *The Making of the Tudor Dynasty*. New York, 1985.

Halsted, Caroline, *Richard III. as Duke of Gloucester and King of England*. Philadelphia, 1844.

Hansen, Mark, *The Royal Facts of Life: Biology and Politics in Sixteenth-Century Europe*. Metuchen, N. J. and London, 1980.

Henneman, John Bell, *Royal Taxation in Fourteenth-Century France: The Captivity and Ransom of John II, 1356–1370*. Philadelphia, 1976.

————, *Royal Taxation in Fourteenth Century France: The Development of War Financing 1322–1356*. Princeton, 1971.

Herlihy, David, *Medieval Households*. Cambridge, Mass., 1985.

Holdsworth, Sir William S., *A History of English Law*. 17 vols. 5th ed. reprint. London, 1966.

Huizinga, Johan, *The Waning of the Middle Ages*. Garden City, N. Y., 1954.

Jacob, E. F., *Essays in the Conciliar Epoch*. 3rd ed. Manchester, 1963.

————, *Essays in Later Medieval History*. Manchester, 1968.

Jenkins, Elizabeth, *The Princes in the Tower*. New York, 1978.

Jolliffe, J. E. A., *The Constitutional History of Medieval England*. London, 1937.

Jones, Richard H., *The Royal Policy of Richard II: Absolutism in the Later Middle Ages*. Oxford, 1968.

Jordan, William C., *Louis IX and the Challenge of the Crusade*. Princeton, 1979.

Kantorowicz, Ernst, *The King's Two Bodies*. Princeton, 1957.

Keen, Maurice, *Chivalry*. New Haven and London, 1984.

Kendall, Paul Murray, *Richard the Third*. New York, 1965.

Kern, Fritz, *Kingship and Law in the Middle Ages*. Oxford, 1956.

Koenigsberger, H. G., and George L. Mosse, *Europe in the Sixteenth Century*. New York, 1968.

Lavisse, Ernest, et al., *Histoire de France depuis les origines jusqu'à la Révolution*. 9 vols. Paris, 1901–2.

Levison, Wilhelm, *England and the Continent in the Eighth Century.* Oxford, 1946.

Lewis, Andrew W., *Royal Succession in Capetian France: Studies on Familial Order and the State.* Cambridge, Mass., 1981.

Lewis, P. S., *Later Medieval France: The Polity.* London, 1968.

Luchaire, Achille, *Histoire des institutions monarchiques de la France sous les premiers Capétiens (987–1180).* 2 vols., 1st ed. Paris, 1883.

McIlwain, Charles H., *The High Court of Parliament and Its Supremacy.* New Haven, 1910.

McKisack, May, *The Fourteenth Century 1307–1399.* Oxford, 1959.

Maitland, F. W., *The Constitutional History of England.* Cambridge, 1926.

Major, J. Russell, *Representative Government in Early Modern France.* New Haven, 1980.

Markham, Sir Clements R., *Richard III: His Life & Character.* London, 1906.

Michelet, Jules, tr. Albert Guérard, *Joan of Arc.* Ann Arbor, 1967.

Nicolas, Sir Nicholas Harris, *History of the Orders of Knighthood.* . . . 4 vols. London, 1842.

Olivier-Martin, F.-J.-M., *Études sur les régences I: les régences et la majorité des rois sous les Capétiens directs et les premiers Valois (1060–1375).* Paris, 1931.

Pernoud, Régine, tr. J. M. Cohen, *The Retrial of Joan of Arc.* London, 1955.

Perroy, Édouard, *The Hundred Years War.* London, 1951.

Peters, Edward, *The Shadow King: Rex Inutilis in Medieval Law and Literature.* New Haven, 1978.

Petit-Dutaillis, Charles, *The Feudal Monarchy in France and England.* London, 1936.

Plancher, Urbain, *Histoire générale et particulière de Bourgogne.* 4 vols. Paris, 1739–81.

Pollock, Frederick, and Frederick W. Maitland, *The History of English Law Before the Time of Edward I.* 2 vols., 2nd ed. Cambridge, 1968.

Potter, Jeremy, *Good King Richard?.* London, 1983.

Powicke, Sir Maurice, *The Thirteenth Century 1216–1307.* Oxford, 1953.

Ramsay, James H., *A History of the Revenues of the Kings of England 1066–1399.* 2 vols. Oxford, 1925.

Reeves, Marjorie, *The Influence of Prophecy on the Later Middle Ages. A Study in Joachimism.* Oxford, 1969.

Reynolds, Susan, *Kingdoms and Communities in Western Europe 900–1300.* Oxford, 1984.

Ross, Charles, *Edward IV.* Berkeley and Los Angeles, 1974.

———, *Richard III.* Berkeley and Los Angeles, 1981.

St. Aubyn, Giles, *The Year of Three Kings 1483.* London, 1983.

St. German, Christopher, *Doctor and Student.* London, 1751.

Sayles, G. O., *The King's Parliament of England.* London, 1975.
Scholz, Richard, *Die Publizistik dur Zeit Philipps des Schönen und Bonifaz VIII.* Stuttgart, 1903.
Shaw, William A., *The Knights of England.* 2 vols. London, 1906.
Steel, Anthony, *Richard II.* Cambridge, 1962.
Stenton, Sir Frank, *Anglo-Saxon England.* 3rd ed. Oxford, 1971.
Strayer, Joseph R., *Medieval Statecraft and the Perspectives of History.* Princeton, 1971.
————, and Charles H. Taylor, *Studies in Early French Taxation.* Cambridge, Mass., 1939.
Stubbs, William, *Constitutional History of England.* 3 vols. Oxford, 1880.
Tierney, Brian, *Foundations of the Conciliar Theory.* Cambridge, 1955.
————, *Origins of Papal Infallibility 1150–1350.* Leiden, 1972.
Tout, T. F., *Chapters in the Administrative History of Medieval England.* 6 vols. Manchester, 1920–33.
Treharne, Reginald F., *The Baronial Plan of Reform, 1258–1263.* Manchester, 1932.
Tuck, Anthony, *The Crown & Nobility 1272–1461.* London, 1986.
Ullmann, Walter, *Origins of the Great Schism.* London, 1948.
Warner, Marina, *Joan of Arc: The Image of Female Heroism.* New York, 1981.
Warren, H. L., *Henry II.* Berkeley and Los Angeles, 1973.
————, *King John.* Berkeley and Los Angeles, 1961.
Wedgwood, Josiah C., *History of Parliament.* 2 vols. London, 1936–38.
Wilkinson, Bertie, *Constitutional History of England in the Fifteenth Century.* New York, 1964.
————, *Constitutional History of Medieval England 1216–1399.* 2 vols. London, 1948–52.
Wilks, M. J., *The Problem of Sovereignty in the Later Middle Ages: The Papal Monarchy with Augustinus Triumphus and the Publicists.* Cambridge, 1963.
Williams, D. T., *The Battle of Bosworth.* Leicester, 1973.
Wood, Charles T., *The French Apanages and the Capetian Monarchy 1224–1328.* Cambridge, Mass., 1966.
————, ed., *Philip the Fair and Boniface VIII.* 2nd ed. New York, 1971.
[Wright], Georgia Sommers, "Royal Tombs at St. Denis in the Reign of Saint Louis." Doctoral Dissertation, Columbia University, 1967.

ARTICLES

Armstrong, C. A. J., "The Inauguration Ceremonies of the Yorkist Kings and their Title to the Throne." *Transactions of the Royal Historical Society,* 30 (1948).

Attreed, Lorraine C., "From *Pearl* maiden to Tower princes: towards a new history of medieval childhood." *Journal of Medieval History,* 9 (1983).

Barker, N., and R. Birley, "Jane Shore." *Etoniana,* no. 125 (June 1972).

Benton, John F., "Les entrées dans la vie: Étapes d'une croissance ou rites d'initiation?" *Annales de l'Est,* 5ᵉ série, no. 1–2 (1982).

Blackley, F. D., "Adam, The Bastard Son of Edward II." *Bulletin of the Institute of Historical Research,* 37 (1964).

Branner, Robert, "The Montjoies of Saint Louis." *Essays in the History of Architecture Presented to Rudolf Wittkower,* ed. D. Fraser et al. Vol. I. London, 1967.

Brown, Elizabeth A. R., "*Cessante Causa* and the Taxes of the Last Capetians: The Political Application of a Philosophical Maxim." *Studia Gratiana* [*Post Scripta*], 15 (1972).

Campbell, Gerard J., "The Protest of Saint Louis." *Traditio,* 15 (1959).

Caspary, Gerard E., "The Deposition of Richard II and the Canon Law." *Proceedings of the Second International Congress of Medieval Canon Law.* Vol. I. Rome, 1966.

Chaplais, Pierre, "Le Traité de Paris de 1259 et l'inféodation de la Gascogne allodiale." *Le Moyen Âge,* 61 (1955).

Cheyette, Fredric L., "*Suum cuique tribuere.*" *French Historical Studies,* 6 (1970).

Chrimes, S. B., "Richard II's Questions to the Judges, 1387." *Law Quarterly Review,* 72 (1956).

Cuttino, G. P., "A Reconsideration of the 'Modus tenendi parliamentum.'" *The Forward Movement of the Fourteenth Century,* ed. Francis Lee Utley. Columbus, Ohio, 1961.

———, and Thomas W. Lyman, "Where Is Edward II?" *Speculum,* 53 (1978).

Dunham, William Huse, Jr., "'The Books of Parliament' and 'The Old Record,' 1396–1504." *Speculum,* 51 (1976).

———, and Charles T. Wood, "The Right to Rule in England: Depositions and the Kingdom's Authority, 1327–1485." *American Historical Review,* 81 (1976).

Elton, G. R., "The early journals in the house of lords." *English Historical Review,* 89 (1974).

Evans, Joan, "The Wilton Diptych Reconsidered." *Archaeological Journal,* 105 (1948).

Fawtier, Robert, "L'attentat d'Anagni." *Mélanges d'archéologie et d'histoire,* 60 (1948).

———, "Parlement d'Angleterre et États Généraux de France au Moyen Âge." *Comptes-rendus de l'Academie des Inscriptions et Belles Lettres* (1953).

————, "Les reliques rouennaises de Sainte Catherine d'Alexandrie." *Analecta Bollandiana*, 41 (1923).

Ferris, Sumner J., "The Iconography of the Wilton Diptych." *Minnesota Review*, 7 (1967).

————, "The Wilton Diptych and the Absolutism of Richard II," *Journal of the Rocky Mountain Medieval and Renaissance Association*, 8 (1987).

Fraioli, Deborah, "The Literary Images of Joan of Arc: Prior Influences." *Speculum*, 56 (1981).

Giesey, Ralph E., "The French Estates and the Corpus Mysticum Regni." *Album Helen Maud Cam*, I. Louvain, 1960.

————, "The Juristic Basis of Dynastic Right to the French Throne." *Transactions of the American Philosophical Society*, new series, Part 5, LI (1961).

Hartland, E. Sidney, "The Legend of St. Kenelm." *Transactions of the Bristol and Gloucestershire Archaeological Society*, 39 (1916).

Harvey, John H., "The Wilton Diptych: A Re-examination." *Archaeologia*, 98 (1961).

Helmholz, R. H., "The Sons of Edward IV: A Canonical Assessment of the Claim That They Were Illegitimate." *Richard III: Loyalty Lordship & Law*, ed. P. W. Hammond. London, 1986.

Hope, W. H. St. John, "The Discovery of the Remains of King Henry VI in St. George's Chapel, Windsor Castle." *Archaeologia*, 2nd series, 62 (1911).

Hoyt, Robert S., "The Coronation Oath of 1308: The Background of 'Les Les et les Custumes.' " *Traditio*, 11 (1955).

Jacob, Ernest F., "The Complaints of Henry III against the Baronial Council in 1261." *English Historical Review*, 41 (1926).

Kaeuper, Richard W., "Royal Finance and the Crisis of 1297." *Order and Innovation in the Middle Ages*, ed. W. C. Jordan, C. B. McNab, and T. F. Ruiz. Princeton, 1976.

Kelly, H. A., "Canonical Implications of Richard III's Plan to Marry His Niece." *Traditio*, 23 (1967).

————, "The Last Chroniclers of Croyland." *The Ricardian*, 7, no. 91 (December 1985).

Langmuir, Gavin I., "Community and Legal Change in Capetian France." *French Historical Studies*, 6 (1970).

————, "Counsel and Capetian Assemblies." *Studies Presented to the International Commission for the History of Representative and Parliamentary Institutions*. Louvain, 1958.

Lapsley, Gaillard, "The Parliamentary Title of Henry IV." *English Historical Review*, 49 (1934).

Leclercq, Jean, "La rénonciation de Célestin V et l'opinion théologique en

France du vivant de Boniface VIII." *Revue d'histoire de l'église de France*, 25 (1939).

Levine, Mortimer, "Richard III—Usurper or Lawful King?" *Speculum*, 34 (1959).

Lewis, Andrew W., "Dynastic Structures and Capetian Throne-right: The Views of Giles of Paris." *Traditio*, 33 (1977).

McKenna, J. W., "The Myth of parliamentary sovereignty in late-medieval England." *English Historical Review*, 94 (1979).

[Madden], Sarah Hanley, "L'idéologie constitutionelle en France: le lit de justice." *Annales*, 37 (1982).

Myers, A. R., "The Character of Richard III." *History Today*, 4 (1954).

Ormes, Nicholas, "The Education of Edward V," *Bulletin of the Institute of Historical Research*, 57 (1984).

Pollard, A. J., "The Tyranny of Richard III." *Journal of Medieval History*, 3 (1977).

Reynolds, Susan, "Law and Communities in Western Christendom, c. 900–1140." *American Journal of Legal History*, 25 (1981).

Richardson, Henry G., "The Coronation in Medieval England," *Traditio*, 16 (1960).

Robinson, Chalfont, "Was King Edward the Second a Degenerate?" *American Journal of Insanity*, 66 (1909–10).

Roskell, J. S., "The Office and Dignity of Protector of England with special reference to its origins." *English Historical Review*, 68 (1953).

Ruiz, Teofilo F., "Reaction to Anagni." *Catholic Historical Review*, 65 (1979).

Sandquist, T. A., "The Holy Oil of St. Thomas of Canterbury." *Essays in Medieval History Presented to Bertie Wilkinson*, ed. T. A. Sandquist and M. R. Powicke. Toronto, 1969.

Spiegel, Gabrielle M., "The *Reditus Regni ad Stirpem Karoli Magni:* A New Look." *French Historical Studies*, 7 (1971).

Strong, Patrick and Felicity, "The last will and codicils of Henry V." *English Historical Review*, 96 (1981).

Taylor, Charles Holt, "Assemblies of French Towns in 1316." *Speculum*, 14 (1939).

Tout, Thomas F., "The Captivity and Death of Edward of Carnarvon." *The Collected Papers of Thomas Frederick Tout.* 3 vols. Manchester, 1934.

Treharne, Reginald F., "The Mise of Amiens, 23 January 1264." *Studies in Medieval History Presented to Frederick Maurice Powicke*, ed. Richard W. Hunt et al. Oxford, 1948.

Turner, G. J., "The minority of Henry III, Part I." *Transactions of the Royal Historical Society*, new series, 18 (1904).

Viollet, Paul, "Comment les femmes ont été exclues de la succession à la couronne de France." *Mémoires de l'Institut de France,* 34² (1895).

Wood, Charles T., "The Deposition of Edward V." *Traditio,* 31 (1975).

————, "England: 1216–1485." *Dictionary of the Middle Ages,* ed. Joseph R. Strayer et al. Vol. 4. New York, 1981– .

————, "Personality, Politics, and Constitutional Progress: The Lessons of Edward II." *Studia Gratiana [Post Scripta],* 15 (1972).

————, "*Regnum Francie:* A Problem in Capetian Administrative Usage." *Traditio,* 22 (1967).

————, "Richard III, William, Lord Hastings and Friday the Thirteenth." *Kings and Nobles in the Later Middle Ages,* ed. Ralph A. Griffiths and James Sherborne. Gloucester, 1986.

————, "Who killed the little princes in the Tower? A Ricardian murder mystery." *Harvard Magazine,* 80, no. 3 (January–February 1978).

Wormald, Francis, "The Wilton Diptych." *Journal of the Warburg and Courtauld Institutes,* 17 (1954).

Index